ENGAGING SPACES

People, Place and Space from an Irish Perspective

Jim Hourihane lectures in geography at St Patrick's College, Drumcondra, Dublin. He devised and acted as consulting editor of the Thomas Davis Lecture series – **Engaging Spaces** – broadcast by RTÉ in Ireland and by National Public Radio (NPR) in America. He has written and edited many books in geographical and environmental education.

ENGAGING SPACES

People, Place and Space from an Irish Perspective

Edited by Jim Hourihane

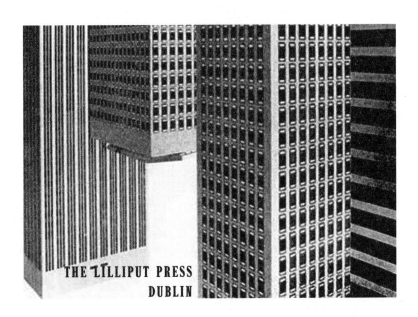

THE LILLIPUT PRESS
DUBLIN

First published 2003 by
THE LILLIPUT PRESS LTD
62–63 Sitric Road, Arbour Hill,
Dublin 7, Ireland
www.lilliputpress.ie

A CIP record for this title is available
from The British Library.

1 3 5 7 9 10 8 6 4 2

ISBN 1 84351 034 0

Published with the support of the Heritage Council and
the Research Committee, St Patrick's College, Drumcondra.
The editor also wishes to acknowledge the support
of Urban Institute Ireland.

Set in Perpetua
Printed in Dublin by Betaprint

Contents

Illustrations between pages 50 and 51

Foreword

The eight essays that make up this book are stimulating, exploratory, strongly argued and clearly written. They will make readers consider both the spaces in their own minds and the little and vast spaces of the world(s) about them. The eight writers confront the fascinating mysteries and clarities of space, moving from the county and the region to dreams, nightmares and rural idylls, to the political character of urban areas, to the effect of globalization on the sense of belonging, and hence of loyalty, to a place.

Space is both physical and mental. It can seem like a vast absence or a presence that crushes or consoles, intimidates or inspires. Space can be a liberating cliff-top full of warm memories or a dark, cold room that can almost freeze a heart with fears familiar yet inexplicable. Space can be a stage where the leading actor is Original Sin or a schoolboy convinced that the silliest, most sinister creation of the human mind is algebra or geometry, or both. Space is science and poetry meeting at a crossroads. Space is the smell of a lover's skin and the setting for Danny Pat Danaher's conviction that ten glasses of whiskey and six pints of Guinness per day are the only answer to the world's ugliness and greed. Space is a billion stars winking knowingly at Jupiter and a mucky pool in the corner of a small field. Space is the horror of foul congestion and the thrill of limitless possibility.

This thrill, this excitement of the possible generated by an awareness of the actual, is precisely what makes these essays so fascinating.

Though written by eight different people, the essays echo each other in unexpected, illuminating ways. The essays have in them, in their perceptions and wonder, something of the marvel of space itself in all its complexity. The book has a sense of journey in it, and also a sense of intense, even passionate exploration. It is a world reaching out to other worlds. Readers will, I believe, thoroughly enjoy this exploratory journey. More importantly, they will make their own unique and deeply personal discoveries.

Brendan Kennelly

Introduction

We shall not cease from exploration
And the end of all our exploring
Will be to arrive where we started
And know the place for the first time.
Through the unknown, unremembered gate
When the last of earth left to discover
Is that which was the beginning;
At the source of the longest river
The voice of the hidden waterfall
And the children in the apple-tree
Not known, because not looked for
But heard, half-heard, in the stillness
Between two waves of the sea.

T.S. Eliot[1]

The exploration of the environments within which we exist can fall into many categories. Exploration may be highly planned or quite casual. It may last for a long or for a short period of time. It may be quite local and immediate or far removed in distance from our usual place of living. There is a common unifying thread in all of our environmental contacts, however. They all feed into a complex and elaborate model of environmental interaction that informs and guides our knowledge and behaviour.

The title of this book of eight essays, *Engaging Spaces*, poses a dialectic. It suggests that spaces engage us but that we also engage spaces. This dual process of engaging spaces has never before been so potentially bewildering in the history of humanity. Speedy and cheap travel, allied to virtually instantaneous communications, has resulted in a number of unprecedented challenges and opportunities. Many more people can now see places and spaces far removed from their own localities. Even as recently as half a century ago such localities, unless emigration determined otherwise, would have been the containers within which their full life-spans were lived out. These localities would have been intensely known and, although limited in extent, would often have nourished people emotionally in a way rare in the early twenty-first century.

The differences in the traits that form individual cultures are becoming increasingly blurred as globalization – first expressed in largely economic terms and impacts – becomes more pervasive and deeply rooted. A process that had its origins in the most advanced economies and very large multinational and transnational corporations is now much truer to its name – it is global in extent. It is also global in its ability to influence the lives of individuals, and not always in positive and enhancing ways. As globalization further establishes itself as a dominant economic and political philosophy, it is vital that we have an informed and informing context within which to position it, ourselves, and our sense of space and place.

Spaces and places matter in our lives. Spatial awareness and culture pervade much current research on humanity, its decisions and directions. Our world and our sense of it are hugely shaped by the relationship between the spaces of our physical world, those of the built world and those of the mind. We need to question how we think and act. How does our spatial engagement affect our emotional lives? What are the relationships between space and place, space and time, time and place? Irish consciousness of space as a people living on an island has begun to change profoundly over the last decade or so. Global forces have brought with them many possibilities and potential problems. At the same time our awareness of the need to appraise and redirect our national spatial development has grown.

Geography's redefinition and re-embrace of the importance of space has been labelled the 'spatial turn'. It is both grounded in, and a reaction to, the writings of several eminent philosophers. Heidegger's phenomenology and existentialism examined 'being' and, implicitly, space.[2] Bachelard's *Poetics of Space*, again phenomenological in nature, examined the house and its associations with being and image.[3] Michel Foucault's analysis of time and space did, ultimately, result in a critical re-evaluation of space that had been neglected for generations.[4] Finally, the writings of Henri LeFebvre were both a part of, and a trigger for, much post-modernist thinking on spatial practices.[5] The spatial turn within geography owes much to the writings of two geographers over the last thirty years: David Harvey[6] and Edward Soja.[7] Both are urban geographers but their work transcends any attempt to compartmentalize them – they range widely across the three related strands of space, time and place, and in turn assess the critical nature of modernity and post-modernity within society.

Many people rejoice in their ability to escape, even if only for a day, the headlong rush towards urban life and living. Equally, the potential to escape from a lonely and isolated rural life, again, if only for a day, reinvigorates others. The more complete person is likely to have a wide framework for understanding spaces – the wild and primeval, the cultured rural landscape and the urban environment with its interlocking maze of challenges. In our past, even the recent past, most people living in Ireland were rural in nature. The urbanization of the Irish population and the counter-urbanization back into rural areas bring their own challenges. The pressures on each of the layers of space around us need to be understood. They are, after all, part of our heritage – both natural and built – and it is important that we assess where we are going.

Continuity and change in landscapes, places and spaces seem, at initial reading, to be mutually contradictory. Geographers have always been fascinated by their co-existence, and by their management at sensitive and balanced levels. What is intriguing is that even though we all assess places and spaces as individuals, there is often a considerable degree of overlap between our different perspectives. Irish people, while they are now likely to be part of the majority of the population who are urbanized, may often only be a generation removed from the land. It is also very likely that we collectively share an ability to receive information through our senses and perceive the environments around us in quite sophisticated ways. We perceive our environments at many levels, not least on a limbic-intuitive level. The limbic-intuitive mode of perception operates on a non-cognitive level, drawing from stored ancestral information. Its cultural roots are likely to be very deep indeed within Ireland, since our past was so fundamentally linked with the land and its related earthy lifestyle.

The essays here were originally scripted as a Thomas Davis Lecture series bearing the same title, *Engaging Spaces*. They were broadcast by both RTÉ in Ireland and National Public Radio in the USA during the summer of 2002. The publication of the book on this, the fiftieth anniversary of the first Thomas Davis series, is particularly apposite. Over the years the Thomas Davis series has served to question and query as much as to inform. The eight geographers who have reconstituted and extended their original radio scripts continue in this tradition.

Given Thomas Davis's iconic status for a new Ireland it is particularly appropriate that time/history is what differentiates spaces from places. Spaces become places with the passage of time and, quite probably, the intervention of people. At their simplest level, we can map space and photograph place. To this end, a number of photographs have been chosen to represent significant aspects of the places and spaces discussed in the essays.

The essays move sequentially outward from the spaces inside our heads to those that denote our limits of ordinary access and travel – the global. I begin by looking at how we conceive space and internalize it within our framework of day-to-day behaviour. Patrick Duffy argues that a relocalization of our spatial behaviour and interests is taking place. Ruth McManus examines the co-existence of dreams and nightmares within the urban environment. Desmond Gillmor assesses the longevity and importance of the county as the unit of space to which people in Ireland pay such continuing allegiance. Mary Cawley contrasts the rural idylls of today with those posited by Classical Greeks, the Romantics and the builders of early Irish nationhood such as Thomas Davis himself. Desmond McCafferty questions the importance of what in many senses is the most enduring of geographical units, the region. Yvonne Whelan decodes the symbolic spaces of urban areas and demonstrates that such landscapes are often contested and highly political. Joseph Duffy ranges through a world without frontiers, and questions whether our sense of belonging to a particular place is threatened by the global standardization of foods, built environments, currencies, and so forth.

We are all clearly part of planet Earth. While our spheres of contact with places and spaces may vary, it is essential that at this historical juncture we draw a breath, informed once more by the cultured geographical perspective of T.S. Eliot:

Home is where one starts from. As we grow older
The world becomes stranger, the pattern more complicated
Of dead and living. Not the intense moment
Isolated, with no before and after,
But a lifetime burning in every moment
And not the lifetime of one man only
But of old stones that cannot be deciphered. [8]

1. Spaces in the Mind

Jim Hourihane

'Space: the final frontier.'
One wonders did Denis Tito allow these words to cross his mind
as he was blasted into space in April 2001? He had paid the Russian
space agency twenty million dollars for just over a week in space.
It was an expensive week but when he returned to Earth he
described it as 'a trip to paradise'. Tito's trip to space, or paradise,
allowed him to enter the annals of history. He became the world's
first 'space tourist'.

Geographers might find this ironic. We are all space tourists.
We are so from birth to death. But there is a difference, of course,
in the spaces we tour: Denis Tito toured astronomical space; we
tour Earth space.

Earth space is the focus of this Thomas Davis series. Geography
is the discipline most associated with the study of this type of space.
If we tease out the etymology of geography, we begin to understand both its origins and its concerns.

The word geography comes from two Greek words, *ge* and
grapho, that mean 'I write the earth'. It is a global aspiration and it
is certainly not a modest undertaking. The Greeks were the first

geographers. They mapped their world and the spaces they knew. Greek philosophers also reflected on the notion of space. Aristotle developed a theory of place that he called 'topos'. The word and the concept are still central to geography today. Topography refers to the shape and form of landscapes.

Before he died in 1984, the French philosopher Michel Foucault wrote, 'The present epoch will, perhaps, be above all the epoch of space.'[1] Now, at the start of the twenty-first century, we have finally begun to pay space the attention it deserves. Spaces in our cities, our towns and our rural areas are under huge pressure. A growing population, a dynamic economy and an uneven geographic spread of economic development have all led to these pressures.

Our lives are rooted in time and space. Historically, and I use the word in more than one sense, time was felt by many social theorists to be the factor that helped to explain our existence. Karl Marx,[2] Emmanuel Kant[3] and many other philosophers claimed that time/history was central to the development of society.

Before his conversion to the importance of space Foucault wrote, 'Time was rich and full of life. Space was fixed and dead.'[4] This division is curious. We exist in both time and space. As we live our moments of time, we do so within space. We are quite incapable of doing anything unless we have a sophisticated set of spatial relations. We think, just to name a few spatial terms, about near and far, inside and outside, north and south, separated and joined. We take these spatial concepts and structures for granted. If we did not have them we would be fixed in one place. Quite simply, we would be incapable of moving. In such a scenario, the space we occupied really would be the final frontier – we could not move outside it!

So what is this space that so preoccupies us at the moment? It is the space that tempts us all to ask for 'space to breathe'. It is the space that allows auctioneers to put up the 'for sale' sign. Apart from the fact that they are both spaces, these have little else in common.

Space is complex and as a term, as a concept, it means different things in different situations. Geographers use the term space in three ways. First, space to breathe – that is space as a mental construct. Secondly, what teenagers might call their own space – that is space as a lived space. Thirdly, space as land for sale – that is space as a physical form. Each of these has a part to play in our lives.

The poet Brendan Kennelly identifies the significance of each of these concepts of space in 'Clearing a Space':

> A man should clear a space for himself
> Like Dublin city on a Sunday morning
> About six o'clock.
> Dublin and myself are rid of our traffic then
> And I'm walking.
>
> Houses are solitary and dignified
> Streets are adventures
> Twisting in and out and up and down my mind.
> The river is talking to itself
> And doesn't care if I eavesdrop.
>
> No longer cluttered with purpose
> The city turns to the mountains
> And takes time to listen to the sea.
> I witness all three communing in silence
> Under a relaxed sky.
>
> Bridges look aloof and protective.
> The gates of the park are closed
> Green places must have their privacy too.
> Office-blocks are empty, important and a bit
> Pathetic, if they admitted it!
>
> The small hills in this city are truly surprising
> When they emerge in that early morning light.

Nobody has ever walked on them,
They are waiting for the first explorers
To straggle in from the needy north.

And squat down there this minute
In weary legions
Between the cathedral and the river.
At the gates of conquest, they might enjoy a deep
Uninterrupted sleep.

To have been used so much, and without mercy,
And still to be capable of rediscovering
In itself the old nakedness
Is what makes a friend of the city
When sleep has failed.

I make through that nakedness to stumble on my own,
Surprised to find a city is so like a man.
Statues and monuments check me out as I pass
Clearing a space for myself the best I can,
One Sunday morning, in the original sun, in Dublin.[5]

How do humans develop a sense of space? Are we born with it
or is it acquired? If we look at ourselves as simply being part of the
animal kingdom then our space is inherited – it is genetic and in
our nature. Some writers like Ardrey,[6] Morris[7] and Lorenz[8] argue
that human spatiality is largely innate and inherited. There would
be clear benefits of such a genetic transfer. Space provides social
organization and stability for animals and could do the same for
humans.

The alternative view, as written about by Hall,[9] is that we learn
about space from the culture groups to which we belong. This view
emphasizes an ability to transfer spatial knowledge on an environmental basis. These opposing views are often referred to as the
nature/nurture arguments on spatial ability.

Rejection of the nature argument poses a major problem. Our evolutionary background cannot be completely discarded. It is reasonable to assert, however, that the environments within which we grow are of primary importance. If I were pushed as to which of the two views – nature or nurture – to choose, I would choose nurture. The fact that children and adults operate so differently in a spatial sense suggests such behaviour is learned.

Much of our knowledge about how children learn about space comes from the work of Jean Piaget. His book *The Child's Conception of Space*[10] was published nearly half a century ago. Many of his ideas have stood the test of time. He seemed to suggest that spatial intelligence was a different form of intelligence. Piaget argued that all studies of human thought must begin with the individual who is attempting to make sense of the world. Howard Gardner, in his book *Frames of Mind*,[11] maintains, 'There is persuasive evidence for the existence of several relatively autonomous human intelligences.' One of these is spatial intelligence. Gardner suggests that Western civilization places a heavy emphasis on two of the other intelligences – the logical/mathematical and the linguistic. Other societies – for example, island cultures in the Pacific – value spatial intelligence to a greater degree.

It would be interesting to combine Piaget's thoughts about making sense of the world with Gardner's recognition of spatial intelligence. Geography can act as a prism and as a focus for such ideas.

As stated, geography is concerned with the study of Earth space. Geographers differentiate between spaces that move and spaces that are fixed. Personal spaces move. As you sit reading this book, you have personal space around you. When you move, your space moves with you.

Space has many uses. It helps us, literally, to be people. It preserves our individuality and our privacy. We are not aware of our personal space unless somebody else invades it. Our personality affects our personal space. Imagine a party scene where extroverts and introverts meet. The extrovert flits in and out of everybody's space. The introvert jealously guards the little bit of space he or she has. Moods and expectations matter. Friendlier people tend to stand close together in space while formal business transactions tend to be conducted at a more removed level of space.

The situations we find ourselves in also matter. Imagine going to an important football match or other such sporting event. The entrances and the exits are jammed. Nobody seems to mind having space invaders around. In fact, it gives rise to much good-natured banter. Though packed into a relatively small space, people do not feel crowded. They tolerate less space and do so because they are in a setting where less space is expected.

On the other hand, it is sometimes possible to feel crowded in open spaces, such as a beach, and where there are relatively few people. We can measure density. We cannot measure the feeling of being crowded. That happens in our minds and, like most negative psychological constructs, it is notoriously difficult to come to terms with. A physical lack of space is neither good nor bad in itself. If we feel crowded, however, the sensation is almost always negative.

Cultures vary in how they deploy space. The contrast in the spatial behaviour of people from Mediterranean countries and those from more Northern European countries is quite fascinating. Is it due to the sun and the climate? Is it because people from the Mediterranean countries spend far more time out of doors? Teenagers especially are much more casual and assured in how they use their personal spaces in Mediterranean countries. We are improving here in Ireland. Older Irish people still tend to be more reserved, while younger people are far freer in how they engage with the world.

Regardless of where we come from and of our stage in life, we all have rules about what is and is not appropriate. It is intriguing to see people protecting their privacy and space on crowded buses and trains, especially at rush hour. They preoccupy themselves with newspapers and books. Quite often, they do not lift their heads until journey's end. These defence mechanisms create a sense of detachment for people when their personal space is lessened and slightly threatened. It is even more striking when an individual on a bus or train tries to read a neighbour's reading material, invading the personal space barrier represented by the newspaper. Often the offended traveller adopts a further defence mechanism and closes the paper even more tightly around the body. Rush-hour travellers also avoid eye contact, eliminating any possible gesture that could be interpreted as an invitation for conversation.

In these strategies to buy spatial privacy, we try to maintain a sense of self-identity. In towns and cities we come into contact with large numbers of people on a daily basis. The more private we manage to be, the more likely we are to control those we interact with. We are saving energy – psychic energy.

It is also interesting to observe the way we drop our guards on occasions. In extreme weather, such as heavy snow, a far friendlier atmosphere prevails between people in the spaces they occupy. They begin to say hello. They might even speak with strangers. But when the snow melts, they retreat again behind their walls.

People tend to defer hugely to public figures in terms of the space allowed them. Are they regarded as needing more space because they have a spatial aura around them saying, 'Keep out'? Or is a stored memory activated from our more primitive past in which smaller creatures yield space to larger, more important animals? Again, the nature/nurture debate is announced.

Teenagers often speak of their 'own space', tending not to differentiate between, say, their bedroom spaces that they regard as sacrosanct, and their personal spaces that move with them. When we use the word space in contexts like this, we describe what is called lived space, and here there is clearly an overlap between spaces that move and spaces that are fixed.

Traditionally, geographers have always studied fixed spaces, usually called areas or territories – perhaps, at times, to the exclusion of equally important mobile spaces such as personal space.

Some studies of personal space have been conducted at a microspatial level and tell us much about how we function as people. How many directions for journeys in Ireland seem to involve pubs? The pub is central to Irish cultural life, but this is only part of the explanation. Other factors may be equally important. Pubs tend to be hard to miss – they are generally housed in bigger buildings than normal. They are usually named. In addition, they are usually located in well-chosen places – what geographers would call strategic locations – where we make navigational decisions. Pubs, therefore, are ideal cues for triggering decisions about the directions and distances that make up our journeys.

When people leave one place and go to another they do not behave randomly. They use maps that they carry around in their minds. These mental maps contain signals telling people where to turn, how far to go before they turn again, and so on, until they reach their destination. Places make a visual impact on the mind and these make up a large part of the stored mental maps. More subtle aspects of the spatial environment also feed into these maps. Sounds may register. Passing trains, running water and heavily trafficked roads may all contribute to our decision-making process. Smells may also be significant but they tend to leave their mark for all the wrong reasons. Our mental maps are extremely personal. Yet, if we tease out their components and compare them with other people's maps, there are considerable overlaps. As a species we share many of the spatial cues stored in our minds.

We cannot store all of the information that spaces hit us with. We need to be selective and discard large chunks of it. Reading any space is much like reading a piece of written text; as little as 20 per cent of it registers but that is usually quite enough to allow us to operate within our spatial environments. If we find that our map is not working, we change the information we have stored, feeding it back into our mental maps and then, hopefully, we operate in a more successful manner.

It is instructive to watch people constantly trying to improve decision-making strategies for their journeys. In recent years many roads running through residential housing estates have had ramps put down on them to deter, or at least slow down, the 'rat runners' who divert through them. Earth space is clearly a finite quantity when it comes to squeezing extra cars onto already busy roads and streets.

How does our spatial learning, information and behaviour help us develop life-spaces and lived spaces as people? Some features seem to be specific to some groups of people. Others seem to be more universally applicable.

'When in Rome, do as the Romans' appears to be sound and sensible advice adopted by generations of people. It also describes the very individual nature of the lives and living spaces of different culture groups. Eric Erikson,[12] the psychoanalyst and anthropologist, regards humans as relatively plastic and pliable animals. In his analysis, they depend heavily on learned as opposed to instinctive behaviour, and become obsessively attached to their own native tribal cultures. It may well be that territorial spacing helps cultures to evolve in the way biological species do. Certain characteristics appear and develop in particular spatial environments, partly because people adapt to that environment, and partly because an actual culture develops and emerges over a period of time.

Other life-spaces are more universal. If we begin literally at home, we have the first layer of space – familial space, often marked by boundaries such as walls or fences. There is clearly a legal basis to the privacy that people can enjoy inside these boundaries. People make their homes; they modify them and gain greatly from being 'homed'. One of the most revealing ways of looking at the positive aspects of having such a space is to think of the alternative – being homeless.

People personalize their home-spaces by creating gardens and by painting their homes in a variety of colours. Grey – the colour we most associate with Irish winters, can at least be tempered by bright and vibrant colours to give home-spaces the stamp of individuality and personality. The Irish are slightly anarchical when it comes to reconciling, or perhaps not reconciling, their own colour choices with those of their neighbouring spaces, painting blues side-by-side with greens and many other colours of the rainbow. It is a way of making spaces our own. Irish planners are slow to be prescriptive, and people create large-scale, multi-coloured pictures that seem to jump off the canvas provided by the landscape.

Analysts now observe that many people see their cars as a logical extension of their home-space. We drive around protected by a ring of steel and it forms a space within which we can feel safe and sometimes, unfortunately, aggressive. Road-rage is very much linked to perceived ownership of a little bit of road space for a little bit of time. Disputed spaces do not just exist between countries.

If we move outwards from the home, we encounter a series of concentric zones with which and within which we interact. Neighbourhood spaces may be urban or rural, with the latter becoming more and more urbanized as time goes by. These spaces have their own personalities and have been well documented in Irish literature.

John B. Keane's play *The Field* wonderfully captures the importance of territory and points to the contrast between rural and urban spaces in the voice of Bull McCabe: 'That field is mine! Remember that! I'll pay a fair price. God Almighty! 'Tis a sin to cover grass and clover with concrete.'[13]

Within the rural or the urban we may also have our economic spaces – the places where we work and our recreational spaces – the places where we relax and rest. We also relate to many other critical layers of space – political, social and cultural. Counties provide us with further layers of identity and belonging. Our national space again gives us membership of a setting whose uniqueness appeals to us at many levels – not least attachment to known and familiar places and spaces.

Geographers are clearly interested in large-scale, fixed spaces such as countries and continents, which formed much of the geography that we learned in primary and second-level schools. Macro-spatial studies of large units of territory contrast sharply with the more micro-spatial analysis of personal space and mental maps.

Territoriality delineates boundaries, borders and contested spaces: the Middle East is one such instance, so too is Kashmir between India and Pakistan. In Northern Ireland, the so-called peace lines separate community spaces closely monitored by the people who live in them.

Globalization has its supporters and, as we have seen at several recent G8 and EU summit meetings, its critics. Regardless of what side of the fence we are on, or even if we claim to be sitting on it, globalization is changing the spaces around us. Ireland has benefited hugely from it in economic terms but is vulnerable to global downturns that seem removed from our control. Globalization also polarizes the world we live in, as the rich become richer, the poor poorer.

The world around us is changing, and doing so more rapidly than at any other point of human history. The space within our world cannot change, but the ways we use it can. Absolute space remains the same but the relativity between units of this space is changing profoundly. We live in a shrinking world in which travel is easier, cheaper and faster. Large cities and economies are being fragmented, the division between rural and urban becoming increasingly blurred, and people are seeking attachment to more human scales of existence.

The geographer David Harvey characterizes post-modernity as an era of 'acceleration in time and space compression'.[14] At one level that sounds like science fiction. The reality, however, is as Harvey describes it. We live in what might be described as the start of virtual space – with global forces bringing every kind of change and perhaps also greater similarity between places and far less particularity in our spaces.

Towards the end of *Finnegans Wake*, James Joyce wonders what it would be like to be lost at sea:

> Where are we at all? and whenabouts in the name of space?
> I don't understand. I fail to say.
> I dearsee you too.[15]

We could well pose the very same questions about the Earth spaces we inhabit. We first need to know where we are, and then move onwards to where we would like to be.

2. Change and Renewal in Issues of Place, Identity and the Local

Patrick Duffy

In 1936 my father attended seventy-seven dances in his home parish in Monaghan. Some were impromptu dances at home when neighbours came in or cousins arrived for summer holidays. They were mainly house dances, held in kitchens or outbuildings, with a smattering held in local parish halls.

His diaries chronicled the unfolding daily life of the local community and illustrated the intensity of life at local level from his perspective as a young man in the 1930s and '40s. This was a world of walking and talking, cycling, visiting, churchgoing, football meetings and dances, with people working in fields and farms and bogs – all within a fairly limited range in the parish. There were important local linkages with the outside too – fair-days, football matches and 'the pictures' in Castleblayney, which were accessible by bike, bus or hackney car. For travel further afield in this largely car-less countryside, frequent bus services between Monaghan or Castleblayney connected with the train station and Dublin or Belfast.

It was a world where the intensity of *local* life was in striking contrast with today. Now, the orbit of activity is much more widely spread out. A degree of what we could call 'de-localization' has accompanied the deepening globalization of recent decades. The house dance in the 1930s, for instance, was one measure of the depth of local space and local allegiance and the connections of family and place. Clearly in situations of such local social life, marriages were still strongly localized. In my grandfather's generation, in the early decades of the twentieth century, most people in the countryside married within a cluster of townlands in their own parish. Jump forward a generation or two and as car mobility increased, so the 'marriage distance' gradually expanded, so that today's national and international marriage and relationship networks reflect linkages with a much wider world.

Anthropologists and folklorists have long recorded all these indicators of the localness of living in the Irish countryside – reflected in things like the céilidhe houses, dances, the 'joins' or mutual aid co-operation and harvest meithealls between farms, and the station masses, all of which dwindled away to insignificance from the 1960s onwards. Beyond these social manifestations of locality, material life also reflected the primacy of local self-sufficiency. Traditional or 'vernacular' houses, shops and outbuildings, for example, were built from local materials (of thatch or slate, stone, clay or timber) in distinctive local idioms and were another measure of localness, which contrasts with today's standardized bungalows, lawns and leyland cypress hedges. The enhanced value that attaches to surviving traditional cultural artifacts today is a reflection of the distinctiveness of such lost local legacies.

The sometime poet of rural life Patrick Kavanagh was the great apologist for the local and his poem 'Epic' is its celebration. Important places, he insisted, were local.

> I have lived in important places, times
> When great events were decided, who owned
> That half a rood of rock, a no-man's land

> Surrounded by our pitchfork-armed claims.
> I heard the Duffys shouting 'Damn your soul'
> And old McCabe stripped to the waist, seen
> Step the plot defying blue-cast steel –
> 'Here is the march along these iron stones'
> That was the year of the Munich bother. Which
> Was more important? I inclined
> To lose my faith in Ballyrush and Gortin
> Till Homer's ghost came whispering to my mind
> He said : I made the Iliad from such
> A local row. Gods make their own importance.[1]

Kavanagh's celebration of the local was written about 1930s Monaghan. He was ahead of his time in unashamedly and publicly celebrating local places at a time when the 'City' and urban places either here or overseas were the principal markers of modernity and progress. Ironically, like tens of thousands in following decades, Kavanagh himself abandoned Ballyrush and Gortin for Dublin. It would seem that when local life and culture were most vibrant, pressures to change – from the outside and from the inside – were increasing rapidly. Urbanization was impinging on rural areas from the outside, emigration was haemorrhaging them from within. And local communities themselves were uninterested, indeed ashamed, of any label of localness, which often meant backwardness and deprivation – except for Kavanagh perhaps.

The following discussion engages with the idea of the local in two ways. Firstly, it looks at the meaning of the local through ideas about a sense of place, identity and belonging, memory and home. It might be suggested, for instance, that these local spaces are *placeful*, instead of some localities which might be characterized as rootless and *placeless*. Secondly, it examines how this meaning of the local is read and translated through a territorial template of material places. Here we look essentially at local space as *landscapes* – of fields and farms, roads and houses, townlands and parishes and, indeed, as streets and neighbourhoods, named and claimed by local communities to make sense to them.

We can summarize some meanings of the local in terms that are familiar to many. The local is often our first place, a place of first memories and first lessons in the importance of space and place. Memory is embedded in place, laden with associations for family, neighbour and community. *Here* is where I grew up, *there* is where I went to school, *there* is the last resting place of family or ancestors. Growing old is like climbing a hierarchy and knowing a range of ever more distant locations and places. Earliest memories are of learning the first practical exercises in scale, location, distance, a place-anchored experience that has been described graphically for rural localities by Seamus Heaney:

> The rooms where we come to consciousness, the cupboards we open as toddlers, the shelves we climb up to ... the secret spots we come upon in our earliest solitudes out of doors, the haunts of our first explorations in outbuildings and fields at the verge of our security ... At such moments we have our first inklings of pastness and find our physical surroundings invested with a wider and deeper dimension. [2]

Heaney's is a very particular rendition of the power of place, especially local place, in our lives, and expresses a kind of organic link between people and place, where time and space are inextricably interwoven in memory and experience, 'the replayed shards of feeling arising from a particular place'. [3]

The local is also about community and belonging, a place 'where everybody knows your name' (the yearning for belonging in the ultimately placeless community of the city pub in *Cheers*), where identity, home, kin and friendship relations are important. As Carson Mc Cullers said: 'to know who you are, you have to have a place to come from'. [4]

Traditionally, and especially in rural communities, there was a high level of familiarity with the topographies of place and people.

Both were known intimately and homely placenames and nick-names were manifestations of this familiar knowledge. This is a place of belonging celebrated in John Denver's song which invokes three powerful words – home, place and belong – in one refrain: 'Take me home country roads, to the place I belong.'

In this way, landscape becomes place through interaction with its occupying community, which helps it acquire a depth of social meaning, and helps to embed it in the community's consciousness and memory. Homesickness and nostalgia are often associated with leaving such well-*known* places, being displaced to new and unfamiliar landscape associations.[5]

The local is also about roots and continuity in the relationship between people and place, for example, being 'born in the same room as my father and grandfather'. This is a frequent reminiscence of many people born in the Irish countryside in the early decades of the twentieth century. In these cases, past time is important, and memories are handed down, connected to places and landscapes shared with foreparents. Familiar lives have passed through these landscapes, therefore, indeed have helped to build, plant, to make and shape them. This making-and-shaping has frequently featured in the imagery of poets and artists, such as John Hewitt:

> Once alien here my fathers built their house,
> claimed, drained, and gave the land the shapes of use ...

Or more recently, Willie Doherty's republican reflection on the stone walls of the West:

> They represent the blood and sweat of countless generations.
> For all this
> land is 'made' land, hand made.[6]

And so local place is culturally significant and deeply territorial. It is about material physical space, where activity space or 'taking part in the landscape', for instance, is most intense. This is the space that we travel up and down, back and forth, every day – routine space where the tangible form and texture of landscape, like houses and buildings, fields and hedges and road networks, are most familiar, most intimately named and known.

The significance of the material landscape is best seen in the search for roots, for personal and family identity, in a physical place – a common quest especially by visiting Americans to Ireland wanting to see where their foreparents came from. RTÉ's *Sunday Miscellany* some years ago described a journey which two brothers from Manchester made to visit the village their grandmother and her small children had left in Romania at the beginning of the twentieth century.[7] They were motivated by their father's story about the long journey across Europe and the place he dimly remembered as a child. In describing their return to Romania, the brothers demonstrated the significance of local landscape in our lives: they 'discovered' their identity, for example, by seeing and sensing this forgotten place – their grandfather's grave, the village and its unpaved streets, the railway where their grandmother had started her journey, the roadside villages and the fields where she had worked almost a century earlier, all of them physical expressions of this revisited landscape. It was a feeling akin to meeting long-lost relatives who had lived in and moved through this place. Touching the very stones and earth and the furniture of their ancestral landscape was an emotional experience like people seeing a new-found birth mother for the first time.

In what ways are these local spaces translated into places? We can talk about a territorial hierarchy of places in the Irish countryside – from field and farm to townland and parish, nestling around small towns, up to the county and beyond, which largely remains valid as a spatial frame of reference. We can think of it as a sort of lattice of places that are part of the vocabulary of the local landscape. Just as the text of a book cannot be read until we know the words, so the townland and parish are part of the vocabulary for knowing the local countryside. How could we survive in this countryside, let alone understand where we live, if it did not have townlands, parishes, counties, not to mention fields and farms?

Agents of 'localization' work through this territorial lattice: postal addresses, for instance, are by townland. There are more than 60,000 townlands in Ireland – there are 1800 in Monaghan, 1000 in Armagh and so on, a vast and complex geometry of little local places. The Post Office and the postman or woman continue as important agents of local social interconnection. The postman on his bicycle used to be a daily presence linking every household in the community. In 1936 he was even delivering the mail on Christmas Day. Today's deliveries are more impersonally made by van over more extensive postal districts. Current proposals to close local post offices, in the interests of efficiency, are popularly perceived as hitting at the very heart of locality. The post office is regarded as the vital link between the local and the national.

The Church operates through the townland-parish framework. In the 1930s the Catholic Church played a fundamental role in cementing the local community together, with a multiplicity of well-attended services throughout the year – benedictions, holy hours, novenas, devotions, stations of the cross. And Sunday masses, where lists of names of people and townlands, regularly intoned as familiar badges of identity, were public affirmations of the primacy of local place and people. These were especially highlighted in funeral 'offerings' and quarterly collections of monies for the parish, and the mispronunciation of the dialect of local placenames by visiting clergy was an amusing demonstration of the 'outsider' status of visitors. Social studies of rural communities in the 1940s–'70s frequently zoned in on the significance of class and gender relations expressed within and outside the church: Kavanagh's *Tarry Flynn* was a percipient observer of these geographies in the 1930s. The modern decline in churchgoing must have important ramifications for the meaning of locality in this sense.

Fair days and markets in towns were the traditional meeting places of localities engaging with the outside world of dealers, buyers and sellers on a regular, but sometimes infrequent basis. Of course, towns play an even more important role today in the social and economic life of the local places surrounding them, one which reflects a more diversified rural community and urban economy, as well as a convergence of urban and rural lifestyles.

But the primary template of locality in the Irish countryside must be the farm and field. Even though the numbers of farms (and farmers) are rapidly reducing, the reality is that almost all of the space of rural areas is still owned by farmers – and their farms are subdivided into the most familiar feature of the local landscape – the tens of thousands of fields. The look, shape and texture of local places are very much a product of fields and their hedges, walls and fences. All the changes taking place in rural housing today, all the growth in 'non-locals' or 'blow-ins' in rural populations, are happening within the landscape spaces of farms and fields. What is a new house site in the countryside but part of a field sectioned off, sold on and built upon?

An important measure of localness is the way in which local places were and are named, intimately and in great detail, by their occupants. This process applied equally to city areas, though here street naming was usually the prerogative of developers or Local Authorities. Children in city neighbourhoods, however, were adept at naming the minute local spaces where they played: in Ballyfermot, before the city engulfed many of the open spaces, there were the Backers, the Gaels, the Naller, the Ranch, the Californian Hills, the Tarmac, many of which over time were absorbed into the official lexicon of placenames.[8] Such informal local naming practices were an expression of the closeness of links between people and place at the local level.

Apart from the 60,000 plus townland names, there are tens of thousands of minor names in the countryside, mostly 'unofficial' names known only at the local and familial level, many of which are now slipping out of local memory. Probably the most universal process was the naming of the fields by farm families, usually labelling the landscape by its location *vis-à-vis* each farmhouse or farm. Thus, for example, common patterns would be the Far Field, the Top Field, the Bottoms, or we find them named by local qualities – the Furry field, Well Field, Brick Field, the Three-Cornered Field, the Sixteen Acres, Above-the-House, Below-the-House and so on. In parts of the West of Ireland, many are in Irish, like Garraí Mhór, Garra Iochtar, Lug na Misceáin, Poll na Hinse, Páirc an Tobar. Field names can be seen, perhaps, as representing a key to reading and understanding a very local world, which is largely inaccessible to outsiders, where the shape and aspect and size and individuality of the fields, intimately known to their owners, are identified at this grassroots spatial level.[9] Along the seashores and lakeshores, where local agricultural land uses blend into marine or estuarine activity, there is a rich legacy of names on every rock, inlet and local landmark. The townland of Portacloy in north Mayo, for instance, has dozens of such names: Barr na Spince, Leac na mBáirneach, Cladach na Cathaoireach, Na Gearrachaí Beaga, Slis na gCriosach, Uaigh na Madaí, Gob a' Chóthra etc.[10]

Townlands, which are fossilized property units from the six-teenth and seventeenth centuries whose evolving names were recorded as 'official' places by the Ordnance Survey in the 1830s and '40s, are fundamental spaces of identity. There is a poetry and rhythm in their names, which is redolent of local dialect and place, frequently reached for in Kavanagh's writing and aptly summed up in the words of the poet John Montague:

> Beragh, Carrickmore,
> Pomeroy, Fintona –
> placenames that sigh
> like a pressed melodeon ...[11]

The question is, how many of these expressions of locality are still valid? How relevant are they for many of us and for many places today? How have they been altered? To what extent have we been 'de-localized'?

These broad expressions of local space show variations in meaning and significance from place to place in different parts of the country. While a universal process of globalization has been taking place, there is also variety in the way local places are experiencing change, especially with the arrival of more and more 'non-locals' to open out places – which must be one of the biggest contrasts with the 1930s, '40s and '50s, when 'local worlds' were dominant and largely self-sufficient socially, culturally and perhaps economically.

So there are different manifestations of 'locality' in the West, the Midlands, and areas of open countryside, which contrast with other areas like the commuter zones around towns and suburban areas which are more open to outsiders, more fluid socially and less integrated locally perhaps. The population census for 2002 shows Dublin's commuter belt expanding far into the midland region, with assumptions being made about long commuter trips to work in the capital and limited linkages to localities. But emerging evidence suggests that a re-localization of these new communities is taking place. Ratoath is a rapidly expanding suburban community 30 km north of Dublin city centre. Its 'village character, country feel, friendliness and sense of community' endure as strong components in its emerging sense of place and the local orientation of its population. Most of its social, recreational and shopping activity is focused on a fairly constrained local area, though one that is strongly car-based.[12]

One of the easiest ways to understand the significance of locality and place and its importance for identity is to contrast social and economic patterns and processes today with how they were a couple of generations ago. Looking back helps to provide a kind of benchmark against which to measure the nature of change and the meaning of something like local place and identity today.

In what ways has the organic connection with place and locality decreased over the decades? The widespread housing in rural areas today (nearly half of all new houses, for example, are being built in the countryside) would seem to indicate living, thriving localities, hustling and bustling with people. Indeed this is the case that is made by localities seeking to open up planning processes. But how many today in such local areas have a local allegiance or a local commitment? To what extent are 'dormitory' suburbanized countrysides developing in many areas?

My father's daily journey to the school where he taught was by bike in the 1930s. During severe winter weather he came, in his own words, 'straight home'. But during the spring and summer months, his return journey frequently took a longer and more roundabout route, as he 'called into' houses, or more often, as he met people on the road and stopped for a chat.

In fact, it was very much a pedestrian world as it had been for centuries, where the scale of community was defined in walking distances, 'shank's mare', where meeting and talking were an important part of the connectedness of the local. The world of *Tarry Flynn* in the 1930s, or any other novelist's representation of the rural at that time, is one of local sounds, of people, animals, horse carts trundling along roads and lanes, with time to talk. It was also, of course, often a world of intolerable intrusion by watching and gossip, a notable feature of literary representations of the time.

The hand wave or salute to passing traffic in remoter rural areas today is a remnant of the passing greeting and leisurely chat of the pre-car era. The car and later the television isolated people in their local spaces. More than a quarter-century ago Hugh Brody commented on the significant growth of 'privacy' in rural households: the traditional role of neighbours' comings and goings was being replaced by a modern emphasis on individually private, isolated and socially independent households.[13]

Today, at another extreme in time and space, we can see how motorwayed landscapes signify the altered relationships between people and place, cutting through or sweeping across the grain of the local, where instead of walking or cycling or driving in and through local spaces, we are swept by and over them. In these instances, there is increasing disconnection from local spaces, which are unrecognized places on a blur of signposts. As one commentator has remarked about such landscapes, 'the M25 doesn't really exist – there is no "there" there ... the road and its borders are metaphors of circulation and containment, dreams of escape and inevitable return'.[14] The ultimate in placelessness are the reductionist landscapes identified by numbered motorway junctions: where Celbridge will be identified with Junction 3 on the M4, Duleek with Junction 8 on the M1.

Our 'activity space' is much larger than it ever was. The huge rise in car ownership means that people now range over longer distances to work, to shop, to play – well beyond local horizons. And local commitment to place is more elusive and ambiguous. 'Where are you from?', an inquiry which is laden with enormous social as well as geographical meaning, may soon become as meaningless as it is in many new world landscapes where a highly mobile population renders it irrelevant.

Some have referred to a process of 'de-localization' taking place, where there is a clear disconnection from locality. The internet and multiple television channels, for example, seem to have made the world dominantly global – thereby eclipsing the local entirely. One reflection of this may be the way the American television and movie industries are leading to a global convergence of cultures, reflected in a universalizing of values, tastes and lifestyles. Popular/rock music's global culture knows no bounds. At a more superficial level, it may also be leading towards a smoothing of regional accents among the young. More and more people may now also identify with non-existent places and spaces, 'virtual communities' in cyberspace, which override all boundaries of locality and render the local irrelevant.

And can we talk of local areas in Ireland, like parts of the US, which are perceived as 'placeless'? There are, no doubt, suburban landscapes where rapid changes have taken place, where there is no connection with the landscape by its inhabitants. These places have little meaning, no memories, no name even. A sort of 'landscape amnesia' prevails.

Perhaps there are examples of this too in many rural landscapes in Ireland which have been depopulated and abandoned and which have reverted to wilderness, haunted by the slumbering ghosts of people who once lived and loved there. In the West there are such lost landscapes, forgotten fields among the whins and heather and lazy beds of the mountains.

Even at this most local level in the hierarchy of places in Ireland, changing farm practices have reduced the knowledge of local space. Tractored agriculture has little use for field names bestowed when these local spaces were ploughed and harvested for hours or days on end with horse or scythe. Rural work patterns have changed relationships between people and their locality. As Michael Viney has observed in west Mayo: 'Flocks of sheep that, twenty years ago, were driven past the gate by a man and a dog now proceed routinely ahead of the farmer's car (the dog, on occasion, riding in the passenger seat). The end of manual turf-cutting ... has cancelled a whole seasonal procession between the townlands and the bog'.[15] In County Down, three generations of one family have shown a successively contracting knowledge of townland place-names in their district, with the grandfather knowing a wide range of townlands, while the grandson was only aware of his own town-land name.[16] So it would seem there is a much reduced connect-edness today with the landscape of farms and fields and laneways.

So we could ask – are local places important anymore ? Do they matter today? Our world today has stretched over other spaces and experiences and, as Seamus Heaney has noted, 'We are no longer innocent, we are no longer just parishioners of the local.'[17] Although our relationship with the local has been irreversibly altered in the past couple of generations, he suggests that we still need to be grounded in a local dimension, in a sense of place.

Perhaps associations with local space are more complex today. There is still a need for grounded placeness. We still have to belong some*where*. Is it just that the kind of belonging may be different now? Social change inevitably means revisions or modifications to the relationship as reflected, for instance, in emerging communities like Ratoath in the metropolitan fringe of Dublin.

It does seem that we are now seeing a turnaround and a resurgence of interest in the diversity and the particularity of the local – the ordinary, the everyday and the homely in terms of living space. The writer Dermot Healy said, 'Now places and dialects are opening out again to the world.'

So maybe we are seeing a 're-localization' taking place? This turnaround is reflected in local studies and history courses, in rising interest in local landscapes as reflected in the best-selling *Atlas of the Irish Rural Landscape* published in 1997, and also the evident rise in local heritage tourism.

Ironically the outsider or tourist gaze may have stimulated a response by locals that has helped to redefine their relationship with their locality. Many townlands in west Mayo and Connemara now have their names prominently displayed on carved stones by the roadside – a pride in place that has been energized by tourism and an interest in heritage. And a contrast to fifty or more years ago when townlands and intimate countrysides were hidden places known only to locals and of little interest to anyone else.

In a preface to a book on Ulster townlands, Seamus Heaney refers to his own personal feelings about the idea of the local townland when as a young man he read John Hewitt's poem 'The Townland of Peace' in Magherafelt library. The very sight of the word 'townland' appearing, as he said, in a 'fume of affection and recognition', on the 'official paper' of a book was a public affirmation of the local landscape and sense of place. He talked about a 'premonition of demarginalisation' passing over him – the townland coming out of the margins and into the light.[18] This is why the abolition of townlands in Northern Ireland by the Post Office authorities over twenty years ago was resisted in so many places. It was an example of the erosion of local identities by a bigger 'global' technology – computerized postal codes – which struck at the heart of local identities.

So, interest in local landscape is emerging almost as an antidote to the placelessness and facelessness of global culture. Local cultural differences that are grounded in local experiences are now increasingly prized. There is a new awarenesss of the value of the inherited artifacts and landscapes which surround us. No doubt commercial tourism has now commodified heritage, as well as the 'local' culture and the local landscape. And the EU actively supports the maintenance of cultural diversity, as it is reflected, for example, in local landscapes and places. The implementation of the Rural Environment Protection Scheme throughout the country is a validation of changing popular attitudes to local landscapes and places, and the radical reconstruction of the CAP will significantly alter relationships between rural farm population and landscape in many localities.

One reflection of the continuing importance of the local has been the enduring popularity of the GAA. Indeed the GAA from its beginnings attached its organizational structures to the architecture of parishes, townlands and counties, and probably helped to preserve and promote a local sense of place over the decades. Many of today's Gaelic sports clubs are using the World Wide Web to consolidate their local allegiances beyond the bounds of their localities and in newly-emerging suburban and ex-urban communities like Ratoath, it is a crucially important local integrating agent.

Local Radio in the past ten years has also been one of the most significant agents of local identity and local renewal. Ironically, the 'wireless', which in the 1930s, '40s and '50s helped to open up localities to the national world beyond their horizons, is now helping, through local stations, to nurture local identities. Local advertising, news and information (including funeral arrangements, a lasting mark of local commitment), music and requests, have significant listener allegiances. Local newspapers too have consolidated their position as badges of identity. Many are now on the web, so that Mayo people in Chicago or downtown San Francisco can drop into the *Mayo News* and keep up with local affairs back home. Although music is a universal global language, changing by the year, the vibrancy of traditional music is a reflection of a resurgence of the local. Nurtured by Comhaltas Ceoilteoiri Éireann, Feiseanna, etc. over the years, it is now thriving in a commercial and community sense.

We have almost certainly come full circle through all the big changes – we've probably seen a reaction against the placelessness of the global and a search for the connectedness of the local. And local cultures are taking what they find useful in the outside world (like modern technology) and using it to further their own ends. While it (seemingly) reduces the local, it can also nurture and reinforce it.

The Irish Folklore Commission realized the importance of the local and how rapidly changes to it were taking place as long ago as the 1930s. Its scores of collectors spent lifetimes recording the little bits and pieces of life that add up to the texture and meaning of local places and landscapes, which now form a valuable archive of Irish folklife. Like Kavanagh's invocation of Ballyrush and Shancoduff, they focused on the little things that their contemporaries took for granted or thought were unimportant. Time has told us how 'important' were the little places and how 'great' were the 'events' that happened there, manifested in pride in place, local settings of local communities, local culture, local building traditions, accents, dialects, music, all the marks of significance of locality and place. The 1938 Folklore Commission's Schools Collection, based on a successful formula of linking schoolchildren at the time with older inhabitants of the community, could probably not be replicated in the same way for most places today.[19] This is a measure of change and changing relationships in local community, landscape and allegiances in Ireland today. It is no coincidence that the National Museum of Country Life opened in 2001 in Castlebar, presenting the work of decades of collecting by the Folklore Commission and Folklore Department of University College Dublin. It is entirely appropriate that it should open at a time when the local life it recorded has slipped away, but when interest in locality has been revived and renewed.

3. Urban Dreams – Urban Nightmares

Ruth McManus

My mother has always stressed to me the importance of achieving perspective on any given situation. It was good advice to offer a geographer! By looking at something differently, it becomes revealed in a new way. I was reminded of this quite forcefully on a recent flight from Dublin Airport. As the aeroplane climbed, I could look down from the almost cloudless sky and see the city through new eyes. Gazing out the window, the stunning physical backdrop of the city provided by the mountains and the sea was clearly visible. In the middle distance was the city itself and the green fields of rural County Dublin were directly below. It certainly offered me a new perspective, both literally and metaphorically.

What particularly struck me that day, though, was the way in which we humans were creating new spaces in the urban environment. Although I felt that I knew the city, from previous study, field trips, reading and even the 'bird's eye' view available from close scrutiny of maps, my familiarity with the scene was being challenged by new development. Last time I looked, it seemed that the dramatic C-shaped ring of the M50 motorway had encircled the city, marking a boundary between the city and the countryside beyond. This clear delineation was no longer evident as, looking down, it was possible to make out new structures, mostly ware-houses, which had leap-frogged across the road and were eating up the green swards beyond. I have often heard cities described as a kind of monster, eating up the countryside. Now, here in Dublin, that monstrous tendency was quite visible, as the growing tentacles of the city reached out into the rural areas beyond. The green fields, bound by hedges, were being physically consumed by these new, low-rise buildings. In fact, what I was seeing was the creation of new urban space at the edge of the city.

This rather unattractive space – composed of the greyish blocks of the buildings, the greyish concrete of the new roads, and the brown of the soil which had been turned to make way for new foundations – contrasted very sharply with the green of the remaining fields. I began to wonder, as I looked down at this emerging scene, what sort of urban spaces are we creating? We seem to be blithely ploughing on – and that may be an unfortunate choice of verb, given the loss of countryside that is involved – while we are apparently oblivious to any meaningful consideration of the nature of space or place.

Urbanized Ireland

Irish people do not generally consider themselves to be urbanites. If you ask the average Dublin person where they come from, even those born in the city are quite likely to qualify the statement by saying that their parents are from Clare or that they always cheer for the Mayo football team. Few would actually claim to be city people, through and through.

Nevertheless, it is a fact that more people in Ireland live in towns and cities than in the countryside. Since the 1970s, the majority of Ireland's population has lived in urban areas, while the

2002 Census of Population shows that just over two-thirds of people (66.8 per cent) reside in towns. However, a recent study by Amárach Consulting has suggested that Irish people living in urban areas are not as happy as their rural counterparts.[1] This 'Goodness Indicator' measures quality of life on the basis of four key influences – happiness, family life, health and finances. Based on these indicators, it was suggested that people living in Ireland's urban areas have a lower quality of life than those in rural areas. People in Ireland's largest city, Dublin, ranked lowest of all.

Yet cities seem to offer all sorts of opportunities not found in other areas. Why else would people choose to live there? Remember Dick Whittington heading off for the 'bright lights' of London, where the streets were proverbially paved with gold? Many young country lads and lasses have travelled to cities such as Dublin or Cork with similar aspirations. Life in rural Ireland may have seemed dull and predictable, whereas there is a sort of vitality, a 'buzz', associated with urban areas. Maybe one of the problems being highlighted by the 'Goodness Indicator' is that we demand too much, that our expectations of life in the city are heightened. Maybe the reality of the city fails to live up to its image? Perhaps this result is a reflection more of dashed hopes, of fading dreams than of the urban spaces themselves.

In the time that I have been interested in cities, I have noticed an increasing tendency among people to discuss various aspects of urban life. Media coverage and day-to-day conversations frequently turn to questions relating to the shaping of Ireland's cities and towns. But such discussions are almost invariably couched in negativity – the problems of traffic, commuting, lack of planning, suburban sprawl and so on. In fact, what becomes apparent from such discussions is that we are creating spaces for cars, not people, and that our urban areas are felt to be badly planned and less than pleasant places to be in. People appear to feel helpless in the face of considerable urban change, yet tend to ignore their own participation, even complicity, in that change, in terms of their choice of transportation, type of home, and the myriad of lifestyle choices which have required this urban development to occur. Maybe, too, we need to start discussing the ways in which we can work to create urban spaces and places that are perceived in a more positive light.

Part of the reason for poor urban structure may be that we Irish have never really accepted that we can be both Irish and urban at the same time. If we think for a minute of the images that we have of ourselves and the ways in which we tend to project Irish culture to other people, it becomes clear that these images are couched in terms of rural nostalgia. The thatched cottage with the turf fire somehow appears more Irish than the suburban semi-detached house, even though statistically we are far more likely to be living in suburbia than in a rural idyll reminiscent of de Valera's speeches.

Cosy Communities and Urban Escapes

Talking of this rural nostalgia brings us to another of the problems we hear being discussed in relation to urban areas. This is the lack of 'community' and a sense of belonging, particularly in the larger towns and cities. 'Down the country' everybody knows your name, your business, where your forbears are buried. They may well know more about you than you might know about yourself. A community can be a support in times of crisis, but can also force conformity and acceptance of the status quo.

In urban areas, particularly in larger towns and cities, it is possible to become anonymous. For some, this is a frightening thought. Again the newspapers, or urban myth, will supply grizzly stories of fatal attacks or lonely deaths. These tales reinforce the prejudice against urban places – the city is seen as a dangerous place. Bad things happen in cities, whereas there is a perception of safety in rural areas, partly because they are generally less busy, less diverse and less anonymous. And yet, it can be argued that such perceptions are missing the point. One of the wonderful features of living in a larger place, at any rate, is the fact that you can *choose* to be anonymous, you can *feel* the excitement and dynamism of the urban space and interact in new ways as a result.

So anonymity can be an attractive notion, in that you can shape a new identity for yourself, create your own space, free of the trammels of tradition which might hold you back in a rural area. It becomes possible to walk down a street, browse the shops, do some shopping, without every move being noted and reported back to the entire community. Living in an urban context can be liberating. It might inspire you to uncover aspects of self which were kept repressed or hidden – an artistic side or, perhaps, the freedom to express one's sexual orientation. Sometimes, then, living in an urban area can be a rewarding experience or a release from the bounds of convention.

It is also important to realize that there is a sense of community in almost every urban area, but that it takes shape and is played out in different ways than in a rural place. People are not necessarily bound together because of where they live, as in a rural locale, but through other aspects of their lives; perhaps because of a common interest, place of work, leisure time activity, and so on. Community may thus arise more naturally, as a result of common bonds, and it may be possible for people to belong simultaneously to several overlapping communities. that reflect the various aspects of their lived experience. Although cities may appear to be large and confusing, every person will have their own 'activity space' within an urban area. This activity space includes the places you pass through every day on the way to work, to shop, to go to play sports, and so on. Within this space, you are likely to encounter familiar faces, people you nod to on the street, people you say hello to, people who become friends. Maybe what is different in urban places is the greater element of choice in the development of community. You can choose to belong, to get involved, to know your neighbours, or you can opt out. For some people, this *option* is one of the features that makes urban life most palatable, even desirable.

Poverty and In-Migration

Not everyone sees the city as a place of excitement, freedom and liberation. Such concepts may be overrated if you are living in an urban area without the means to enjoy its advantages. To a person trapped in the poverty cycle, living in a city may not hold out much in the way of opportunities. Differences become even more acute in an urban setting because of the juxtaposition of wealth and poverty which is an inevitable aspect of the capitalist city. Indeed, in an urban area you are more likely to be frustrated by seeing other people's affluence, while the cost of urban living tends to be higher than in rural places. This partly explains the success of the various rural resettlement schemes, which enable those reliant on social welfare payments to move to the countryside.

Despite some movement out of cities, however, the general tendency is for increasing numbers of people to move *into* urban areas. The world over, urban areas tend to attract newcomers, be they from the rural hinterland or from farther afield. One of the inevitable outcomes is a greater degree of diversity in cities and towns than in the countryside. People of varying ages, backgrounds, religious persuasions, ethnicities, social status and educational levels are generally mixing together in urban areas. In the past few years, Ireland has begun to experience ever greater levels of diversity, particularly in towns and cities, as increasing levels of prosperity and job opportunities have made this country an attractive destination for immigrants. In a sense, we are seeing our migration history come full circle. The greatest degree of rural to urban migration in Ireland began in the nineteenth century, particularly after the Great Famine of the 1840s. Many of our emigrants finally established themselves in the cities of Britain and North America. Now, with the increasingly globalized patterns of migration, we are receiving large numbers of immigrants, many of whom are fleeing poverty and seeking a better quality of life. These new immigrants have a great potential to enrich our culture and have already begun to create a visual imprint on some of the larger towns, where new shops and businesses are catering for a wide range of tastes.

Increasing ethnic diversity can, of course, lead to a number of outcomes. People may mix happily and take on aspects of each other's culture. Amsterdam's guidebooks, for example, generally recommend the visitor to eat a Rijstafel, a specialist Indonesian meal, while restaurants in the English towns of Bradford and Leicester serve some of the best curries in the world. Sometimes too, people get along by ignoring their differences, rather than embracing change and adapting. What we hear about most, though, is the potential for disharmony that arises from the differences which are most apparent in urban areas. Not too long ago, there were race-based riots in Oldham in the UK, while racially-motivated attacks in Irish urban areas appear to be on the increase.

Often the solution employed is one of segregation, of separating different groups out in space. At its most extreme, this may result in complete separation and subjugation, as in the apartheid townships of South Africa. The tactic employed by many governments and local authorities is to segregate populations through their housing policies, based largely on ability to pay, but also frequently on the basis of ethnicity. The rationale for segregation is to reduce the opportunity for conflict through mixing. But it is possible that segregation actually increases the potential for disharmony. Fear of the unknown can be far greater than distrust of a known group. Does the creation of ghettoes and no-go areas really make things better, or does it simply intensify the problem?

Reputation and the Naming of Spaces

Ghetto is a powerful, evocative word. Yet, increasingly in Ireland, we are hearing talk about the ghettoization that is supposedly occurring in our towns and, more especially, our cities. Despite the increasing discussion of new immigrants, most of the segregation which occurs in Ireland is based on socio-economic status and levels of educational attainment, rather than ethnicity. We seem very willing to label certain places and their inhabitants, generally in negative ways.

Everyone knows the names of the bad parts of any town or city, the areas on the 'wrong side of the tracks', the places where we are most likely to find a clustering of the disadvantaged members of society. Such areas get a bad reputation and it becomes difficult to shake this off. People living in these areas find themselves disadvantaged when they apply for jobs simply because of their addresses. Others find it difficult to get mortgages, because financial institutions are unwilling to invest in certain locations. The physical space, particularly housing, may not necessarily be substandard, but in the public imagination these are 'bad spaces' seen in a negative light. The reinforcement of stereotypes contributes to the negative cycle of disadvantage.

And yet, anyone who has worked in these so-called 'deprived' areas, will tell you of the extraordinary community spirit that often exists there. They will tell you of self-help groups and of a myriad of activities being undertaken by community activists. In many ways, such 'bad' areas have the very community attributes that are so desired by more affluent people. This in itself must be a challenge to the way in which urban spaces and their problems are perceived.

If you cannot move your physical location, at least you can rename that space. Think of the celebrated renaming of Windscale as Sellafield following the nuclear accident there. Less dramatically, when an area gains a certain reputation, local groups can some-

times pressurize the authorities to rename that place in an attempt
to lose the associated negative connotations. Most frequently, the
impetus will come from residents in private housing estates close
to public housing with a similar name who may petition for a name
change. Similarly, when An Post proposed changing the boundaries
of some postal districts on the south-side of Dublin city, locals
objected. They preferred to retain their original postal code, which
was seen to connote a certain social standing.

Perhaps of all these examples of the naming of spaces, the most
interesting is Dublin 4. At its simplest, Dublin 4 is a geographical
space, purely an area designated by the postal service to facilitate
the delivery of mail. What Dublin 4 *symbolizes* is far more important than the physical space, and actually quite different. Dublin 4
is a term used to represent a particular mind-set, generally the
more educated, middle-class, 'liberal' viewpoint. People talk and
write about Dublin 4 attitudes, even when these emanate from
journalists based in other locations. My own experience of the
'real' Dublin 4, when I lived in a house without central heating,
with rudimentary plumbing and a hazardous electrical system, was
a million miles removed from the stereotype. This serves as a useful reminder of the gulf between real and imagined urban spaces.[2]

The New Urbanism – Back to the Future?

The Disney Company is known for manufacturing dreams through
its movies. Perhaps less well-known is the new town that it has
manufactured in Florida.[3] This new town, Celebration, creates a
new form of urban space and is part of a whole movement in the
USA termed the 'new urbanism'. So, what does this modern urban
dream consist of? The nature of this new town of Celebration is
actually quite surprising. This is not a modern metropolis of gleaming high-tech towers and glass skyscrapers. There are no hints of a
futuristic movie in these Florida streets. In order to create what is

perceived as an ideal place, Disney's planners and architects have actually retreated in time. They have re-created the old-style town square; the houses are surrounded by white picket fences and come in a variety of styles — but none of them could be described as modern architecture. All hark back to a time when, apparently, life was led at a gentler pace and community ties were stronger. The dream being sold in Celebration, Florida, is a return to old-style values and it is represented by a pre-1940s architecture and 'safe', pedestrian-friendly urban spaces. The spaces of Celebration are consciously imagined and created to evoke a sense of positive values and well-being.

There is nothing quite like Celebration in Ireland — yet. But some of our more up-market new housing estates are being consciously marketed in ways which owe something to the same search for certainty and community at a time of considerable social change.

Public vs. Private Places — Surveillance and Defensive Space

One of the biggest changes that has taken place in Irish towns and cities in recent years is the increasing tension between what is seen as public space and what is private and restricted. Walk through the main streets of any major urban area and you will notice various physical improvements. Most frequently these take the form of pedestrianized shopping streets, new paving and enhanced street furniture such as litter bins, decorative lamp standards, perhaps even ornamental seating. But looking a bit closer, beyond these cosmetic changes, you might see something a little more disturbing. Almost everywhere within the urban area, you are more or less constantly under surveillance. Ostensibly these cameras exist to protect people and property. Cameras mounted high on walls and lampposts in public spaces are intended to record criminal activity as, for example, in the case of the cameras that

record activity at ATMs. However, the extent to which they may be used for other purposes is questionable. Even the cameras used to monitor traffic flows can be directed to observe a potential offender on the street. Is this constant surveillance likely to lead to increased safety on our streets? Is the use of cameras in this way eroding the public nature of our urban spaces? To me, they're too much like 'Big Brother' in Orwell's *Nineteen Eighty-Four* and raise many questions: Why should I be watched? Who decides on what or who is to be watched? Who is doing the watching?

Whatever your opinion, the invasion of the camera is a reflection of the changing nature of our public spaces. Mirroring a trend seen across the globe, our urban areas are becoming increasingly closed to the casual visitor. Entry is conditional on the observance of certain codes of behaviour, with security cameras and guards used to ensure compliance. This is particularly evident in the privately-run shopping centres which are emblematic of our consumer culture. To most shoppers, the surveillance is barely visible, as they are welcome guests intent on spending money, but to anyone who does not 'fit in' the discovery will soon be made that the reception offered is strictly limited, when they are requested to leave these private precincts. Even where a location is technically a public space, not all members of the public are necessarily welcomed. When I walk through Dublin's redeveloped docklands and financial services area, the IFSC, I become particularly aware of this tension and I find it difficult to feel at ease there.

There is a belief that, in any urban place, the general public has to be protected from those who are perceived to be 'undesirable'. Leave 'them' – and that is a hazy undefined concept – to live among their own, in the ghettoes of our towns and cities. Put them out of sight, refuse them entry to many of our so-called public spaces. And ultimately what happens? We ignore the problem until the dam bursts ... there is an incident ... the bus drivers refuse to travel there after hours, or the fire brigade declares the place to be a 'no-go' area. And the cycle continues. The place becomes more marginalized, its inhabitants even less likely to be accepted outside of their own community. Another world exists within the city or town. It has its own rules, its own sense of order. If a member of a more affluent social group, or with a different skin colour, strays into such an area, he or she is suddenly the one who does not belong! So the place you are in within an urban area can determine your social status in various ways.

Our increasing fear of the 'other' taking over our towns and cities is one of the reasons that so-called 'gated communities' have been developed. In the USA and places like Sao Paulo in Brazil, such gated communities consist of complete housing areas with all the necessary amenities. As the name suggests, all of these amenities are available behind security walls, protected by cameras, trained dogs and armed response units. Of course, it might be argued that such things are only seen on TV, that they only occur in other countries, but I am not so sure. In Ireland we have taken to building walls around new housing estates. Sometimes these are just intended to define that space, to make us see it as an entity. But in other cases, particularly with apartment blocks, security codes are needed to open the high gates and gain access to the spaces of privilege within. I lived for a while in such a secure apartment close to the heart of Dublin. Despite the obvious advantages, I always felt uncomfortable unlocking the gate that separated my home from the world outside. In that moment, when I turned my back on the city at large to retreat into my safety zone, I felt most acutely the differences between people and, inevitably, a vague sense of guilt at my good fortune.

Renewal and Sameness

Fare thee well sweet Anna Liffey, I can no longer stay

And watch the new glass cages that spring up along the quay
Me mind's too full of memories, too old, to hear new chimes
I'm a part of what was Dublin in the rare aul times.

Pete St John's song 'Dublin in the Rare Aul Times' poignantly depicts some of the changes to physical and social spaces that we have already discussed. Since the late 1980s and particularly during the 1990s, many of Ireland's towns and cities have experienced huge physical changes brought about by government tax incentives and general economic prosperity. Initiated by the urban renewal taxation initiatives, construction of city-centre apartments and office space resulted in the revitalization of many formerly run-down urban areas. People, particularly the more affluent, have returned to live in the city centres, and new shops and other facilities have been created to provide for their needs. But one of the outcomes has been the same sort of disconnection described in the song. Urban spaces are changing so fast that one's sense of familiarity and belonging becomes a victim to progress. After the collapse of the Berlin Wall, many streets in East German towns were renamed and rapid reconstruction occurred. The citizens felt lost in places they had lived in all their lives. Sometimes I feel the same walking through Dublin's rapidly changing urban scene.

In bringing about such rapid change, we do not seem to have sufficiently considered the nature of the new urban spaces which we are creating. Indeed, a recent conversation with some English tourists struck me quite forcefully. While quite delighted with their Irish holiday, they remarked that Dublin reminded them of a town they knew in England – not just the range of shops, but even the way it had been pedestrianized, the street furniture, the very 'feel' of the place. With all of this newness, are we losing the essence of our urban places? It may be that we are creating generic cities, places which could equally be situated in any First World country.

The rapidity of change may cause distress as people come to terms with the physical alterations to places with which they were previously familiar. It may also result in social stresses, as the existing community structures are challenged by an influx of new residents and users of urban space. This is particularly true of 'gentrification', the process whereby certain previously devalued areas become increasingly attractive to urban élites, often involving the displacement of poorer people, either directly or indirectly.

Soulless Suburbs?

Moving beyond the city centre, people seem to enjoy criticizing suburban houses and indeed, suburban lifestyles. But the fact is that the majority of people who live in urban areas are not living in the city or town itself, but rather on its outskirts. So most of us are suburbanites rather than true urbanites and, for most people, this is a conscious choice.

A common criticism of our suburban surroundings is their sameness. A visitor from South Carolina was astonished at the fact that all of the houses in a typical Irish suburb were built in exactly the same style, whereas in her own experience of US suburbs the houses were more varied. However, although our houses might all appear the same on the surface, one of the interesting features of suburbia is the way in which people tailor their homes to their own needs. In fact, it is in this personal space that people often come into their own. Some might decry, in superior tones, the 'keeping up with the Joneses' mentality, the perfectly manicured lawns or replacement windows, which appear to connote the middle-class suburb. The simple fact is that it is in their suburban homes and estates that people actually seize control of their own space and actively create the space around them. In many senses, it is in the suburbs that ordinary individuals have the greatest power to mould their surroundings.

So, I would argue that suburbs in themselves are not necessarily a bad thing. What worries me, however, is the way in which they have extended so far into the countryside around our towns and cities. Flying across Ireland it is possible to identify ribbons of new housing stretched out in all directions from the urban cores; ribbons which belonged more to the nearby town than to the rural hinterland. Given the pace of development and apparent lack of planning, I wondered if, some day, there might be nothing left but concrete and cobble-lock paving.

The Future?
We seem to have become an urban nation without noticing or consciously planning for that situation. Yet it is clear to me that the degree and speed of change in our urban areas is throwing up major issues that need to be tackled seriously. People are very quick to complain but appear reluctant to actively participate in potential improvements in urban affairs. Although the system of local government in Ireland is weaker than in many other countries, individuals still have the ability to lobby for positive urban change. We need to accept our urban and suburban realities and to work together to shape a more positive urban experience for all. It is probably time for a more comprehensive approach to urban affairs in Ireland, maybe even a dedicated government department, but I am afraid that such intervention may only finally occur when the tensions we have been considering here reach crisis point.

4. The County:
Designation, Identity and Loyalty

Desmond A. Gillmor

T he county looms large in the Irish sense of place. This applies not just to the physical entity of the county but it extends even to people's traits and characteristics. A popular example is actor Niall Toibin's interpretations of county accents, going from one county to another and picking out the nuances so clearly. So there are accents that are associated with par- ticular counties, even though accents tend to change gradually over space. The gradation in accent can sometimes be quite abrupt, however, as would be found in travelling from south Donegal to north Sligo.

County stereotyping can extend beyond accents or language, to the idea that there are some distinctive county personalities. The characteristics involved are not always complimentary. That is inher- ent in Niall Toibin's portrayal of the Cavan person as a thrifty indi- vidual. The reference is generally to the male, as in the so-called Kerryman jokes. The implication inherent in the Kerryman jokes differs somewhat from the idea of the Kerry person as being intelli- gent and devious. As Kerry story-teller Eamon Kelly said, 'You'd ate a bag of salt before you'd get to know a Kerryman.'

Also at variance with present reality, but intended to be more complimentary, are the designations sometimes applied to certain counties. Cork may be referred to as 'The Rebel County', Wicklow as 'The Garden of Ireland', Tipperary as 'The Premier County', Meath as 'The Royal County' and Wexford as 'The Model County'. The extent to which certain counties are noted for particular products varies in its accuracy. There is a traditional, though diminished, association of Donegal with tweed and other woollen goods. The association of some counties with glassware would relate more accurately to individual towns or factories rather than to whole counties, whether it is Waterford, Tipperary, Cavan or Tyrone. The occurrence of 'Limerick ham' on restaurant menus is rather more frequent than that county's 3 per cent of Irish pigs would justify, and the source of 'Wicklow lamb' is also, perhaps, open to some questions!

Turning to firmer reality, the county is the internal geographical space most often referred to in Ireland. References to people often include their source counties. When asked about where they come from, people most commonly state their county of birth or of residence. For some Dublin residents, it is a combination of these, as in, 'I come from Longford but I live in Dublin.' The attachment to county is not uniformly strong. It tends to be weakest in the larger urban places, such as Belfast or Dublin. People there may see themselves as belonging more to the city than to a county. For the rural residents of north County Dublin, there is the somewhat schizophrenic situation of sometimes being regarded as 'Dublin culchies'.

This attachment to county extends across the oceans and in some respects it may even be intensified amongst Irish emigrants. This may be expressed in death, in that the tombstones of some Irish emigrants in their adopted countries record their counties of origin in Ireland. The emigrant's attachment to county is evident in the membership of the various county associations in New York, with the wide range of social, cultural and sporting activities in which they engage. Even in Dublin, though less pronounced and active, there are some county associations established by migrants to the city. As a reversal of this in a sense, an organization has been formed recently for people from Dublin who have moved to the West of Ireland, an outcome of the growth of counter-urbanization.

Reflecting this Irish attachment to place and county is the tendency for many people on meeting for the first time abroad, or even at home, to be interested in determining the county from which each has come. This provides a locational or reference point and it may lead on to trying to find out and then talking about any people whom they might know in common.

The county figures prominently in many aspects of everyday Irish life. The county of residence is in many postal addresses. Confusion is caused when the address differs from the county of residence, as in some localities in south-west Wicklow and south-east Laois for which the postal address is Carlow. It follows from postal addresses that the counties of residence are given in telephone directory entries. The plates of motor vehicles on roads and parking areas indicate clearly the counties in which they were registered. Many radio and television news items give locational reference by indicating the counties of happenings, whether for instance it was a road accident in Tipperary or snow showers in Antrim. Many travel guides, tourist accommodation publications and other books about Ireland, are organized on a county basis. There are county soil and archaeological surveys. There are books about the history and other aspects of individual counties. Series of such books range from the statistical surveys of counties published by the Dublin Society two centuries ago, to the current series of county histories by Geography Publications, Dublin. Newspaper and radio series may be based on the counties, e.g. 'The State of the Counties' in the *Irish Times* and *Thirty-Two* on RTÉ Radio. Counties are shown on most maps of Ireland. While school students in earlier decades may have been required to learn the chief towns of all the counties, today the county towns are listed on Fáilte Ireland's website. Various competitions are on a county basis. A number of counties have 'County Person of the Year' awards.

Given all this, it may seem surprising that the county was not an indigenous Irish feature. It was, instead, an Anglo-Norman and British institution, imposed on Ireland in association with the gaining of control over the country. In some instances, however, there was an element of continuity where county delimitation was influenced by the pre-existing Gaelic chieftain territories or *tuatha*. This followed from the processes through which conquest occurred and lands were acquired. The O'Rourke lands became Leitrim and the McMahon lands became Monaghan. There was some continuity from the Desmond territory in south Kerry and from Thomond in Clare. This influence is reflected in the Irish name for Tyrone, Tír Eoghain, and the old name for Donegal, Tír Conaill. The provinces, which are comprised of sets of counties, are of course derived from the ancient kingdoms of Ireland. The system of church dioceses predated the counties and, while being mainly monastic in origin, was also influenced to some extent by the secular territorial divisions. This accounts for some of the limited correspondence that exists between diocesan and county boundaries.

The feudal system of shires and liberties, or what became counties, began soon after the Anglo-Norman invasion. This occurred first around the invaders' main urban settlements, so that the bases of counties Dublin, Cork and Waterford had been established by *c.* 1200. Over the following century, the counties of much of the east and south of the country were formed. Sometimes there was a staged process, with larger territories being later subdivided as they had proved to be too big. Thus much of Munster and Connacht were originally shires, which later were divided into smaller county units. Subdivision occurred also in the separation of Westmeath from Meath in 1541.

Counties of Ireland

Much of the present county delimitation in Connacht and Ulster occurred only in the latter half of the sixteenth century. Also Offaly and Laois, originally King's County and Queen's County respectively, were established in 1556. This second main phase of county establishment was under the Tudors and James I, when it was considered to be an integral part of the reconquest of Ireland. Thus it is in those parts of the country which remained 'Irish' for longest that the counties tend to be the most recent. The last of all of the thirty-two counties to be established was Wicklow. In 1606 it was formed from parts of Dublin, Kildare and Carlow.

Subsequently the county system has remained essentially intact, though there have been some changes in county boundaries. These must have created difficulties for the residents at the time. Some of the changes were associated with the Local Government Act of 1898 when, for instance, Ballaghaderreen was transferred from Mayo to Roscommon. Other changes were made at that time in order to include expanding suburbs within the same counties as their towns. In general, however, the county boundaries have remained fixed despite the changing human geographies of the country.

Deriving in part from how they were formed, the counties vary greatly in population, size and shape, and have many peculiarities in their delimitation. In terms of population, the counties range from only 26,000 in Leitrim to over 1.1 million in Dublin. The largest county, Cork, is more than nine times the size of the smallest, Louth. Apart from Cork and Tipperary, the largest counties tend to be along the west coast – Galway, Mayo, Donegal and Kerry. Presumably this is in part because these counties incorporate large tracts of mountain and bog that are only sparsely populated.

The physical landscape has some influence on county layout in other ways. County boundaries sometimes lie along rivers, often minor ones. With regard to major rivers, Antrim is separated from Down by the Lagan and from Derry by the Bann. Much of Kilkenny's eastern boundary is formed by the River Barrow and its southern boundary by the Suir. Most notable of all, however, the River Shannon acts as a county divide along much of its length. It separates Clare, Galway and Roscommon to the west, from other counties of Munster and of Leinster to the south and east. In this respect, 'The Banner County' of Clare has more of its boundary clearly defined than others. It has the sea to the west, and the Shannon estuary and

1. Densely crowded urban environments – the urban dream and the urban nightmare.

2. & 3. Continuity and change in the Irish landscape.

(Top) 4. The daily grind of horse ploughing in the 1960s allowed time for reflection and enjoyment of place. *(Above)* 5. A boundary fixed in stone.

6. & 7. Townland names carved in stone in counties Mayo and Galway.

(Top) 8. Waterford city.
(Above) 9. A grid pattern of housing.

(Top) 10. Small-scale clusters of homes are now emerging on the edges of Irish towns like Skiberreen, Co. Cork. *(Above)* 11. Bantry, Co. Cork, displays a congested street pattern.

(Top) 12. Mountains such as Errigal, Co. Donegal, help to establish identity.
(Above) 13. County loyalty in Co. Kilkenny.

(Top) 14. Malin Head, Co. Donegal. *(Above)* 15. Mizen Head, Co. Cork.

(Top) 16. The landscapes of western Ireland – so loved by tourists from home and abroad.
(Above) 17. Landmark sites, such as the Rock of Cashel, Co. Tipperary, are internationally known.

(Top) 18. Larger, extensive farms have emerged in the Irish landscape.
(Above) 19. The cultural landscape imprinted onto the natural landscape.

(Top) 20. The European Union has helped define the current Irish road network.
(Above) 21. Kilkenny city – growing outward in low-rise fashion.

(Top) 22. The Golden Vale is a region defined by its landscape and its agricultural economy.
(Above) 23. The Burren, Co. Clare, is a region defined by its geology and its landscape.

(Top) 24. The GPO in Dublin city is a building and a space filled with symbolism.
(Above) 25. The James Joyce Bridge in Dublin – a symbol for new internationalism in architecture.

26. The Spire in O'Connell St, Dublin, juxtaposed a new statement of identity on a street charged with memories.

(Top) 27. The developing docklands of Dublin. The architecture is international in style.
(Above) 28. New-style retailing units. Are there any clues that identify this location?

(Top) 29. The interior of the Tesco store in Letinani, Prague.
(Above) 30. The monastic remains of Clonmacnoise on the River Shannon.

river and Lough Derg as its southern and eastern boundaries. While the Shannon separates counties elsewhere, its upper course, where it becomes Lough Allen, splits County Leitrim in two. This division of Leitrim into northern and southern parts has detrimental effects on life and administration, hindering travel and contact between the two separated parts of the county.

As with rivers, mountain ranges can act as both boundary zones between counties and divides within counties. Much of the Cork-Kerry border lies along mountain ridges. The Carlow-Wexford boundary is the Blackstairs Mountains. Parts of Offaly and Laois are separated by the Slieve Blooms, and parts of Derry and Tyrone by the Sperrins. The most striking example of mountains as a divide within a county is Wicklow. The extensive upland mass in Wicklow isolates west Wicklow from the main centres of population and county administration in the east of the county. Mountain barriers add to the isolation of parts of west Donegal, as do the Mourne Mountains in the south-east of County Down.

Despite some alignment of county boundaries with rivers and mountain ridges, most of them are not obvious features nor are they demarcated in the landscape. One might sometimes be aware of passing from one county to another by a change in the road surface or markings. On occasions there are signs on the roadside to welcome travellers to a particular county but more common now are the rather more sombre displays recording statistics of county road deaths in recent years. In general there is little logic to the alignment of county boundaries. Nonetheless there are different loyalties on the two sides of the lines that act as county boundaries.

County boundaries are important as the limits of counties but this significance is enhanced further where they serve also as the divides between other territorial units. The regions of the Republic of Ireland are comprised of groups of counties, so that some of the county boundaries are also regional boundaries. What became in 2000 the most significant division within the Republic of Ireland –

that between the Border, Midland and Western Region and the Southern and Eastern Region – corresponds with county boundaries. The development aids available to either side of this divide are different and there are separate regional assemblies and plans for the two territories. The most notable example of the enhanced importance of county boundaries is in those that became the border between Northern Ireland and the Republic of Ireland. This long, tortuous line is ill-suited to be an international boundary and this unsuitability has been the source of many problems. Yet one of the reasons for the opposition to any changes in the border, such as those proposed by the Boundary Commission of the 1920s, was that any divergence from county boundaries would be undesirable.

It seems that in the delimitation of counties some attention was given to having the county arranged around a central town, particularly during the second phase of county establishment. From a functional perspective, it is advantageous if the location of the county administration in particular is relatively central to the county. Even where this applies, the shapes of some counties determine that parts are less accessible to the centre. The locational disadvantage is greatest where the county town is peripheral to the county territory. In Carlow and Leitrim, the county towns are close to county boundaries, to the extent that part of the built-up area of Carlow town is in Laois and part of Carrick-on-Shannon is in Roscommon.

Returning to landscapes, people may have mental images or pictures which they tend to associate with certain counties. One might think of the Meath landscape as Padraic Colum did when he wrote in his memorable poem 'A Drover', 'To Meath of the pastures …'. These mental images may relate in reality only to parts of the counties concerned. There is much more to County Antrim than the Glens and the Antrim coast road. Armagh as 'The Apple Blossom County' applies only to its northern orchard area. If the limestone of the Burren comes first to mind when people think of a Clare landscape, it relates in reality to only a small part of the county. Picturing Kildare as grazing land with stud farms is to ignore the intensive arable-farming in the south of the county around Athy. Kerry people may often be thought of as living in a mountainous landscape but in reality the bulk of the Kerry population resides on the lowlands of north Kerry, not in mountainous south Kerry and the Dingle Peninsula.

One of the sharpest landscape contrasts within a county is that between east and west Galway. The predominant east Galway landscape is a flat, dry limestone land, with green fields enclosed by regular stone walls and grazed by cattle and sheep. West Galway is what is thought of as Connemara, either barren lowland, in places lake-strewn, or rising abruptly to mountains in the Twelve Bens and elsewhere. On the boundary between the two is Galway city. As is sometimes the case, there are social and cultural differences associated with these different landscape types. Perhaps the distinctiveness of these County Galway divisions were in the minds and memories of emigrants who, in a part of upstate New York, named three adjacent small towns as Galway, East Galway and West Galway.

The differences within County Cork result in it being in some respects almost a microcosm of Ireland. As in the Republic of Ireland, it is dominated by a large capital port city, surrounded by dormitory settlements. The rugged landscapes of West Cork conform with images of the West of Ireland. The productive mixed farming areas of east Cork are more reminiscent of the east of the country. The pastoral north of the county is part of the Munster specialized dairying region.

The mental images that people have of counties result in the development of personal preferences. These concepts of spatial preferences and mental maps were examined some time ago with several hundred Leaving Certificate students who were studying geography in Leinster schools.[1] They were asked to rank the thirty-two counties of Ireland on a map in order of their preferences for spending a two-week summer holiday. The top six counties were, in order, Kerry, Galway, Clare, Cork, Donegal and Mayo. These are all west coast counties. They were followed by those of the coastal south-east together with Sligo. Presumably these preferences resulted from the scenic and recreational attraction of coastal and upland Ireland, along with the cultural appeal of the West. The zone of least desirability for holidays stretched southwards from the counties of central Ulster, through those of interior Leinster, as far as Carlow. When wanting to get away from home for a holiday, Dublin was ranked last, but it was followed closely by Monaghan.

Within the broad Leinster study the residential preferences of Dublin students were also explored. This time they were asked to rank the counties according to their preferences for living in them after they finished their education. Here the position of County Dublin was reversed, the majority of students wishing to live in their home county of Dublin. The fact that it also contained the principal city added to its appeal. The adjacent coastal counties of Wicklow and Wexford were quite highly favoured. Apart from these, the preferred counties for residence were Galway, Cork, Kerry, Limerick and Waterford. Here again, coastal and scenic attractions may have played a role, as did the existence of cities with their varied social and cultural attractions. The eleven least-desired counties comprised all the Ulster counties, with the exception of Donegal, together with Leitrim, Longford and Carlow. This pattern is likely to have been affected by violence in Northern Ireland at the time the study was conducted, together with considerations of political and cultural differences and far less knowledge about Northern Ireland. While the zone of perceived undesirability was more marked in residential than in holiday preferences, overall there were considerable similarities between the two sets of county images.

These mental maps draw attention to differences in the distinctiveness of coastal and inland counties in people's minds. Apart from the greater attraction of the coast for holidaying and living, the poor showing of inland counties in the students' preferences may have been related partly to the fact that these counties were less distinctive in their minds, less well known to them. On their mental maps of Ireland, people may be able to go around the coast naming the counties in succession but they are less likely to be able to locate the fourteen inland counties. Most inland of all is Laois, in the sense that it is the only county that is not bordered by even one maritime county. At least some of the interior counties do not figure so prominently in people's imagination because of their inland location.

Music can contribute to county identity. In traditional music, various tunes have county names, and there are the distinctive musical traditions of counties such as Clare and Sligo. It is in popular and Irish country music, however, that the county looms largest. There are songs such as 'Beautiful Meath', 'Moonlight in Mayo' and 'The Homes of Donegal'. Sometimes it is people from the counties concerned that are highlighted: 'Cavan Girl', 'My Lovely Rose of Clare', 'The Star of the County Down', 'The Men of Roscommon' and 'The Boys from the County Armagh'.

The association with place in song is most emotional when the emigrant is looking back to his or her native county. This is the Irish person's strong attachment to and rootedness in place, and the longing to be back home. This is evident in the following songs:

> There's one county back in Ireland I left so long ago,
> In the province of great Connacht, it's the County of Mayo.
> With its nature and its beauty, in this peaceful land on earth,
> It brings back some happy memories, this county of my birth.
> Let's go back to County Mayo, the pride of all the West.
>
> [from 'Let's Go Back to County Mayo']

> Lovely Laois, I hear you calling,
> In my dreams I hear you say

'Come back home to dear old Ireland'.
Lovely Laois, I'll come back to you some day.

[from 'Lovely Laois']

Last night I had a pleasant dream, I woke up with a smile,
I dream't that I was back again in dear old Erin's Isle,
I though I saw Lough Allen's banks in the valleys down below,
It was my Lovely Leitrim where the Shannon waters flow.

[from 'Lovely Leitrim']

These three songs are about counties as whole units though, as
in the remainder of 'Lovely Leitrim', such songs may include many
placenames from within the county. In other instances, the songs
associated with particular counties are about parts of these counties. Through spatial extension, however, the song has come to be
taken as representing the county. Such songs include 'The Banks of
my own Lovely Lee' for Cork, 'The Rose of Tralee' for Kerry,
'Slievenamon' for Tipperary, 'The Rose of Mooncoin' for Kilkenny
and 'The Curragh of Kildare' for Kildare.

A song in which the focus is on county boundaries, which by
extension emphasizes the importance of the counties themselves as
units of territory, is 'Where the Three Counties Meet':

Lough Rea, O Lough Rea, where the three counties meet,
Longford, Westmeath and Roscommon.

An indication of the importance of songs about counties and
songs representing counties has been the production of several
compilations of Irish county songs. The two-volume album *Paddy
Reilly's Ireland* is composed of a song for each of the thirty-two
counties, as is the more recent GAA compact disc *Songs All-Ireland*.
There are also compilations for individual counties. These are composed of songs about the county, songs about places in it and other
songs associated with the county in some way. Such compilations
include those for counties Donegal, Leitrim, Sligo, Galway, Kerry

and Wicklow. Some counties are richer than others in such songs, though individual initiatives in compiling such collections may also be a factor in accounting for those that exist.

County songs figure on GAA All-Ireland days. It is in the Gaelic Athletic Association that county loyalty is at its height. For many people who normally have little interest in GAA sports, it is a different matter when their county gets to an All-Ireland final. This extends even to some Ulster unionists travelling south to Dublin to support their county in Croke Park. At All-Ireland times, the counties involved are ablaze with the county colours. It is not just the senior All-Ireland and Provincial finals and semifinals that arouse feelings. GAA competitions of all grades are organized on a county basis. Within counties there are various county club championships. The dreams of many GAA players are that their club will win the county championship and that they themselves will play for their county, an ambition similar to that of international representation in some other sports. GAA administration is on a county basis, with counties sending delegates to the Central Council and the Annual Congress. Voting on major issues at Congress is by county. A recent suggestion that County Dublin might be subdivided into north and south for GAA purposes was met with strong opposition. It is ironic that the county, imposed by Britain in the process of gaining control over Ireland, should find its strongest expression and loyalty in the Gaelic Athletic Association, an organization so closely identified with the emergence of Irish national identity.

Local newspapers in many instances play a part in forging county identity and consciousness. They report not just sporting events but all county news and other content. People are bound together by reading the news of their county. The association of local newspapers with counties is reflected in names such as *The Derry Journal*, *Limerick Leader*, *Longford News*, *Offaly Independent* and *The Westmeath Examiner*. While their broadcast range extends beyond an individual county to groups of counties in some instances, local radio stations now also have a role in reinforcing county identity. County names figure in titles such as Cork County Sound, Tipp FM and Radio Kilkenny, or a combination of Louth and Meath in LM FM. These county titles were used, presumably, to give the stations a local identity, recognizing people's place association with their county.

Given that the county was introduced for administrative purposes, it might be assumed that it would have a major role in governance, and that this would contribute much to county identity. County administrative functions were confirmed under the Local Government Act of 1898. At that time county status was granted also to the major cities of Dublin, Belfast, Cork, Londonderry, Limerick and Waterford. This county borough status was given also to Galway in 1986.

Many constituencies for national elections in the Republic of Ireland are organized on a county basis, as either individual counties or combinations of two counties. In the larger and more populous counties with more than one constituency, the county dimension is retained in the constituency names being specified parts of the counties, usually north, south, east or west, as in counties Cork, Kerry and Mayo. In constituencies which combine counties, such as Carlow/Kilkenny and Laois/Offaly, county loyalties are evident in voting patterns. Consequently the larger political parties endeavour to maximize electoral support by favouring a choice of candidates from each county.

The role of the county in public administration has gone in Northern Ireland. There, the counties were replaced by twenty-six district council areas as the units of local government under the Local Authority Government (Boundaries) Act (NI) 1971, which became functional in October 1973. Fermanagh is the only county that remains intact. Many of the former county functions were transferred to organizations with responsibilities for larger areas.

In the Republic of Ireland, the county remains the principal unit of local administration. Yet local government is very weak in Ireland compared with other countries. The county is administered by the elected county council. In Tipperary, however, since 1898 there have been two county councils that separately administer the north and the south of the county. With its growth in population, County Dublin was subdivided in 1994 into three separate administrative units – Fingal, South Dublin and Dun Laoghaire-Rathdown.

The county councils are subject in effect to the control of central administration, through the Department of the Environment and Local Government. This includes financial matters and the recruitment of senior personnel, including the County Manager. The councils can be suspended or abolished by law. Areas of county council responsibility include planning, public housing, water supply, sanitation, roads and traffic, and motor taxation. They are also responsible for public libraries, vocational education, fire services, parks and environmental services, and certain social and community functions.

In some respects, the role of the county in administration has lessened over time. The financial independence of county councils was reduced when the levying of local taxes or rates on private housing and farmland was abolished. A major function in health was removed with the establishment of regional health boards. Some functions may be performed more effectively and efficiently for larger areas or regions.

But there has also been a recent increase in the role of the county. This has followed partly from the provision of new environmental and other services by the county councils. It also results from the increased role assigned to promoting development at a local level and the formulation of county development strategies. This trend is reflected in the establishment of County Enterprise Boards, County Development Boards and County Tourism Committees. Some of the EU LEADER rural development organizations have a county basis. Structures are being put in place to give the voluntary sector a much greater role at the county level. So it seems that in some respects greater power is now being given to the county. Clearly the administrative role of the county fluctuates over time.

One might expect that, overall, the county's place in people's consciousness might lessen with increasing urbanization, regionalization and globalization. Nonetheless the county has become so firmly entrenched in so many aspects of Irish life, and in the minds of Irish people, that county identity, attachment and loyalty will long remain major components of the Irish sense of place and space.

5. The Rural Idyll

Mary Cawley

The concept of a rural idyll, an idealized rustic way of life, may be dated in art and literature to approximately 300 BC when urbanization first began in Classical Greece.[1] Throughout history, as successive waves of urbanization have taken place, townspeople have tended to become physically and spiritually isolated from nature. In reaction, nature and rural society have been elevated to an idealized status in literature and art, and country living has become an aspiration for many, either on a full-time or an occasional basis. This chapter discusses the concept of the rural idyll in the context of some of the ways in which it finds expression in contemporary Ireland. Recognition is given also to the counter-idyll, the often-harsh reality of rural living that an exclusive focus on the idyll ignores. By way of introduction, brief reference is made to some of the ways in which the idyll has been depicted in Irish art and literature since the eighteenth century.

In early eighteenth-century Ireland, following the contemporary practice in England, nature became tamed as great estates were landscaped. In art, the peasantry often appeared as miniscule figures, engaged in their daily tasks, amid expansive sylvan landscapes.

Works by the Irish landscape artist, Thomas Roberts, for example, provide such views of a tranquil nature in which farm workers play a barely identifiable role.[2] The peasant acquired a more realistic, but nobler, status, in both art and literature during the nineteenth century in Western Europe and informed the late nineteenth-century Gaelic revival in Ireland when the rural, and particularly the rural West, became a cultural hearth for the revivalists.[3] The lives and lore of country people, and especially of Irish speakers in Gaeltacht areas, were recorded, collected and archived for posterity by the leaders of the revival including Douglas Hyde and Lady Augusta Gregory. Lady Gregory, Yeats and Synge dramatized rural life. Yeats expressed his personal longing for the simplicity of a self-sufficient island life encapsulated in 'Nine bean-rows will I have there, a hive for the honey-bee', in *The Lake Isle of Innisfree*, written when he was living in London in 1890. The establishment of a National Folklore Commission in 1935 provided an institutional context for the work of folklore collecting which imbued the oral tradition of storytelling and vernacular architecture with a cultural status. During the early decades of the twentieth century, the glori-fication of the 'folk' became associated with the work of the artists Paul Henry, Sean Keating and Charles Lamb who found artistic inspiration in the rural West and depicted a noble peasantry whose faces and bodies bore ample testimony to lives of hard manual labour in fields and on the sea. In a more bucolic vein, Eamon de Valera is often cited as presenting an idyllic vision of the new state in his St Patrick's Day speech of 1943, when he referred to a land of 'cosy homesteads ... athletic youths ... and comely maidens ...'.[4]

It is argued here that the concept of a rural idyll is enjoying a renaissance in contemporary Ireland, following a trend that is pre-sent more widely at an international scale. Four readily identifiable ways in which the idyll finds expression are discussed: the attention that is being given to the protection of the environment and the rural landscape more generally, in reaction to over-intensive land use and problems arising from waste disposal; the re-emergence of small scale food and handcraft production in response to growing markets for non-industrialized products; residential movement, on either a full- or part-time basis, to the countryside in quest of a refuge from an increasingly pressurized life in towns and cities; and the use of rural imagery in the international promotion of Ireland and particular local places as tourist destinations. Evidence is presented relating to these various expressions of the idyll.

Protecting the Idyllic Landscape

Concerns about the protection of the natural environment, arising from the increased amounts of organic and inorganic waste that must be disposed of, have grown significantly in Ireland during the last three decades. There is a heightened consciousness of the damage that has been done to wildlife and its habitats and the threats that have been posed to human health by the increased intensification of land use during the 1970s and eighties. Accession to the European Economic Community (EEC) in 1973 marked a major watershed for methods of Irish agricultural production. From the foundation of the state until the sixties, methods of farming and output had changed only slowly. Underemployment was rife and living standards were low for many until the late fifties. During the sixties, increases in output and advances in methods of production took place as part of the national drive towards economic development and in preparation for membership of the Common Agricultural Policy (CAP).[5] From 1973 on the pace of change accelerated rapidly, as the impacts of the CAP were felt. Survival and success for many farmers depended ultimately on the capacity to embrace capitalization, mechanization, intensification and specialization.[6] The use of fertilizers and insecticides increased dramatically as did animal waste, residues of which escaped, to some extent at least, into watercourses.[7] The number of lakes and rivers registering nutrient enrichment of levels that pose a threat to fish is limited, and Lee has shown that rates of fertilizer application in Ireland are less than in many other European Union (EU) countries,[8] but there is a particular concentration in the north Midlands. Concerns also arose during the eighties about the overgrazing of mountainsides, when the numbers of sheep more than doubled between 1980 and 1990. This sudden increase in numbers was associated with the inclusion of mutton and lamb in the Common Market regime in 1980 and the introduction of premia payments to encourage an increase in the number of ewes.[9]

Concern was emerging not just in Ireland but in the EEC more generally, from the 1970s on, about the loss of wildlife habitats and the reduced biodiversity of ecosystems that were arising from over-intensive land use and waste disposal. A range of environmental legislation and directives was introduced, which included the Irish Wildlife Act 1976 (amended as the Wildlife Amendment Act in 2000), under which National Heritage Areas (NHAs) are protected. At an EU level, the Birds Directive of 1979 (79/409/EEC) provided for the designation of Special Protection Areas (SPAs) and the Habitats Directive of 1992 (92/43/EEC) provided for the designation of Special Areas of Conservation (SACs). Ireland became a signatory to these. There are more than 1700 sites in the state (NHAs, SPAs or SACs) that are designated for protection – either as habitats for flora and fauna or because of their geological interest.[10] Their conservation is particularly important in maintaining the open bog-land and mountainous landscapes, depicted, in late nineteenth-century and early twentieth-century art, as the idyllic West of Ireland.

The Rural Environmental Protection Scheme, known as REPS, which was introduced as part of the reform of the CAP in 1992, has been influential in helping to restore older agricultural landscapes in Ireland, most notably in the western counties. The scheme was designed to reduce farm pollution, extensify production systems, and maintain and enhance the rural environment. It aimed also to provide opportunities for public access and leisure, and education and training in environmental protection and management for farmers. Payments are made to those who comply with the scheme. Because a land management plan must be applied on the farm as a whole but payments apply to a maximum of 40 ha (other than in NHAs, SACs and SPAs where additional reduced payments apply to higher acreages), the scheme is most appropriate for the smaller farms of the West. There has been a high uptake of REPS in western counties where the traditional methods of low intensity beef production aligned well with its requirements.[11] The visible impacts of REPS in the landscape include the rebuilding of stonewalls and dilapidated farm buildings, and the maintenance of boundary drains. All of these contribute to the reproduction of a more traditional enclosed farming landscape evocative of the first half of the twentieth century.

Organic farming has also been introduced during recent decades, partly in association with REPS, and is redolent of more traditional methods of land use in which manual labour played a major role. Organic methods of production promote benign relationships with the environment because they involve the cultivation of land and the rearing of livestock without using artificial fertilizers and pesticides. Instead, crop and livestock rotations, and clover leys, are used to maintain fertility and to control weeds, pests and disease. Organic farming is often a lifestyle choice, inspired by a desire for self-sufficiency, rejection of the urban, and concerns relating to food quality and personal well-being.[12] Organic methods of production are labour intensive, but the prices obtained are usually higher than for conventional produce. Specialist greengrocers and some super-markets deliberately market organic produce as a niche strategy but many producers sell directly to consumers in street markets or through door-to-door sales. The exchange relationship becomes personalized and 'trust' is established which assumes increased importance in the 'risk' society.[13] Knowing the producer, and knowing that the producer shares similar concerns relating to methods of food production, is one of the most powerful forms of quality assurance, particularly in the wake of the health concerns raised by Bovine Spongiform Encephalopathy (BSE) in beef cattle.

Craft Methods of Production

Production and processing in the absence of inorganic fertilizers, growth promoters and artificial preservatives is also the hallmark of a growing number of smallscale local food producers.[14] Wild salmon and trout, and cheeses from the milk of animals grazed on semi-natural grasslands are among the better-known Irish niche food products. Official processing standards are complied with, but the natural qualities of locally available raw materials and the skills of the producer confer distinctive characteristics on the finished product.[15] Sales often occur at the place of production or in street markets and hark back to a pre-supermarket age. As in the case of organic produce, the exchange relationship becomes personalized and that personalization forms the basis for trust in the quality of the product being purchased and creates a willingness to pay a price premium. The consumption of locally produced niche foods is assuming increased importance as part of the visitor experience in locations like West Cork. Some products, in particular Irish farmhouse cheeses, have gained international recognition.

The disquiet that has arisen relating to aspects of industrialized methods of food production and the reversion to small-scale, low-intensity, high-quality output and hand-produced food products find echoes in the sphere of manufacturing also. An increased demand for handcrafted, customized products was documented in many countries during the 1980s.[16] This demand seems to have derived from a reaction against mass production allied with a quest for natural materials and traditional craft techniques, which evoked an idyllic

vision of the rural. As in the case of food products, handcraft production is sometimes associated with the espousal of principles of
self-sufficiency and a return to a simpler way of life. The growing
importance of rural tourism has contributed to the demand for
traditional handcrafts and, indeed, the movement of craft producers
to scenic locations along the south-west coast of Ireland may be
associated with the opportunities presented by tourist demand.[17]

Local craft enterprises had declined during the twentieth century, as mass-produced, often imported, products were introduced. Carpentry survived as an adjunct to the building and construction industry, but many of the major trades had died out by the
fifties. Weaving, lace-making and knitting survived primarily in the
Gaeltacht. Well-known exceptions to the decline of the handcraft
tradition were Waterford glass, Belleek china and Donegal tweed
where craft methods were successfully translated into factory contexts. During the eighties handcraft production began to enjoy a
renaissance on a localized scale in response to growing interests in
traditional household furnishings and natural fabrics, as expressions
of style. The availability of a range of financial supports through
LEADER companies and County Enterprise Boards facilitated the
establishment of small handcraft businesses in the north-west and
the south-west, for example, during the eighties and nineties.[18]
The production of handcrafts is linked to the same revalorization of
natural materials, authenticity and traditional skills that character-
ize the small foods sector. There may be personal links to the producer and the place of production. The consumer is often able to
observe the craftsperson at work and finished products may be purchased in the workshop. The purchase of a coffee mug becomes a
personalized transaction, conducted in a particular place. Drinking
coffee at home later becomes an act of 'souvenir', of remembering.
The coffee drinker has bought into an idyll of rural skill and tradition, practised on the wild, west coast of Ireland, where the hues of
the landscape are captured in the glaze on the mug.

Ironically, the skills associated with many handcrafted items may be traditional, but are also re-introduced. Many well-known craft workers today are, quite possibly, immigrants both to the area where they work and to Ireland. Others are Irish-born but have acquired their craft through study and/or through apprenticeship in Ireland or overseas. The Kilkenny Design Centre has played a particularly important role in this revival. Some of the raw materials may be imported, notably pottery clay, but the act of production links to an age-long tradition and, possibly, a quest for a personal rural idyll by the producer.

The Idyll as Quest: Rural Population and Settlement

The quest for a rural idyll also underlies some of the changes that have taken place in the composition and distribution of the Irish rural population over the past three decades. The early seventies were years of rapid population growth in Ireland when the national total grew by more than 1.5 per cent per year, far in excess of the increases registered in most other European countries.[19] Marked suburban expansion was associated with the larger cities and towns that had been selected as industrial growth centres, and small towns and villages benefited also.[20] This was a period when Irish people returned to Gaeltacht and non-Gaeltacht areas along the west coast to work in newly established industries. Their reasons for returning frequently involved elements of an idyll – the wish to escape from high-density housing, pollution, and the growing social pressures experienced by children in inner-city areas.[21] Retirement migration was made possible by the improved pension benefits available to the post-World War II workforce. Rural residence also became a desirable option as standards of living in the countryside became more closely aligned with those of urban society, following increased public investment in water and sewerage infrastructure.

Marked rural renewal in the remoter countryside was, however, a short-lived phenomenon and began to taper off during the eighties, as recession led to renewed emigration. However, many non-farm families continued to achieve their dream of residing in a detached house in the countryside, within commuting distance of urban-based employment. With the renewed economic growth associated with the 'Celtic Tiger' economy of the nineties, the demand for relatively lower cost, but by no means cheap, housing in accessible small towns and villages has escalated. This movement is stimulated in large part by rapidly increasing house prices in the major cities. Elements of seeking a rural idyll in the guise of a detached house in its own grounds are present also, particularly in scenic areas. Since the mid-nineties, increasing numbers of planning applications for permission to build in more secluded locations have been sought and, indeed, refused.[22]

Economic growth has also brought the dream of a holiday home in the West of Ireland within the grasp of increasing numbers of urbanites. Selected areas on the west coast have, of course, a long-established tradition of holiday home ownership, both among émigrés who retained family properties and non-nationals. Increased affluence during the nineties, meant that many Irish urban dwellers became able to pursue their personal rural idylls by purchasing holiday homes in scenic areas. Inishowen, Gweedore and the Rosses in Donegal have become particularly popular with Belfast and Derry residents. Clew Bay in Mayo, Clifden and Roundstone in Galway, Dingle in Kerry, Glengarriff and the Beara Peninsula in Cork all have enclaves of second-home owners from Dublin and further afield.

Since the seventies so-called 'counterculture migrants', notably from Germany and the Netherlands, have moved in relatively small numbers to remote western areas.[23] Their motives include seeking to return to a simpler way of life, as expressed through the pursuit of organic farming and handcraft production, and they often live in refurbished farmhouses in out-of-the-way places. Some specifically seek untamed nature and places with Celtic associations. Thus,

groups of 'New Age' travellers are found in areas of rural depopu-
lation in the north of the Burren in County Clare, in parts of west
Mayo, and in the hill country of south Sligo, south Leitrim and
north Roscommon. These migrants have been particularly active in
seeking to conserve the more pastoral characteristics of the places
to which they have moved. Common cause has been found with
local conservationists, in opposing proposals for gold mining on
Croagh Patrick and fish farming off the Clare coast at Ballyvaughan,
for example. In 2001, migratory 'Eco Warriors' spearheaded the
opposition to the felling, for road-widening, of naturally regener-
ated oak wood at Coolattin in County Wicklow.

Since the nineties, a rural idyll has been offered as an option to
urban families, often Local Authority tenants, by the non-profit
Rural Resettlement organization based in County Clare. Frequently,
these families seek to leave behind environments characterized by
unemployment, economic deprivation, crime and drug abuse. They
seek a better environment for themselves and, especially, for their
children. The dwellings offered for occupation may be in isolated
places where population decline is endemic. Issues of 'community'
are central to the ethos of Rural Resettlement, such as contributing
to local population increase, supporting local primary schools, and
facilitating the integration of the newcomers into existing structures.
By 2002 several hundred families had made a successful transition
from Dublin to refurbished farmhouses in the rural West.[24]

The Use of the Idyll in Tourism Promotion

The rural idyll is used in very deliberate ways to promote Irish
tourism internationally. Posters depicting the characteristic mountainous, lake-studded landscape of the West of Ireland, as painted
by Paul Henry, were used in the early decades of the twentieth century by Irish and English railway companies to attract tourists to
newly-constructed hotels along the west coast. Film played a role

in popularizing these landscapes in North America. The dramatic scenery and simple yet noble way of life based on land and sea, depicted in *Man of Aran* (1934) and *The Quiet Man* (1952), helped to perpetuate particular imagery in the Irish-American mind which had been inherited from parents and grandparents who left Ireland in the early decades of the twentieth century. The landscapes and lifestyles captured on film undoubtedly reinforced the would-be tourist's consciousness of a wholesome and simple way of life. The picturesque, whitewashed, thatched cottage with red or green half-door, which has long been an icon of rural Ireland, though outdated still retains some currency. Increasingly, it is being recreated in holiday villages. It is also reappearing, either as an authentic reconstruction, as at Bunratty Folk Park, or as a recreation in a growing number of themed visitor attractions. Sometimes, the cottage is humanized through the telling of the story of the 'family'. This may involve a dramatized reconstruction rather than the history of any particular family. Idyll may be moving into the realm of myth.

The dramatic coastal and mountainous scenery of the west coast is still the single most dominant image in Irish tourism promotion.[25] Bord Fáilte (now Fáilte Ireland) surveys show that, following visits to heritage sites, outdoor activities dominate among the types of recreation in which tourists engage while they are in Ireland – walking, angling, golfing, cycling, river cruising. On the 2003 Fáilte Ireland website, the would-be tourist is invited to 'live a different life' and Ireland is promoted as 'friendly, beautiful [and] relaxing'. There continues to be an emphasis on the traditional – lobster fishing from a currach, red-sailed boats off the west coast, line-fishing from a cliff top, set dancing outside a thatched pub.

Rural Realities: the Counter-Idyll

For farmer, fisherman or other rural producer, there are the facts of daily life in the countryside against which the idyll may be

viewed in a cynical way. 'You can't eat scenery' expresses a truth
for many owners of small farms in mountainous areas of the West
of Ireland. Even when scenery is being consumed in the guise of
tourism, long-established inhabitants may lack the resources and
the know-how to reap the major rewards and may actually become
part of a product that is sold by others – mere actors on the rural
stage. Consciousness of the reality of rural life should underpin the
discussion of the idyll as spectacle.

Oliver Goldsmith presented the counter-idyll of dispossession
for the eighteenth-century peasantry, which accompanied enclo-
sure and estate development, when he referred to 'trade's unfeel-
ing train' usurping the land and dispossessing the swain, in *The
Deserted Village*. Synge exposed the counter-idyll in the underlying
violence that is present in *The Playboy of the Western World*. In the late
nineteenth century, the West of Ireland was a place of poverty,
where recovery was slow in the wake of the Famine and land
reform was just beginning. When Eamon de Valera made his
famous St Patrick's Day speech in 1943 more than 20,000 Irish
men and women were leaving the country each year, and more than
100,000 were dependent on dole payments.[26] The boom in agricultural prices following accession to membership of the EEC in
1973 was short-lived, and many farm families experienced a
marked decline in their standard of living in the late seventies, and
a painful process of re-adaptation during the eighties. The number
of farms was almost halved between 1970 and 2001 (from 280,000
to 146,000) and further decline is anticipated. Less than one-quar-
ter of farm families can now hope to gain an acceptable income
from farming alone.[27] Most of the other three-quarters receive
part of their income from off-farm work, or from state transfers of
various kinds. As recession impacted from the mid-seventies on
and public expenditure was cut, access to public transport and
many other services declined for rural residents more generally. A
proposal to deliver mail to mail boxes at the end of lanes, rather

than to the door, is one of the most recent cost-saving measures that was averted only by loud protest.

Tension is increasing between private property rights and landscape and habitat conservation. An Taisce has become progressively more active in landscape protection through the number of proposed housing developments that it appeals to An Bord Pleanála.[28] The desire for one rural idyll is conflicting with another and gives rise to accusations that the countryside is being preserved for second-home owners. The reproduction of a more traditional rural landscape through REPS is not without problems. This relates partly to the cost of having the agri-environmental plan prepared, and partly to the bureaucracy of complying with its provisions. The issue of access for leisure purposes has become a matter of concern for some farmers. They may not reap any financial benefit from the visitors and, if gates are left open by unthinking hikers, livestock may roam onto public roads and cause accidents.

The building of holiday homes and refurbishment of existing properties by outsiders may benefit the local economy through sales of land, house construction and repair. Increasingly, however, the cost of land and housing is moving beyond the grasp of young local people who have to migrate elsewhere in search of affordable housing. Weekend visitors may bring their supplies with them and contribute little to local businesses. The transition for Local Authority tenants from a highly urbanized environment to the remote rural periphery is not always easy. There are inherent problems relating to the reduced availability of services, the absence of adequate public transport, the absence of a family support network, and limited employment opportunities. New issues are also emerging relating to housing and immigration (notably the housing of travellers and integrating migrant workers and asylum seekers into local society). At a more general level, recent survey research from the Economic and Social Research Institute reveals the persistence of poverty among the elderly and the unemployed, in small towns and villages.[29] There is, therefore, a counter-idyll that will, increasingly, have to be addressed.

Conclusion

The rural idyll exists in art and literature as an idealized rustic way of life. It exists in people's minds, is actively sought, and is also manipulated and constructed for economic purposes. The realization of the idyll is not accomplished without problems, however, and we should not forget that there is a counter-idyll, which represents the daily reality of life for many people in rural Ireland. Perhaps the greatest challenge today is to seek to ensure that the idyll does not revert to being the preserve of a privileged minority, as it has been in the past, by default or design. Long-established residents need to become more aware that the resources they control are part of a national heritage. Equally, occasional visitors, recent residents and conservationists need to realize that both the reality and the image that are being protected are constructed from the private property rights of local people.

6. Rediscovering Our Regions

Des McCafferty

A recent article in a weekend magazine enquired whether the ancient nine-county province of Ulster had any meaning in contemporary Ireland. Thinking initially in terms of literature, the author wondered whether there could be said to be a distinctive *Ulster* poetry. She then went on to pose the question more broadly. 'Is there an Ulster?' she enquired. 'Is there anything that carries the adjective that can be seen and touched and photographed, apart from an Ulster fry?'

The article caught my attention for a number of reasons, but in particular because its author appeared to assume that provinces correspond to regions, and therefore should possess some degree of unity or sameness. In the author's words, they should 'hang together'. The requirement of internal cohesion is indeed central to the notion of a region, but the designation of provinces as regions is rather more questionable, and appears to be indicative of a general confusion in the public mind about regions. Despite this confusion, the concept of the region has been central to recent debates about public spending and investment in Ireland, particularly that which is co-financed by the European Union. Moreover, the publication last autumn of the eagerly anticipated National Spatial Strategy has presented an opportunity for this, the least well developed of our territorial concepts, to acquire a new significance in Irish public policy and planning.

Regions, Regionalism and Regionalization

So, what exactly are regions, and what are the factors that have led to their recent prominence in public policy debates? The concept of the region is essentially a geographical one, and geographers were the first academics to place the study of regions at the centre of their discipline. The geographical study of regions was at its height in the first half of the twentieth century. With the completion of the polar expeditions and the other great explorations, geographers turned to the task of describing the newly charted territories as well as the older known world. The central concept and unit of analysis that they employed for this purpose was that of the region.

Over the years, the concept evolved in terms of its meaning. Initially, regions were conceived of as blocks of territory that showed a strong degree of internal uniformity relative to surrounding areas. This uniformity might be expressed in the natural environment, the cultural (i.e. man-made) environment, or, ideally, both together. The list of characteristics on which regional divisions have been based includes topography, climate, agriculture, industry, population, way of life and so on. Regions defined in this way are referred to as formal regions. An example within Ireland might be the Golden Vale dairying region in north Munster, where, as Horner observes, the twice-daily milking routine is a major regulator of farming activity, and, ultimately, lifestyles.[1] A country in which formal regions have been especially well developed historically is France, with its rich tapestry of distinctive landscapes or pays. Regions such as Provence and Brittany are distinguished not just by their topography, but also by their land use and settlement patterns, their architecture, lifestyles and customs.

However, in France as elsewhere, the modernization of agriculture and improvements in transportation and communications in the years after the Second World War contributed to the erosion of formal regions. These improvements included the construction of the motorway network and the development of television and other mass media, which together greatly increased the movement of people, goods, information and ideas across traditional regional boundaries. The advent of the welfare state, with its emphasis on the common provision of services such as education and healthcare, was also a factor in the reduction of regional distinctiveness within states.

In response to these trends, a new concept of the region evolved. Increasingly, in the new era of greatly enhanced mobility, it made more sense to see regions as areas that exhibit some degree of self-containment or cohesion with respect to the movements of people and commodities. Regions defined in this way are termed functional regions. Thus we might speak of the Dublin functional region as the area corresponding roughly to the commuting hinterland of the capital. This version of the regional concept allows for change over time. With the pace of development in the eastern part of the country, the Dublin functional region is today considerably larger than it was even a decade ago. It now extends over much of Leinster, including a large part of counties Louth, Meath, Westmeath, Offaly, Laois, Kildare and Wicklow. Modern geographical thinking allows functional regions to have not just one, but several focal points, each one generating and attracting various forms of social interaction. The only requirement is that the intensity of such interactions within the region is significantly greater than across the regional boundary. Functional regions of this kind are referred to as polycentric regions.

Both formal and functional regions are defined on the basis of objective criteria. However, in a third version of the regional concept, regions are defined on a more subjective basis. A vernacular region is one that is identified as such by its inhabitants, and perhaps also those from outside the region. In other words, it is a region first and foremost in the mind, an integral part of a people's self-identity. The American South – extending from the Carolinas to Texas and from Tennessee to Florida – is a good example. The degree of popular identification with regions is measured in the concept of regionalism, and two of its characteristics can be noted at this point. First, regionalism is often based on a shared and distinctive historical experience; and second, it can vary considerably, even within countries. In some countries regionalism seems to grow in strength as distance from the capital city increases. A recent opinion poll suggests that the UK is a good example of this phenomenon.[2]

Whether this is also the case in Ireland is unclear, due to lack of survey information. However, a more pertinent observation is surely that, while Irish people identify strongly with the county or smaller units of area such as the parish or townland, there does not appear to be a similar sense of identification with the region. For example, think of someone from Donegal who has recently arrived in Dublin, and is asked the usual question used in Ireland to establish identity – 'Where are you from?' That person is most unlikely to reply, 'I'm from the north-west,' or 'the Border Region'. Likewise, if we were to poll the inhabitants of, say, a medium-sized town such as Mullingar or Tuam, on the question of what region they live in, it is doubtful if we would get any kind of consensus. Most Irish people would probably not be able to name any regional entity in response to this question.

Clearly then, regionalism is not well-developed in Ireland. There are several reasons for this. First, as noted by one of Ireland's earliest regional chroniclers, the geographer T.W. Freeman, complex variations in geomorphology, vegetation and land use within small areas make the task of regional delineation quite difficult.[3] The weakness of regionalism in Ireland is also partly due to the absence of any significant, territorially based, cultural and ethnic variation, such as we find in many of the other states of the European Union.[4] The Basque country and Catalonia in Spain, Flanders in Belgium, Scotland and Wales within the UK, Brittany and the Languedoc region in France are all prominent examples.

Important as these aspects of the geography of the country have been, arguably the most significant reason for the lack of regional consciousness in Ireland is that we have never had a regional tier of government or public administration. States build nations, in the sense that the institutional apparatus of the state helps to establish a common sense of identity and loyalty among its citizens. The most important of these nation-building state institutions is probably the government itself. In similar fashion, a strong regional administration can promote popular identification with, and loyalty to, the region. Indeed central governments' appreciation of this, and fear of its effect on national unity, has often been expressed in political opposition to regional devolution. For examples of this, we need look no further than Spain, during the Franco era, or postwar France under various Gaullist regimes.

It is significant therefore that, in Ireland, government is highly centralized. The high level of centralization relative to our European neighbours and the problems arising from it have long been recognized, even by central government itself, and have led to the setting up of a succession of expert committees, commissions and task forces to report on the possibilities for greater decentralization. These include: the Advisory Expert Committee on Local Government Reorganisation and Reform (also known as the Barrington Committee), which reported in 1991;[5] the Reorganisation Commission, which reported in 1996; the Devolution Commission, which reported in 1996 and 1997; and the Task Force on the Integration of Local Government and Local Development, which reported in 1998 and 1999.

While these various initiatives have led to some changes in *local* governance, the most notable being the establishment of county and city development boards, not much has changed at the regional level. Here a major institutional vacuum existed up until 1993, when Regional Authorities were established under the provisions of the Local Government Act of 1991. Even then, the new bodies were entrusted with only a narrow range of functions, and their members indirectly elected by and from the constituent local authorities, rather than by popular franchise. It is not surprising, therefore, that they have so far failed to capture the public imagination. It is doubtful, in fact, if more than a minority of the population is aware of the existence of the Regional Authorities, or the functions they perform. It has not helped either that many public bodies continue to divide the national territory for their own purposes without any reference to the Regional Authority areas. The Barrington Report highlighted the need to harmonize these multiple regional divisions if regional loyalties are to be properly developed.

The weakness of both regionalism and of administrative regionalization in Ireland reflects the relative unimportance of regions as economic entities. Strong regions that command the loyalties of their inhabitants, such as Lombardy in Italy, are often associated with vibrant regional economies. Likewise, Ulster's identity was in large part forged by industrialization based on the linen and shipbuilding industries in the nineteenth century. In the Republic of Ireland, industrialization came much later, and when it did, it was based largely on a dependence on foreign capital. Many of the firms that located here in the post-1960s wave of foreign investment had few links to the local economy. Instead they tended to be outward looking, both for sources of input and for their markets. None of this helped to generate a strong sense of regional identity, nor did it stimulate demands for regional devolution.

The Persistence of the Region

In spite of all these difficulties, the idea of the region as a basis for organizing public services as well as civil and commercial life has persisted in Ireland. Over the years there have been repeated calls for a greater emphasis on the regional aspect of economic development, and, associated with this, for the creation of new regional structures, up to and including regional governments.[6]

There are several sources of these demands arising both within and without the state. Outside Ireland, the Council of Europe and the European Union have been strong advocates of regional devolution. The concept of a 'Europe of the Regions', which both organizations have helped to promote, envisages a politically and economically re-invigorated Europe, in which the pressures of globalization are mediated and regulated by supranational institutions, while the delivery of public services is increasingly devolved to democratically elected, regional-level bodies.

The institutions of the European Union, especially the Commission and the Parliament, have had a particularly strong influence on the development of regional structures in Ireland. Our heavy reliance, until very recently, on European financing of our development plans has given these bodies considerable leverage in this respect. In 1988, a major reform of the structural funds, associated with the passing of the Single European Act, provided for a doubling of aid to less-developed areas, including Ireland, provided that satisfactory development plans were submitted to Europe. The reform simultaneously emphasized the need for central governments to consult regional interests in the preparation of these plans.

The Irish government responded with some alacrity to these promptings, by setting up a regional consultative structure based on a division of the country into seven regions, which were used in the consultation process underpinning the preparation of the National Development Plan 1989–93. Significantly though, these regions differed from an earlier set of nine physical planning regions

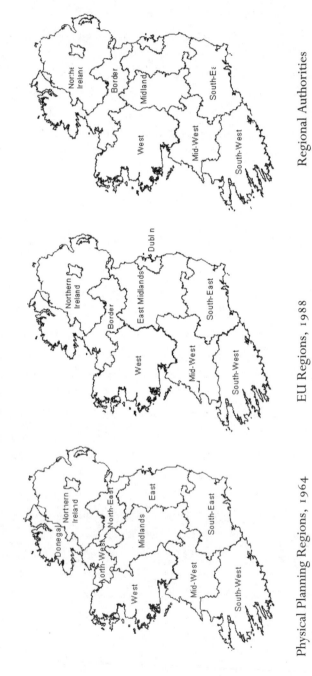

Regionalizations in Ireland

Regional Authorities

EU Regions, 1988

Physical Planning Regions, 1964

established in the 1960s, and in turn they themselves were re-cast when the eight Regional Authorities were established in the nineties (see figure).

More recently, the EU again assumed a central role in the development of Irish regional structures, when the rapid growth of the Celtic Tiger economy in the late nineties resulted in the country as a whole no longer qualifying for priority (Objective 1) status under the structural funds. In order to retain as much of the Brussels largesse as possible, the government created two new 'super-regions' in November 1998. The Southern and Eastern Region extends from Dublin along the east coast and includes all of Munster; the remainder of the country comprises the Border, Midlands and West (BMW) Region. Despite its acronym, this region is characterized by a significantly weaker level of economic activity, and therefore has retained Objective 1 designation. However, the real story of this most recent regionalization concerns the way in which the division became the subject of some contention between the Irish and EU authorities. Continuing the regrettable tendency to constantly revise regional boundaries, which has been one of the main factors undermining the role of regions in public affairs, the government's original proposal for the division included both Clare and Kerry in the BMW region. This would have entailed the new regional boundary cutting across the established Regional Authority areas. Significantly, the EU authorities showed themselves to be more serious about regionalization than the Irish government, by insisting that the integrity of the existing regional structures be respected.

Along with these external factors, there have been domestic reasons for a renewed interest in regions. Among these is a growing recognition that the governance needs of a modern society increasingly require a more decentralized form of government. There is some international evidence to suggest that higher levels of decentralization are associated with greater prosperity: countries with strongly developed local and/or regional government, such as the Scandinavian countries and Germany, also enjoy relatively high living standards. The nature of this relationship is not fully understood, but one possible explanation is that decentralization leads to improved economic performance by promoting local initiative as well as more responsive and innovative government.

One of the areas in which the link between regionalization and development is most apparent is that of industrial policy. In recent years there has been a growing recognition that reliance on one-off foreign direct investment is not a sound basis for sustainable economic development. This has been brought into sharp focus by the global economic downturn that began in 2001, and that has resulted in significant job losses across the country. A recent international survey conducted for the American *Foreign Policy* magazine found that Ireland was the most globalized country in the world, based on an index that takes into account four different aspects of globalization. One of these is economic integration, as measured by, *inter alia*, trade, foreign investment, and income flows. Given Ireland's high level of integration into the global economy, it was inevitable that the changing external economic environment would adversely affect us. However, it is also apparent that many of the recent job losses were in branch plants that had little or no economic ties to the localities and regions in which they were located. Factories that are disconnected from their host economies in this way will always be likely targets for job losses, or outright closure, when reduced international demand leads to a reduction in output.

Recognizing the problems of branch plant investment, the Industrial Development Authority has now adopted a new approach to industrial promotion. Central to this is the concept of industrial clusters, which is based largely on the writings of the American economist Michael Porter.[7] Clusters are networks of inter-linked, highly innovative firms in high-technology industries, together with supporting financial and research institutions, economic and business associations, and government agencies. Modern thinking is that industrial policy stands a better chance of success when directed towards the promotion of these industrial networks rather than the attraction of stand-alone developments. A great deal of international research has focused on clusters in the last few years, much of which suggests that there is a greater likelihood of success when they are organized regionally, and based on the indigenous resources of each region. In turn, this points to the desirability of having regional governments, which would be best able to identify and provide the kind of supports, including policy co-ordination, that clusters need in order to flourish.

Finally, the case for regionalization in twenty-first-century Ireland has been strengthened by the pressures exerted on the country's infrastructure as a direct result of rapid economic growth. There are many ways in which these pressures are evident. Probably the issues that have gained the most attention in the media are the rapid increase in house prices, especially in Dublin and the other urban centres, and the worsening traffic congestion on our roads. These problems are closely related, of course. Many of the new workers are young people who have been unable to afford housing close to their employment in the larger urban areas. Consequently, they are forced into long-distance commuting, effectively substituting travel costs for housing costs. The economic and social effects of large volumes of out-commuting on smaller towns and rural areas are not yet fully researched, but it is likely that, on balance, they are negative. What are certainly evident are the environmental pressures resulting from badly planned housing developments. In general, problems in water supply and in waste disposal are likely to emerge as among the most serious faced by the country in the years ahead. Together all these growth pressures have highlighted the need to pay some attention to the regional spread of development across the country.

Regions in the National Spatial Strategy

The government's response to this need was first signalled in the National Development Plan 2000–2006.[8] The Plan committed the government to producing a National Spatial Strategy (NSS), which would act as a blueprint for the long-term geographical distribution of population and economic activity. The development of the NSS was underpinned by extensive research and public consultations. The research programme covered a wide range of factors impinging on the territorial development of the state, but unfortunately the time available to the researchers was quite restricted. In addition, there is the problem that both the quality and quantity of data available at local and especially regional level is quite poor. In so far as this is due to the weakness of regional structures, it is possible to discern a strong element of chickens coming home to roost!

The strategy was published in November 2002, and is intended to be 'a twenty year planning framework designed to achieve a better balance of social, economic, physical development and population growth between regions'.[9] In recent years there have been major policy statements in relation to various non-spatial aspects of development in Ireland. These include the National Anti-Poverty Strategy, and the Strategy for Sustainable Development, which relate to the social and the environmental dimensions of development respectively. The National Spatial Strategy (NSS) now complements these by providing for the geographical dimension. As such, it is potentially one of the most important initiatives in regional and spatial planning in the history of the state.

The NSS is designed to help achieve the objectives of existing economic policy (increased productivity and international competitiveness), social policy (improvement in the quality of life for all sections of society), and environmental policy (enhancement of the country's natural and cultural heritage). In addition, the strategy has the explicitly spatial objective of fostering balanced regional development. Significantly, this is defined as 'developing the full potential of each area to contribute to the optimal performance of the state as a whole – economically, socially and environmentally'.[10] It is clear, therefore, that balanced regional development does not mean that every area of the country must have similar levels of population, investment, and economic activity. Rather, each area is to be facilitated to reach its capacity for development based on its existing population and other resources. This approach is sensible, in that it is neither possible nor desirable for levels of development to be identical everywhere.

The means by which the spatial strategy aims to achieve balanced regional development is through the promotion of new roles for selected larger centres of population as either 'gateways' or 'development hubs'. The concept of gateways emphasizes the role of the largest centres in attracting external investment into the country, and communicating the benefits of this to the wider regions in which they are located. Because gateways need to possess a minimum level of population, infrastructure and services, only nine have been designated. These include the cities of Dublin, Cork, Limerick, Galway and Waterford, as well as the towns of Dundalk and Sligo. In addition, the midland towns of Athlone, Mullingar and Tullamore are jointly designated as a gateway, and it is envisaged that by linking with Derry, Letterkenny can also fulfil this role. There is a similar number of development hubs, which are conceived of as medium-sized towns that are well connected to gateways and that will act to spread growth to even smaller towns and the rural areas. Two of the hubs are also based on linking together neighbouring centres: Ballina-Castlebar in the west, and Tralee-Killarney in the south-west.

The fact that the number of gateways and hubs is necessarily limited (though greater than what some commentators have suggested is optimal) means there is a danger that the NSS will be seen as favouring certain places over others. It may be perceived as being all about selecting winners and losers. Such a view was expressed, in the immediate aftermath of the strategy's publication, by public representatives from several non-designated towns. But although the designation of centres is the aspect of the spatial plan that has attracted most public attention and comment, the document in fact sets out a more inclusive vision of the territorial development of the state, in which all places have a role to play. The joint designation of centres as gateways or hubs is one way in which this inclusivity is expressed. More generally, it is promoted through a strong emphasis on co-operation and complementarity between places at regional level. The research for the strategy included an examination of functional regions, using data on travel to work, schools, shops, and social facilities, and these regions featured prominently in a public consultation paper on the strategy.[11] While they receive little mention in the NSS itself, there remains a strong emphasis throughout on the regional dimension, with one chapter devoted to a detailed elaboration of how the statutory regions will participate in future territorial development.

The success of the strategy will depend critically on securing the envisaged co-operation between places. This will not be easy, given that relations between neighbouring urban centres in Ireland have traditionally been marked more by a spirit of competition than of co-operation. In recent times this has been evident, for example, in considerable squabbling over the programme for the decentralization of the public services, and over infrastructural development, notably the routing of new motorways. This state of affairs reflects the strength of localism and the weakness of regionalism in this country. Ultimately, therefore, what is needed for the NSS to succeed in its vision of a more balanced spatial structure, is the development of a stronger regional consciousness and sense of regional identity amongst the public at large and its elected representatives.

Conclusion

Ireland currently stands at a critical juncture in terms of the territorial development of the state. Until now, regions have had a very low profile in public administration and policy, and indeed in the public imagination. The National Spatial Strategy has the potential to change this situation significantly. Its suggested mechanisms for spatial development, together with the broad thrust of industrial and environmental policy, point to the desirability of an enhanced role for regions in Ireland. Regions may yet emerge as key forums for democratic decision-making about where people live, where they work, and what kind of services and lifestyles they enjoy. This vision of localities and regions that are more self-reliant, and less dependent and focused on the capital city, is surely one worth striving for. However, given the on-again off-again, opportunistic and ad hoc nature of official engagement with the regions in the past, it's probably wise to temper optimism with a degree of caution – at least for the time being.

7. Symbolic Streetscapes:
Interrogating Monumental Spaces of Dublin

Yvonne Whelan

On 21 October 1805 Lord Nelson fell mortally wounded at the Battle of Trafalgar. Four years later in 1809, crowds gathered in the centre of Dublin to watch in eager anticipation as a tall Corinthian column, topped with a statue of the dead admiral, was unveiled in the middle of Sackville Street. Those jubilant scenes stand in marked contrast to the events that took place over a century and a half later in 1966, the year that marked the fiftieth anniversary of the 1916 Rising. Then, in the early morning of 8 March, explosives that had been planted at the base of the Nelson monument rocked Dublin's most central thoroughfare, O'Connell Street, and the figure of Nelson came toppling to the ground. The site remained vacant until December 2000 when the Irish government announced that a new monument, the 'Spire of Dublin', was to be erected on the site of the old pillar. This steel structure, striking for its overtly apolitical nature, is now set to transform the streetscape and create an innovative symbolic space in the heart of Dublin. It will stand tall alongside a range of other monuments erected in previous centuries to commemorate heroes of earlier ages and political causes.

In many ways the story of Nelson's Pillar captures in microcosm the broader narrative of Dublin's iconography as it evolved before and after the creation of the Irish Free State in 1922. Prior to independence it was just one of many monuments, street names and public buildings that represented in concrete form Ireland's place *within* the British empire. They stood as tangible signs of Dublin's status as the 'Second City', a phenomenon that was further reinforced by visits to the country of various members of the British royal family. On these occasions cities and towns were lavishly decorated, royal processions through urban spaces were symbolically planned, gigantic temporary structures were erected and addresses of welcome were carefully crafted. This, however, is only one reading of what had become a much more complex iconography by the late nineteenth century and one that embodied the fraught political context that then prevailed. In fact, various strands of Irish nationalist, republican and socialist opinion also used the cultural landscape to express resistance and opposition to empire and to assert that Ireland laboured under a malign form of colonial rule from which every effort should be made to break free.

This essay takes the reader back to that contested iconography, charting retrospectively the ways in which the symbolic 'text' of the city was scripted before and after 1922. Particular attention is paid to the role of public statuary in contributing to the contested narratives of identity that then prevailed. As a study in historical and cultural geography, this research can be situated within a broader body of literature that has highlighted the powerful role of landscape as a site of symbolic representation integral to the imaginative construction of national identity. In recent years cultural geographers have begun to focus their research on space as a setting for the exercise of power. The fact that our world is an accumulation of spaces, as much as an accumulation of the experiences of time, has been recognized. As the geographer Cole Harris suggests, drawing upon the work of Foucault, 'Social power is no longer conceived apart from its geographical context. Such power requires space, its exercise shapes space, and space shapes social power.'[1] One of the geographer's tasks, therefore, is to decode the many, layered meanings embedded in the symbolic spaces in which we live.

Recent developments in the sub-field of cultural geography have paved the way for an approach to the cultural landscape as a depository of symbolic space and time. Drawing on the art historian's iconographic method, the symbolic meaning inherent in the urban landscape has come into sharp focus. As Cosgrove argues, 'All landscapes are symbolic ... reproducing cultural norms and establishing the values of dominant groups across all of a society.'[2] Landscapes on the ground and as represented in various surfaces have come to be regarded as deposits of cultural and symbolic meaning. The iconographic method seeks to explore these meanings through describing the form and composition of landscape in their social and historical contexts. Moreover, geographical iconography accepts that landscape meanings are unstable, contested and highly political.[3] Hence, both cultural and historical geographers have begun to explore the powerful role of public statues as symbols of power and signifiers of memory and identity rooted in the cultural landscape. The objects of a people's national pilgrimage, monuments 'mark deeper, more enduring claims upon a national past as part of the present ... Monuments may become both historical symbols of nationhood and fixed points in our contemporary landscapes.'[4] Sandercock points out that we erect sculptures to dead leaders, war heroes and revolutionaries because 'memory, both individual and collective, is deeply important to us. It locates us as part of something bigger than our individual existences, perhaps makes us seem less insignificant ... Memory locates us, as part of a family history, as part of a tribe or community, as a part of city-building and nation-making.'[5] The very qualities that make public statues so valuable in building popular support, however, also make them a useful target for those who wish to demonstrate opposition. Consequently, monuments have been erected to challenge the legitimacy of governments and objectify the ideals of revolutionary movements. This is particularly so in the case of post-colonial countries emerging from beneath the shadow of colonial rule.

Interrogating Symbolic Spaces of Dublin

In Ireland, monumental spaces have proved to be a potent symbolic commodity, not least during the twentieth century when the Irish Free State came into being and the six counties of Northern Ireland became a separate political entity. In the mid-nineteenth century a visitor to the city would have found themselves in a landscape peopled with a variety of figures cast in stone. Statues that had been erected during the eighteenth and nineteenth centuries commemorated a myriad of figures closely connected to the British administration, from kings and queens to members of the military establishment. In the heart of the city Kings William III, George I and George II, Lord Nelson and the Duke of Wellington each occupied dominant positions and were representative of a broader, country-wide trend to represent in stone the link with empire. Points of physical and ideological orientation, these monuments comprised one dimension of a monumental landscape that was consistently augmented over the course of three centuries. Located in prominent sites and unveiled with displays of much ritual, pomp and choreographed ceremony, these statues contributed to the creation of a one-sided symbolic landscape from which figures of Irish nationalist politics were notably absent. They were a feature of many towns and cities throughout the United Kingdom and Commonwealth countries where they confronted inhabitants on a daily basis and represented empire in the domain of the cultural landscape. While these monumental initiatives may have inspired loyalty and served to cultivate a sense of belonging to empire, drawing citizens into closer

communion with the imperial project, they also acted as focal points
for demonstrations of nationalist resistance. In Ireland they increasingly became sites of protest and contestation rather than of loyalty
to empire. For example, the monument dedicated to King William
III in College Green was repeatedly defaced in the late nineteenth
century and often daubed with paint in acts of political protest.

By the mid-nineteenth century the 'one-sided' nature of
Dublin's monumental landscape, from which figures of Irish politics and culture were notably absent, was clearly apparent. As was
noted in the *Dublin University Magazine*:

> Dublin is connected with Irish patriotism only by the scaffold and the
> gallows. Statue and column do indeed rise there, but not to honour
> the sons of the soil. The public idols are foreign potentates and for-
> eign heroes ... No monument exists to which the gaze of the young
> Irish children can be directed, while their fathers tell them, 'This was
> to the glory of your countrymen.'[6]

These sentiments were echoed in the columns of *The Nation* where
it was observed:

> We now have statues to William the Dutchman, to the four Georges
> – all either German by birth or German by feeling – to Nelson, a
> great admiral but an Englishman, while not a single statue of any of
> the many celebrated Irishmen whom their country should honour
> adorns a street or square of our beautiful metropolis.[7]

In the second half of the nineteenth century, the 'supremacy in
statuary' which imperial statues enjoyed was challenged both geo-
graphically and numerically by the unveiling of monuments dedicated to figures drawn from the contrary sphere of Irish culture, literature and nationalist politics. Throughout the country local organizing committees were established that set about erecting monuments to their respective leaders and heroes. In Dublin, monuments
were erected in honour of Daniel O'Connell and C.S. Parnell, both
of whom had been to the fore of constitutional politics during the

nineteenth century. Equally, men who had led sections of the population in violent revolt and sought the creation of an independent
Irish republic were honoured, among them William Smith O'Brien.
By way of sharp contrast, statues dedicated to figures of the British
administration were erected in increasingly peripheral locations
such as the Phoenix Park or the private domain of St Stephen's
Green. Contentious debates often accompanied plans to erect monuments as committees sought out prized locations, engaged native
sculptors and planned elaborate unveiling ceremonies which invariably drew enormous crowds. During the unveiling of the O'Connell
monument, for example, we are told of how:

> The eve of one of Ireland's greatest days has now arrived. Every ele-
> ment of success attended the centennial and O'Connell celebration.
> Numbers, strength, enthusiasm, and all the adjuncts, natural and arti-
> ficial, of popular triumph wait upon tomorrow's festival … if the
> O'Connell bronze, whose heroic beauty will be revealed to the pop-
> ulace tomorrow, could speak, it might tell them, too, that many mon-
> ster meetings of the past looked down upon them, Tara Hill and Mul-
> laghmast, the meetings of the Funeral, the Foundation Stone, and the
> centenary stand before the people for comparisons with tomorrow's.[8]

The erection of each of these monuments on Sackville Street
marked a significant turning point in the evolving symbolic geography of Dublin's monumental landscape. With the exception of
Nelson's Pillar, a dominant and much-contested symbol of empire,
each of the other monuments was unveiled in the latter half of the
nineteenth and the early twentieth century and effectively created
a nationalist monumental landscape in the heart of Dublin. In
terms of the individuals whom these monuments sought to commemorate, the geographical positions they were afforded and the
choreography of the unveiling ceremonies, they are indicative of a
broader change in the politics of power in late nineteenth-century
Dublin. Their unveiling, together with the not always successful
insistence on using native, resident sculptors, can be interpreted as

an attempt by various committees to challenge the ideology represented in the statues that had been erected in the eighteenth century and which had become both outdated and outmoded amid the
changing political and cultural context. Moreover, these sculptural
initiatives also point to the increasing power and nationalist complexion of the city's governing authority, Dublin Corporation, consideration of which is essential in any assessment of the symbolic
geography of Dublin before independence.

In the mid-nineteenth century, Dublin underwent a revolution
in municipal government, which paved the way for a new and
reformed Corporation. Prior to the passing of the Municipal Corporations Ireland Act in 1840 and the Dublin Improvement Act in
1849, the city's municipal authority was 'orange-dominated ... the
voice of Ascendancy and bigotry, operating under the principle of
self-election and absolute control of admission to the franchise'.[9]
The municipal reforms paved the way for the subsequent domina-
tion of the council chamber by nationalist-minded Roman Catholics
at the expense of conservative, unionist members. Throughout the
remainder of the century many issues of little municipal significance
but of great political and religious controversy were debated in its
chamber.[10] The political composition of the Corporation also
served to alienate the Dublin Castle administration and from 1880
members of the authority boycotted official functions, although
relations temporarily thawed with the arrival of the pro-Home Rule
Viceroy, Lord Aberdeen. The nationalist agenda of Dublin Corporation ensured that it became firmly established 'as a body with
wider political interests, a type of substitute for the lost Parliament
of College Green'.[11] This 'substitute Parliament' played a key role
in granting permission for statues to be located on particular sites.
Its willingness to sanction the erection of nationalist monuments in
prominent locations was matched only by its reluctance to afford
similar locations for statues that had a more loyalist bent. Much less
conspicuous sites were granted to statues of, for example, the Earl

of Carlisle, Lord Gough, Prince Albert and the Duke of Eglinton and Winton. This trend continued into the early decades of the twentieth century, most explicitly demonstrated when a monument to Queen Victoria was unveiled in the relative seclusion of Leinster House while a statue of Charles Stewart Parnell was unveiled at the head of Sackville Street.

The erection of the Sackville Street monuments, for example, in the latter half of the nineteenth century signalled the onset of a new era in the symbolic geography of Dublin. These statues stood alongside the pillar dedicated to Lord Nelson in an uneasy juxtaposition and served as a challenge in stone to the prevailing Castle administration and to the monumental landscape of imperial power that had been constructed centuries earlier. It is striking that these figures, drawn almost exclusively from Irish political, cultural and religious circles, should be unveiled in the heart of a city that remained a part of the British empire. After all, the head of state was the British monarch, who was represented by his viceroy, although the real power rested with the chief secretary for Ireland, upon whose advice the viceroy acted. From his offices in Dublin Castle, the chief secretary supervised the administration of a country that was politically and culturally deeply divided. Ireland may have been a colony of the British empire, but its status as a colony was deeply ambivalent.[12]

By 1922, the symbolic fabric of the capital had come to embody and reflect the struggle for superiority, victory and ultimately power that persisted between Britain and one of its kingdoms, Ireland. This struggle was played out through the medium of the public statuary and left turn-of-the-century Dublin in something of a schizophrenic position. On the one hand it was a city of the British empire and capital of the kingdom of Ireland within the confines of the United Kingdom of Great Britain and Ireland, and the canvas upon which the British administration set out to paint a picture of union and loyalty. On the other it was a city under the local governance of the strongly nationalist Dublin Corporation, which attempted to assert a tangible sense of Irish national identity upon the urban landscape in the years before 1922. With the Home Rule movement reaching a crescendo, and political independence in the offing, Dublin's streetscapes stood on the cusp of monumental change. In the decades that followed the 1916 Rising and the establishment of the Irish Free State, the demands placed upon the symbolic landscape altered accordingly as the new administration set about the nation-building process.

Carving New Symbolic Spaces: Iconography after Independence

> The great thoroughfare which the citizen of Dublin was accustomed to describe proudly as the finest street in Europe has been reduced to a smoking reproduction of the ruin wrought at Ypres by the mercilessness of the Hun. Elsewhere throughout the city the streets have been devastated, centres of thriving industry have been placed in peril or ruined, a paralysis of work and commerce has been imposed and the public confidence that is the life of trade and employment has received a staggering blow from which it will take almost a generation to recover.[13]

The Easter Rising began in April, 1916, signalling the onset of several years of destruction, death and civic unrest, punctuated by the War of Independence and culminating in the Civil War. Once the fighting had ceased, the administration of 'Independent Ireland' set about the business of political and economic development. Although the leaders of the first generation after independence evoked an image of Irish society that was almost exclusively rural, various aspects of the cultural landscape did play a significant role in marking the transition towards independence. The Rising of 1916, together with the War of Independence and the Civil War, provided a host of new heroes to stand upon pedestals throughout the city and country. In their geography and iconography, these monuments carved out a visible landscape of memory as a testament to the new political situation. Over the course of succeeding decades, figures like Michael Collins, Arthur Griffith and later Kevin O'Higgins were commemorated in a cenotaph erected at the rear of Leinster House. Other leading figures of the 1916 Rising were also to find positions of public prominence in the capital, among them Countess Markievicz, to whom a monument was erected in St Stephen's Green in 1932, and Sean Heuston, who was commemorated in the grounds of the Phoenix Park in 1943.

As the cradle of the 1916 Rising, it might be expected that Sackville Street, which was formally renamed O'Connell Street in 1924, would be important in the symbolic construction of national identity. Initially the authorities were preoccupied with the reconstruction of the large portions of the street that had been destroyed during the years of war. Once the process of reconstruction was set in train, O'Connell Street assumed a central role in the annual spectacle that marked the commemoration of the rebellion. The fact that the thoroughfare was already lined with an array of public statues, however, meant that the number of new sculptural initiatives was limited. The erection of a monument of the ancient Celtic warrior Cuchulainn took place in 1935. It was dedicated to all those who had died in the Rising and its unveiling on 21 April 1935 in the General Post Office, the nineteenth anniversary of the Rising, brought thousands of citizens out onto the streets of the capital to witness the military parade that accompanied the civil ceremonial. On the fortieth anniversary of the Rising in 1956, the Custom House memorial was unveiled, in memory of the members of the Irish Republican Brotherhood who had died in the War of Independence when the Custom House came under attack on 25 May 1921. In the same year, a site on the north-side of the city at Arbour Hill was given over to the formal commemoration of the dead of the 1916 Rising. The Golden Jubilee 'celebrations' in April

1966, involved a two-week, country-wide commemorative celebration to honour those who took part in the Rising and 'to empha-
sise its importance as a decisive event in our history'. While special
ceremonies took place at provincial centres all around the country,
a number of significant statues were unveiled in the capital,
together with the formal opening of the Garden of Remembrance,
just north of O'Connell Street.

The 1916 Rising was not, however, the only impetus behind
public sculpture in Free State Dublin. On the contrary, other earlier rebellions, including those of 1798 and 1848, also shaped the
monumental landscape. In September 1945, the centenary of the
death of the Irish poet and patriot Thomas Davis was the catalyst
for a display of Irish nationalism on the streets of the capital when
the foundation stone of a statue in his honour was laid in St
Stephen's Green. The Fenian leader and poet Jeremiah O'Donovan
Rossa was also commemorated with a monument on 6 June 1954.
Afforded prominent geographical positions, these monuments
stood in contrast to the somewhat anachronistic monarchical figures erected some decades before and whose future became
increasingly uncertain as time passed.

During the decades after 1922, those monuments that did not
fit so easily with the ideology of the new regime were wiped clean
from the landscape, demonstrating the significance of 'forgetting'
as much as remembering in the nation-building process. Symbolic
spaces that did not conform to a notion of the Irish Free State as a
Catholic and nationalist nation were willfully destroyed or officially
removed as a testimony to their symbolic potency. It would seem
that the people and the events that these monuments focused attention upon had become part of what Osborne refers to as 'the ideological bric-a-brac' of a former era. Among those destroyed or
sold to foreign interests by the state were the statues of Kings
William III, George I and George II, along with monuments dedicated to Lord Gough, the Earl of Carlisle and the Duke of Eglinton

and Winton. In 1948, the statue of Queen Victoria was removed from the grounds of Leinster House in a symbolic gesture that coincided with Ireland's departure from the Commonwealth. It was later to re-emerge in the Australian capital, Sydney, in 1988, as a gift from the Irish government on the occasion of the bicentenary of white settlement in Australia. Perhaps the most famous monument to be removed from the cultural landscape after independence, however, was Nelson's Pillar.

On the night of Easter Monday, 1966, the fate of Nelson's pillar was finally decided when it was badly damaged in an explosion, a month before the fiftieth anniversary commemoration of the 1916 Rising:

> The top of Nelson Pillar, in O'Connell Street, Dublin, was blown off by a tremendous explosion at 1.32 o'clock this morning and the Nelson statue and tons of rubble poured down into the roadway. By a miracle, nobody was injured, though there were a number of people in the area at the time ... Gardai set up a cordon around the city and checked on the movements of members of the Republican movement, but it appeared that the pillar had been shattered by an explosion which had been set some time previously ... The demolition of the pillar was obviously the work of some explosives expert. The column was cut through clearly just below the plinth, and the debris fell closely around the base of the monument, with some stone being hurled just as far as the entrances of Henry Street and North Earl Street.[14]

The editorial of the *Irish Times* on March 9, 1966, observed that:

> Ever since it went up it has been the subject of controversy. It blocked the traffic; interrupted the view of the street, and when we attained our sovereign independence, it was as odd to have Nelson up there as it would be to have had an Austrian general's statue in the principal thoroughfare of Milan.[15]

The bombing was widely thought to have been carried out by a splinter group of the Republican movement, known as Saor Uladh,

Yvonne Whelan

many of whose members came from Northern Ireland and who had a number of adherents south of the border also. Shortly after the initial explosion, the government, under the direction of Seán Lemass, gave authorization for the blowing up of the remainder of the pillar a week later, occasioning in the process considerably more damage to the surrounding area than the initial blast.

After the army demolition of the pillar, the Nelson Pillar bill came into being, providing legislation that dealt with the inevitable legal aftermath of the demolition. The pillar had after all been maintained by trustees, and they were also the recipients of the admission fees to the pillar. By the terms of the Nelson Pillar Act, the trustees were awarded £21,750 in compensation in respect of both the pillar's destruction and its removal, while other compensation covered the loss of admission revenue and legal costs. The site on which the pillar stood was vested in Dublin Corporation and the Nelson Pillar Trust was accordingly declared terminated. Section Four of the Nelson Pillar Act of 1969 conferred on the pillar's trustees an indemnity to cover any suit that might be brought against them for not restoring the Nelson monument.

The debates that accompanied the reading of the Nelson Pillar bill in both the Dáil and Seanad make for entertaining reading. During the second-stage reading in the Seanad the debate was virtually monopolized by Owen Sheehy-Skeffington. He touched on a feeling shared by many Dubliners in his statement:

> When in 1966 the pillar was half blown down by a person or persons unknown, I, as a Dubliner, felt a sense of loss, not because of Nelson – one could hardly see Nelson at the top – but because this pillar symbolised for many Dubliners the centre of the city. It had a certain rugged, elegant grace about it ... The man who destroyed the pillar made Dublin look more like Birmingham and less like an ancient city on the River Liffey, because the presence of the pillar gave Dublin an internationally known appearance.[16]

Towards a Postmodern Iconography

The capacity of the seemingly innocuous public statue to engage with popular public opinion, to shape ideals and political values and to contribute to the nation-building process, was made patently clear in Dublin in the decades before and after independence. The various state-sanctioned monumental initiatives created a visual landscape that served to fix in the minds of citizens the memory of people and events that marked out the path to political independence. As Bhreathnach-Lynch writes, 'One important reason to rush to create 'new' heroes and revive 'old' ones lies in the need a newly independent nation has to establish quickly its own sense of national identity ... The promotion of new heroes suggested not only a positive, affirming self-image but also implied that another such age would emerge in the near future.'[17] The bitter and contentious Civil War that followed the emergence of the Irish Free State, however, meant that commemorative practices in Dublin and more widely across Ireland were lacking in direction from central government. As Fitzpatrick points out:

> The Irish Free State emerged from four bitter conflicts, between Irish and English, Catholics and Protestants, 'constitutional nationalists' and 'separatists', and finally 'Treatyites' and republicans. The rulers of the new state represented a sub-group within Catholic and nationalist Ireland, their triumph being bitterly resented by many Irish protestants as well as by Catholic republicans and unreformed constitutionalists.[18]

This political discord inevitably raised problems for commemorating the past and often flared up during unveiling ceremonies, such as occurred at the Civil War commemoration ceremony and at the unveiling of the 1916 monument in the General Post Office.

Nevertheless, a host of figures drawn from the disparate strands of Irish nationalist politics did find their way onto the streets and green spaces of the capital after 1922. This 'scripting of national memory' stands in marked contrast to the de-commemorative practices that also prevailed after 1922 and saw older icons of empire unceremoniously bombed from their pedestals or sold by the state to foreign interests.

Since the 1960s however, there has been a tangible shift in the nature of Dublin's iconography, a product of the growing distance from the independence struggle, the inevitable cultural maturing of the state and perhaps influenced also by the political situation that developed in Northern Ireland. The much more low-key commemoration of the 1916 Rising, for example, and the absence of any displays of nationalistic military might, stands in marked contrast to the earlier state-sponsored 'celebrations' that characterized previous ceremonies. Meanwhile, those monuments that were once erected with such ceremony as symbols of a nationalist ideology would seem to have lost much of their symbolic potency. Many of Dublin's citizens would be hard-pressed to name the statues that line O'Connell Street, figures which might now be considered anachronistic features of the cityscape. It would seem that such spaces no longer retain the powerful significance they once possessed. This raises some interesting issues regarding the contemporary iconography of the island's space. In many ways the new 'Spire of Dublin' speaks volumes of the cultural and political climate that now prevails in Ireland. As the centrepiece of O'Connell Street's integrated action plan, it is intended to become the signature of the city in the twenty-first century, a Dublin version of Paris's Eiffel Tower or Sydney's Opera House. This monument is striking for a number of reasons, not least its utter simplicity, its ahistorical nature and complete lack of any political association. These combined to make it, in the eyes of the judging panel, 'an ideal emblem for the current time'. In these respects the 'Monument of Light' stands in marked contrast to earlier emblems of nationhood that marked the Free State's symbolic geography after 1922. It captures in microcosm a much broader, paradigmatic shift that has taken place in Irish political and cultural life during the modern period.

It is a shift from dependence to independence, from the modern to the post-modern and from being an inward-looking island on the periphery of Europe to an outward-looking contributor to the European super-state in an era of globalization. It symbolizes the changing conception of culture that now prevails and which transcends narrow ethnic boundaries. This conception recognizes that Irish identity crosses over the simple binary oppositions of Catholic and Protestant, nationalist and unionist, republican and loyalist and is contested along new axes of differentiation.

This essay, in focusing upon a case-study of Dublin, has confirmed that cities are indeed constructed landscapes, shaped by sets of agents that are caught up in a web of social, cultural and political circumstances. The argument that every landscape is 'a synthesis of charisma and context, a text which may be read to reveal the force of dominant ideas and prevailing practices, as well as the idiosyncrasies of a particular author', is particularly true in the context of Dublin before and after 1922.[19] We have seen that public monuments to royal monarchs erected in the Irish capital acted as important focal points around which political and cultural positions were articulated. This study contributes to a broader literature, as yet under-represented in the Republic of Ireland, which recognizes that public monuments are an important lens through which to explore the symbolic meaning of the urban landscape, especially those shaped amid the turbulent political transition from the colonial to the post-colonial.

8. No Frontiers, Diversity within Unity:
Borders and the Identification with Place

Joseph Brady

T he business of living requires an engagement with space: we travel to work, go shopping or go on holidays. Each activity involves, at the very least, overcoming the friction of distance and the physical movement from one space to another. This process may hardly register with us; we may barely notice the spaces through which we move. However, with some spaces there is a deeper level of engagement, and they become places. These places have a meaning for us over and above the mere fact of their relative location. The meaning and the relationship in many cases is personal but there are some places with which the engagement is societal and is one with which we, as citizens, are expected to identify. One such space is the national territory, defined in spatial terms for us by the presence of borders. The border separates us from the outside world and identifies what is ours and what belongs to the other; those outside. It is often more than a physical barrier; cultures can take very different paths on either side and so the physical space contained within the border can become a cultural space. We then come to identify with the physical space in cultural terms. As we become more globalized and as frontiers diminish, we receive cultural influences from a far greater geographical range than ever before. The question that arises is whether we are responding to a global culture by changing or even losing our attachment to particular places.

Borders and National Identity

The importance of borders used to be emphasized by the elaborate ceremonial involved in making a crossing. I recall my first visit to the Soviet Union in the early 1980s. As one of a long line of would-be visitors, I presented myself to a young unsmiling border guard who scrutinized my passport and visa for what seemed an eternity. He looked backwards and forwards several times from me to my documents. It went on so long that I felt it was inevitable that he was going to find some fatal flaw that was, at best, going to deny me entry. This impressed on me that I was now, very much, in a different county.

Borders have always been important because of the degree to which space has been contested. People have fought about where to draw lines on maps from the dawn of time and there can be few places on earth that have not seen conflict. We do not have to go very far back in time to recall the convulsions that occurred in Europe and resulted in two world wars in the twentieth century. The Balkans remain as contested today as they were in the nineteenth century. Much of the instability in today's Africa results from the manner in which its internal borders were drawn. They reflected the balance of power between competing European powers rather than any local sense of place or territory. The boundaries that emerged after the Berlin Conference of 1885 were generally based upon geographical features, especially rivers and watersheds, and astronomical or geometrical lines. They remain just as contentious today.[1]

Within secure borders, nations could develop their identity and

enhance those aspects of life that made them different to those on
the other side of the border such as language, culture or the side of
the road on which we drive. It might extend even to the recording
of time and the calendar used: Russia did not adopt the Gregorian
calendar until after the 1917 Revolution. Borders also served to
restrict the impact of foreign influences, if the ruling authorities so
wished, as in communist Albania where the outside world was all
but excluded. The land within the border could then take on precious, mystical characteristics – it became the fatherland or moth-
erland. It was from this that people drew their strength; it was this
that gave them their identity, their sense of who they were and, of
course, it had to be defended. Horace's phrase 'Dulce et decorum
est pro patria mori,' 'It is sweet and proper to die for your country,'
was until recently, one of the aphorisms learned by any schoolchild,
just as she or he might have been taught the lines from Walter
Scott's 'The Lay of the Last Minstrel':

> Breathes there the man, with soul so dead,
> Who never to himself hath said,
> This is my own, my native land!

This expectation that people will accept this merging of their
identity with a specific place is widespread and cuts across different
political and cultural systems. Of course, the acceptance is not
unchallenged, as the poet Wilfred Owen, killed in the last moments
of World War I, made clear in his 'Dulce et Decorum Est':

> If in some smothering dreams you too could pace
> Behind the wagon that we flung him in,
> And watch the white eyes writhing in his face,
> His hanging face, like a devil's sick of sin;
> If you could hear, at every jolt, the blood
> Come gargling from the froth-corrupted lungs,
> Obscene as cancer, bitter as the cud

Of vile, incurable sores on innocent tongues,–
My friend, you would not tell with such high zest
To children ardent for some desperate glory,
The old Lie: Dulce et decorum est
Pro patria mori.

Borders and the Economy

The border, therefore, is what sustains and defines us as a people. At a more prosaic level, frontiers have been used to constrain trade and business. They have been the means whereby vital national interests have been protected, insulating strategic businesses from competition by tariffs and others forms of tax. Economists tell us that these practices promote inefficiency and damage prosperity. By contrast, their absence permits nations and regions to specialize in what they do best and free trade ensures the necessary flows of goods and services. Thus, the theory goes, we all benefit when nothing inhibits the operation of the market.

This kind of specialization also creates an interdependency that weakens the ability of any country to wage war. The European Coal and Steel Community, the forerunner to today's European Union, was established in 1951 by six countries – Germany, France, Italy, Luxembourg, Belgium and the Netherlands. At an economic level, it aimed to rationalize an inefficient industrial sector by managing it supranationally. Member nations of ECSC agreed to a unified market for their coal and steel products, lifting restrictions on imports and exports and between 1952 and 1960 iron and steel production rose by 75 per cent and industrial production rose 58 per cent. The motivation behind the community was even more radical at another level. Coal and steel were the essential tools of war and these tools were now shared between the six members in a way that made a war between them almost impossible to contemplate.[2] In his declaration to the international press on 9 May

1950 (9 May is now Europe Day), Robert Schuman announced that the ECSC would 'change the destinies of those regions which have long been devoted to the manufacture of munitions of war, of which they have been the most constant victims'. This was the first step towards more integration that led to the EEC, the EC and latterly the European Union or EU.

The EU in which we now live is spoken of as a 'Europe without frontiers'. We have seen the removal of barriers to commerce and the replacement of national regulations by community regulations. The nations of the EU function less and less as independent economic units and there are relatively few aspects of economic life in which a country can act unilaterally. In addition, social matters are increasingly subject to European rather than national control. The conditions under which we work are becoming more similar across Europe – a major exception being the United Kingdom.

Europe Without Frontiers

There are also physical manifestations of the weakening of frontiers. Borders, even those of the Soviet Union, were always leaky, but in many parts of Europe they barely exist any more. In Strasbourg the journey from France to Germany simply involves a walk over a bridge. It is about as unimpressive a transition as can be imagined and it is even harder to imagine that this is Alsace, a land that was for so long, so bitterly contested by those two nations. Even where border crossings still exist, most lack any real sense of being a frontier, at least for citizens of the Union who can move freely from place to place.

Other aspects of difference between EU states have weakened. When people speak of travel plans, the conversation will now frequently turn to the question of language and to the reassurance, 'Oh, you won't have any problems there, everyone speaks English.' Fortunately, perhaps, there is still no single European language but language is less and less of a barrier – especially within European cities. It has encouraged many people to set up a home away from home. In Dublin there are now quite a number of 'one-stop shops' selling villas in Spain. This has been facilitated by greater prosperity but it also reflects the fact that abroad is no longer as foreign as it used to be. It is like home but with more sun.

On 1 January 2002 we lost another facet that emphasized our differences. Currency was always part of what set one place apart from another. It was a barrier to business, certainly, but on a personal level it also emphasized the otherness of the place. These people, this place, were different, there was a new arithmetic to be mastered. The euro has ended all this. More than many other EU initiatives, the euro has made a major contribution to the smoothing out of perceived differences between places. It is hard to overemphasize the impact that this has made on travellers within the Eurozone and it is not just in practical terms. There is a comfort, an ease, of having our own currency in our pockets. The symbolism of the euro currency, or at least the notes, emphasizes the desire for unity. The map of Europe on the notes is one without borders. The drawings are not specific to any place. They reflect European space but are not tied to any particular European place.

It might be argued that only travellers experience these changes. For those who do not travel internationally, this makes little difference. However, borders work both ways and in this freer environment we are open to outside influences to an unprecedented degree. This has coincided with the process of globalization. The rhythms of business are global. They shift as the sun moves across the planet, creating global business centres in cities devoted to commerce: places like New York, London, Tokyo, Singapore and increasingly Shanghai. These cities are so much part of an international, transnational network that they are virtually detached from their countries. They are placeless city-states whose absolute location does not matter – all that matters is their pattern of connectivity. Similarity in these cities extends to the kinds of buildings in which business takes place. There is little that differentiates the office blocks of London from those of Singapore.

Nowhere is really outside these global trends. Increasingly, the companies that employ many of us and supply us with a great variety of goods and services are part of large transnational operations. This ensures that we too can enjoy the range of goods and products that other people have. Some products are truly universal. There are few places where Coca-Cola and McDonald's have not reached. So pervasive are these brands that some writers have chosen to christen this new globalized world as 'McWorld'.3 The 'Big Mac' will be pretty much the same in Dublin as it is Berlin or Madrid. This is some people's idea of hell – going to a foreign place and eating in an international fast food restaurant, but others like the sameness, the comfort of knowing that there will be nothing strange or even threatening about the experience.

Globalization

The effect of globalization on us as consumers is multifaceted. It affects the things we buy, the food we eat. It also affects where we shop and the landscapes, the cityscapes, in which these items are offered. Many people fear that the impact of these changes is to make every place the same. The link between a person and their place will be weakened, even sundered. People will become placeless, lack identity, and, so the argument goes, will be alienated from a source of spiritual strength.

Let us turn first to the question of urban landscapes. Town centres in Europe have grown and developed over a thousand years, through the medieval and Renaissance periods. Many have been shattered by revolution and war, and each is the sum total of its experiences. It is this totality that has given the towns their character and therein lies their charm. Into these have come the international chains of shops with the same look, the same approach and the same products. Trends in style, merchandizing and layout are so internationalized that the business of shopping is universal. You can wander into a supermarket in most parts of Europe and you will know the 'rules', i.e. how to use the place. In fact, you may well be shopping with the same company as at home.

People do not necessarily see this in negative terms. Conservationists and planners may lament the loss of the distinctive architecture of town centres and its replacement by an undistinguished international style of building – essentially featureless boxes – but many shoppers like being able to shop in the same stores as people in Paris, Madrid, Milan or Berlin. It can, however, lead to a sense of towns being anywhere, anyplace.

Bill Bryson, puts it nicely in *Down Under* when he describes his first impressions of Alice Springs, which is located almost in the centre of Australia.

> Nearly all guidebooks and travel articles indulge the gentle conceit that Alice retains some irreproducible outback charm – some away-from-it all quality that you must come here to see – but in fact it is Anywhere, Australia. Actually it is Anywhere, Planet Earth. On our way into town we passed strip malls, car dealerships, McDonald's and Kentucky Fried Chicken outlets, banks and petrol stations. Only a scattering of Aborigines strolling around the dried bed of the Todd River gave any sense of exoticism. We took rooms in a motor inn on the edge of the modest town centre. My room had a balcony where I could watch the setting sun flood the desert floor – or at least I could if I looked past the more immediate sprawl of a K-mart plaza across the road.[4]

And, indeed, if there is anything that is turning Ireland into 'Anywhere, Planet Earth' it is new shopping centres. Compared to our American cousins, Europeans were slow enough to adopt them – it was the late 1960s before the first arrived in Ireland at Stillorgan, Co. Dublin, but we have made up for it since. It is hard to think of a more standardized urban form than the shopping centre and from one end of Europe to the other, they are the same. Granted there are little architectural flourishes that add some variety and the mix of units has to be adjusted to suit particular markets. For example, Irish centres must offer food retailing if they are to survive – a feature not essential in the United Kingdom. But this does not alter their essential role – giant temples to retailing designed to service large numbers of people travelling by car. Some are large enough to rival cities. For example, the Trafford Centre outside Manchester is about two years old. It has about 130,000 square metres of shopping space, over 280 shops, 35 restaurants, a 20-screen cinema and free parking for 10,000 cars.5 Moreover it will continue to grow. For all its size, however, it lacks a distinctive character despite its marble floors and ceiling murals; its like can be seen right across Europe.

The Czech Republic, which will join the EU in 2004, is an interesting example of the diffusion of the international retail model. Recently there has been a surge of shopping-centre building on the outskirts of its cities, driven by non-national companies – British, German, Austrian, Scandanavian. One of the first advertising boards you see on leaving Prague's international airport heading for the city is for a large, Tesco-anchored centre. The Czechs had no experience of large-scale retailing under Communism; shops were small and local and people wondered if they would take to this massive-scale retailing. They did so and with some enthusiasm. On a fieldcourse to the Czech Republic some time ago, we visited the Tesco shopping centre in Letinani, north of Prague. It was expansive and bright, with a small range of stores, a big Tesco and a gigantic car park. There was nothing wrong with it: the range of goods was excellent, the price of beer seriously tempting, but it was no different to countless others elsewhere. With a change of the signs it could have been Dublin.

It is not that we have been unwilling participants in this process of standardization. All the evidence is that we, as consumers, like what is on offer. We like the range of stores and we like the range of goods. The cereal shelf in any supermarket offers a vast choice: every class and kind of puffed rice, oat flakes, corn and bran are available. Exactly the same range is available in any similar store anywhere across Europe.

Local and Global

The local is increasingly being replaced by the global. Fruit and vegetables never go out of season. Older people can remember that certain fruits and vegetables were associated with particular times of year. New potatoes were eagerly awaited as last year's crop took on an increasingly sad appearance. There was a season for apples and oranges, grapes and plums. Now these items are always available. The wheels of industry and distribution ensure that as the Irish potatoes pass their best, they are replaced by those from Italy or Cyprus or even North Africa. It is unnecessary to depend on our uncertain summers for tomatoes because they are available all year. North and West African estates produce all-year round vegetables and even flowers for demanding European consumers. Imports to the EU from the ACP African countries – essentially non-Mediterranean Africa excluding South Africa – in 2000 comprised cut flowers and bulbs to the value of €259 million and a further €138 million worth of leguminous vegetables. (The fact that these countries might be better employed growing food for their own populations is a discussion for another day.) The range of products on offer in our stores is more and more exotic. It cannot be that long since most Irish people would have known nothing of mango, star fruit or prickly pear, let alone how to eat them. Yet you will now find these and other exotic fruits in many fruit shops. Fewer and fewer things are exclusive to particular places. It used to be that when you went abroad, certainly to the Continent, that you would find something – a wine, a cheese or a beer – that was different and distinctive. This helped mark the difference between that place and home and pointed out the distinctiveness of both places. This is now much more difficult to do. We are all aware of the great selection of wines available in Irish stores but consider too the range of beers on offer and their geographical origin.

Our daily experiences are becoming more like those of other places and theirs are becoming more like ours. Ethnic restaurants proliferate. We have exported the Irish pub so that everyone else can have 'a unique local experience'. It is not just that the range of food that we eat is getting wider and more international. It has been suggested that food is another of the means whereby we assert our identity. Studies undertaken among Irish emigrants suggest that they seek out Irish products and good Irish meals as a way of maintaining a link with home.[6] It is more than simply a taste for a particular product and a desire for salted butter in a Europe where salt is not used in butter. As Kneafsey and Cox put it:

> This suggests that food consumption practices can help to reflect and constitute Irishness. People choose particular foods both because they are Irish and they know those foods from home, and because they want to restate that Irishness, usually within the domestic sphere of the home.[7]

If this is so, then it can be equally argued that the greater internationalization of our food palette is weakening our link with our home place.

Home is more and more like other places and other places are more and more like home, and many of us like it like that. As mentioned, there has been an upsurge in people buying villas in Spain, and South Africa is becoming an important market for holiday homes. Yet it is not the attraction of a different country, language, culture or food that makes these so attractive. People are not seeking to engage with another culture and live a different life. Rather it is because so much is the same.

A Sense of Place?

This suggests that much of what made states distinctive places has disappeared. Those individualizing elements of culture and life nurtured and developed within secure borders have been weakened and we have adopted a more global form of lifestyle. Without these supports, our sense of belonging has been weakened and our attachment to places such as the national territory has diminished. We are on the road to becoming placeless.

It would be difficult, though, to accept this argument to any significant degree. If anything, we may well be developing new attachments to places and though becoming global, we may be becoming more local. A sense of place involves complex interactions, operating at a number of different spatial scales. The visible expressions of national borders may have weakened to the point of irrelevancy, and we may all be citizens of Europe, but most of us see ourselves simultaneously in national terms. I can be European and also Irish. I can be Irish and still hope that Dublin wins the All-Ireland. This struck me while driving through a well-to-do area of Holland, outside Haarlem near the sea. The houses comprised substantial villas, big even by Irish standards, and many had large gardens. More than a few sported a tall flagpole flying a Dutch flag. Certainly, we were in the EU but this was still the Netherlands and these people were asserting their distinctiveness. And this was so despite all of the shared experiences, the same TV programmes, the same international cultural icons and the widespread facility to do business in English. It would be hard to argue that the French have become less French or the Italians less Italian. Could anyone suggest that it would be possible to abolish national football teams and try to send an EU team to the World Cup? Many aspects of our lives and daily experiences are now similar to those in other lands but many remain different. In other words there can be diversity within unity.

In the past, we were required to identify with our national territory much more than other spatial units such as the county or the townland. The key place to which we belonged was the state and it was to this that we owed and paid our allegiance. The supremacy of the national territory has been weakened by the addition of a layer above it – a European layer of identification. We have yielded sovereignty in many different areas and our states cannot command the same level of loyalty as before. We are citizens of the European Union, whose passport we carry. We are about to see the emergence of a European constitution. However, this new layer or supranational state does not command the same response from us as was the case with our own state. That kind of allegiance has yet to be built. In this changing spatial scale, sub-national or regional identities have emerged or re-emerged. In the past, these were often suppressed in the process of nation building when diversity was seen as a threat. It was important that there be one land, one people and perhaps one leader. In its extreme form it echoed throughout Nazi Germany as 'ein Volk, ein Reich, ein Führer'. In order to allow the EU to function, countries have less control over their own economic matters, social affairs and even foreign policy. As long as nothing threatens this new, more expansive sense of sovereignty, it is possible to permit diversity to assert itself within nations.

A case in point is that of Catalonia in Spain. Under Franco, the region was depressed and underdeveloped. In order to attain national integration, Catalan was suppressed, as was Basque, and its use prohibited in public and discouraged in private. Castilian was imposed as the official language. In modern Spain, Barcelona has now emerged as an important European commercial centre. It has all of the trappings of an international city – you can do business there in English and all of the elements of global culture are there too. Yet Barcelona has become more local. People prefer to speak in Catalan when doing day-to-day transactions. The city is the capital of a strengthening regional culture and no one sees a contradiction in being local as well as global. It depends on what is appropriate to particular circumstances. Of course, this assertion of a regional identity has occurred within the boundaries of a larger state. There are as many Catalan speakers outside Catalonia as within it. It is unlikely that accommodation of emerging regional identities will stretch to altering national boundaries, at least in the near future. This might push the unity in diversity idea a little too far.

Most of us still have a need to belong somewhere, to be from somewhere. We may be becoming part of a more homogenized Anglo-American culture; we may be less parochial; but we are a long way from seeing ourselves merely as citizens of Europe, let alone of Planet Earth. When we have to, we can find other elements, other badges that allow us to identify with the places that matter at the spatial scale that is important to us at the time. Sometimes it may be important to be Irish, other times the scale may be smaller. It may be important to be from Dublin as distinct from Cork. Yet again, precisely where in Dublin may be the issue. At a sub-national level, it can be argued that people from rural areas have a stronger attachment to place where there is the continuity of a shared past. It is argued that people in cities have a weaker sense of place and that urbanization is as much a threat to losing identity as globalization. Certainly urban dwellers identify less with the parish – they know their local landscape less well but they still identify with place. This identification is less ingrained and more ephemeral. It is not to do with ancestral values but more to do with good and bad areas, known and unknown, easy to commute to or not. Where one lives in the city matters and it becomes part of what defines us, whether we like it or not! Try persuading an estate agent that an address is just a relative location, something without meaning or value. For example, within Dublin, it would make abundant sense to introduce a system of postcodes such as in the UK or in the United States, but this has not happened because of what existing postcodes convey. 'Dublin 4' or 'Dublin 6W', or the differentiation of '6W' from 'Dublin 6' speaks volumes, conveys all kinds of meanings about the places they define; a meaning that in the case of 'Dublin 4' extends far beyond the city of Dublin.

Globalization and the EU have weakened our fundamental attachment to place and territory only a little in my judgment. We have embraced the global in many aspects of our daily lives but we still retain many, if not most, of our more local characteristics. The Euro coins are not a bad metaphor for this. In contrast to the notes, where the emphasis is on unity, the coins emphasize diversity within unity. While the obverse of each coin is the same no matter where the coins are minted, each state has been permitted to place national symbols on the reverse. Some states such as Ireland have chosen clear statements of national identity – the Harp and Éire. The Italians in contrast have chosen images of their art and architecture.[8] Nonetheless the tension between national symbols on one side and common European symbols on the other reflects the tension between subsidiarity and integration at EU level, between the desire to do things our own way and the need to have a single approach. We may be less likely to go to war with our EU neighbours to defend our national territory but we still value our national identity, in which place still plays an important part.

We must also remember that only internal EU boundaries have been dismantled. The border around the EU is as strong as ever and is likely to be strengthened even further. We have added yet another scale to the sense of our spatial identity. We now have a larger territory to defend. And we should not forget that there are also people on the other side of the frontier. For them, there is still the experience of the unsmiling border guard.

Notes

INTRODUCTION

1. T.S. Eliot, 'Four Quartets: Little Gidding', in *Collected Poems 1909–1962* (London 1963).

2. M. Heidegger, *The Question of Being*, translated by W. Kluback and I.T. Wilde (New York 1956).

3. G. Bachelard, *The Poetics of Space*, translated by M. Jolas (Boston 1958).

4. M. Foucault, 'Of Other Spaces', *Diacritics*, 16 (Spring 1986) 22-7.

5. H. LeFebvre, *The Production of Space* (Oxford 1991).

6. D. Harvey, *Social Justice and the City* (London 1973). D. Harvey, *The Condition of Postmodernity* (Oxford 1989). D. Harvey, *Spaces of Hope* (Edinburgh 2000). D. Harvey, *Spaces of Capital* (Edinburgh 2001).

7. E.W. Soja, *Postmodern Geographies: The Reassertion of Space in Critical Social Theory* (London 1989). E.W. Soja, *Thirdspace* (Malden, Ma and Oxford 1996). E.W. Soja, *Critical Studies of Cities and Regions* (Malden, Ma and Oxford 2000).

8. T.S. Eliot, 'Four Quartets: East Coker', in *Collected Poems 1909–1962* (London 1963).

1. SPACES IN THE MIND
JIM HOURIHANE

1. M. Foucault, 'Of Other Spaces', *Diacritics*, 16 (Spring 1986), 22–7.

2. K. Marx, *A Contribution to the Critique of Political Economy* (New York 1967). K. Marx, *Capital*, three vols (New York 1967). K. Marx, *The Economic and Philosophic Manuscripts of 1844* (New York 1964).

3. I. Kant, *Critique of Pure Reason* (n.p. 1781).

4. M. Foucault, 'Of Other Spaces', *Diacritics*, 16 (Spring 1986), 22–27.

5. B. Kennelly, 'Clearing a Space', in *A Time for Voices* (Newcastle on Tyne 1990).

6. R. Ardrey, *The Territorial Imperative* (New York 1966).

7. D. Morris, *The Human Zoo* (London 1969).

8. K. Lorenz, *On Aggression* (London 1966).

9. E.T. Hall, *The Silent Language* (New York 1959). E.T. Hall, 'A System for the Notation of Proxemic Behaviour', *American Anthropologist*, 65 (1963), 1003–27. E.T. Hall, *The Hidden Dimension* (New York 1966). E.T. Hall, 'Proxemics', *Current Anthropology*, 9 (1968), 2–3, 83–95.

10. J. Piaget, *The Child's Conception of the World*, translated by J. and A. Tomlinson (Boston 1984). J. Piaget and B. Inhelder, *The Child's Conception of Space* (London 1956).

11. H. Gardner, *Frames of Mind: The Theory of Multiple Intelligences* (New York 1983).

12. E. Erikson, *Identity and the Life Cycle* (New York/London 1994). E. Erikson and J.M. Erikson, *The Life Cycle Completed* (New York/London 1998).

13. J.B. Keane, *The Field* (Cork 1997).

14. D. Harvey, *The Condition of Postmodernity* (Oxford 1989).

15. J. Joyce, *Finnegans Wake* (New York 1999).

2. CHANGE AND RENEWAL IN ISSUES OF PLACE, IDENTITY AND THE LOCAL
PATRICK DUFFY

1. P. Kavanagh, *The Complete Poems of Patrick Kavanagh* (New York 1972), p. 238.

2. S. Heaney, 'The Sense of the Past', *History Ireland*, 1, 4 (1993), 33.

3. I. Hunt, 'Familiar and Unknowable', in W. Doherty (ed.), *Somewhere Else*, catalogue Tate Gallery 1998, p. 49.

4. Quoted in S. Heaney, 'A Sense of Place', *Preoccupations: Selected Prose 1968–1978* (London 1980), p. 135.

5. Many of these aspects of local identity and belonging are represented in some evocative writings by *Irish Times* journalists about their home places, whether in city or countrysides in Ireland, England and the USA: 'Back Home Series', *Irish Times*, July 2003.

6. J. Hewitt, 'Once Alien Here', in *The Selected Poetry of John Hewitt* (Belfast 1981), p. 20. W. Doherty, 'They're All the Same', *Somewhere Else*, p. 22.

7. RTÉ, *Sunday Miscellany*, RTÉ radio, April 1998.

8. Brendan Bartley, NUIM, personal communication.

9. P. Duffy, 'Unwritten Landscapes: Reflections of Minor Placenames and Sense of Place in the Irish Countryside', in H. Clarke, M. Hennessy and J. Prunty (eds), *Surveying Ireland's Past* (Dublin 2004 [forthcoming]).

10. U. Mac Graith, *Dún Chaocháin* [cd rom]; see also S. O Cathain and P. O Flanagan, *The Living Landscape: Kilgalligan, Erris, Co Mayo* (Dublin 1975).

11. J. Montague, 'Last Journey', *Selected Poems* (Oldcastle 1995), p. 171.

12. M.P. Corcoran, J. Gray, M. Peillon, 'New Urban Living: A Study of Social and Civic Life in Irish Suburbs', Interim report to Royal Irish Academy, Department of Sociology, NUIM (2003).

13. H. Brody, *Inishkillane: Change and Decline in the West of Ireland* (London 1973), pp. 144–5.

14. Brian Dillon's review of *London Orbital: A Walk Around the M25* by Iain Sinclair, *Irish Times*, 14 December 2002.

15. Michael Viney, 'Another Life', *Irish Times*, 15 September 2001.

16. Personal communication, Brian Turner, Ulster Local History Trust.

17. Heaney, *Preoccupations*, pp. 148–9.

18. S. Heaney, Preface in T. Canavan (ed.), *Every Stoney Acre Has a Name: A Celebration of the Townland in Ulster* (Belfast 1991), p. xi.

19. Department of Irish Folklore, Schools Collection, University College Dublin.

3. URBAN DREAMS – URBAN NIGHTMARES
RUTH McMANUS

1. Amárach Consulting, 'Quality of Life in Ireland: A Study for Guinness UDV Ireland', (Dublin 2002).

2. D. Massey, J. Allen, and S. Pile (eds), *City Worlds* (London/New York 1999). N. Smith, *The New Urban Frontier: Gentrification and the Revanchist City*, (London/New York 1996).

3. www.celebrationfl.com (Official website for Celebration, Florida).

4. THE COUNTY: DESIGNATION, IDENTITY AND LOYALTY
DESMOND A. GILLMOR

1. D.A. Gillmor, 'Mental Maps in Geographic Education: Spatial Preferences of some Leinster School Leavers', *Geographical Viewpoint*, 3 (1974), 46–66.

5. THE RURAL IDYLL
MARY CAWLEY

1. C. Glacken, *Traces on the Rhodian Shore: Nature and Culture in Western Thought from Ancient Times to the End of the Eighteenth Century* (Berkeley 1967).

2. A. Crookshank and The Knight of Glin, *Ireland's Painters* (New Haven 2002).

3. C. Nash, 'Irish Placenames: Postcolonial Locations', *Transactions, Institute of British Geographers*, 21, 4 (1998), 457–80.

4. J. Lee and G. Ó Tuathaigh, *The Age of de Valera* (Dublin 1982).

5. D.A. Gillmor, *Agriculture in the Republic of Ireland*, Akademiai Kiado (Budapest 1977).

6. S. Lafferty, P. Commins and J.A. Walsh, *Irish Agriculture in Transition: A Census Atlas of Agriculture in the Republic of Ireland*, Teagasc in association with the Department of Geography, National University of Ireland, Maynooth (Dublin and Maynooth 1999).

7. Environmental Protection Agency, *Ireland: A Millennium Report* (Wexford 2000).

8. J. Lee, 'Some Aspects of Sustainability in Relation to Agriculture in Ireland', in F. Convery and J. Feehan (eds), *Assessing Sustainability in Ireland*, Environmental Institute, University College Dublin (1996), pp. 71–85.

9. D.A. Gillmor and J.A. Walsh, 'County-Level Variations in Agricultural Adjustment in Ireland in the 1980s', *Geographical Viewpoint*, 21 (1993), 25–44.

10. Environmental Protection Agency, 'Ireland: A Millennium Report' (Wexford 2000).

11. H.J. Emerson and D.A. Gillmor, 'The Rural Environmental Protection Scheme of the Republic of Ireland', *Land Use Policy*, 16 (1999), 235–45.

12. H. Tovey, 'Food, Environmentalism and Rural Sociology: On the Organic Farm Movement in Ireland', *Sociologia Ruralis*, 37, 1 (1997), 21–37.

13. B. Adam, U. Beck, and J. Loon (eds), *The Risk Society and Beyond: Critical Issues for Social Theory* (London 2000).

14. C. Cowan and R. Sexton, *Ireland's Traditional Foods: An Exploration of Irish Local and Typical Foods and Drinks* (Dublin 1997).

15. B. McIntyre, M. Henchion and E. Pitts, *Regional Images and the Promotion of Quality Food Products* (Dublin 2001).

16. D. Miller (ed.), *Acknowledging Consumption: A Review of New Studies* (London 1995).

17. M.E. Cawley, S. Gaffey and D.A. Gillmor, 'The Role of Quality Tourism and Craft SMEs in Rural Development: Evidence from the Republic of Ireland', *Anatolia: An International Journal of Tourism and Hospitality Research*, 10, 1 (1999), 45–60.

18. *Ibid.*

19. Central Statistics Office, *Census of Population Volume 1, Areas* (Dublin 1982).

20. M.E. Cawley, 'Population Change in the Republic of Ireland 1981–1986', *Area* 22, 1 (1992), 67–74.

21. F. McGrath, 'The Economic, Social and Cultural Impacts of Return Migration to Achill Island', in R. King (ed.), *Contemporary Irish Migration* (Dublin 1991), pp. 55–69.

22. Department of the Environment, *Planning Statistics 1998* (Dublin 1999).

23. U. Kockel, 'Counterculture Migrants in the West of Ireland', in R. King (ed.), *Contemporary Irish Migration* (Dublin 1991), pp. 70–82.

24. R. Kirwan, 'Resettlement Group in Talks with County Housing Plans', *Limerick Leader*, 5 January 2002.

25. B. Quinn, 'Images of Ireland in Europe: A Tourism Perspective', in U. Kockel (ed.), *Culture, Tourism and Development: The Case of Ireland* (Liverpool 1994), pp. 61–73.

26. J. Lee and G. Ó Tuathaigh, *The Age of de Valera* (Dublin 1982).

27. Teagasc, *National Farm Survey 2001* (Dublin 2002).

28. F. McDonald, 'Objectors Win Almost Half of Their Appeals to An Bord Pleanála', *Irish Times*, 23 November 2001.

29. C. O'Reardon, 'Inequality in the New Irish Economy', in S. Cantillon, C. Corrigan, P. Kirby and J.P. Flynn (eds), *Rich and Poor: Perspectives on Tackling Inequality in Ireland* (Dublin 2002), pp. 111–49.

6. REDISCOVERING OUR REGIONS
DES McCAFFERTY

1. A.A. Horner, 'Geographical Regions in Ireland – Reflections at the Millennium', *Irish Geography*, 33, 2 (2000), 134–165.

2. BBC Press Office (2002), http://cgi.bbc.co.uk/pressoffice/pressreleases/stories/2002/05_may/08/devolution_poll.shtml.

3. T.W. Freeman, *Ireland: A General and Regional Geography*, 4th edn (London 1972).

4. The obvious exception to this, the Gaeltacht area, does not possess one of the fundamental characteristics of a region, viz., spatial contiguity.

5. Advisory Expert Committee, Local Government Reorganisation and Reform (Dublin 1991).

6. Muintir na Tíre, *Towards a New Democracy? Implications of Local Government Reform* (Dublin 1985). European Parliament, 'Report on the Regional Problems of Ireland', EP Doc A2–109/87 (Luxembourg 1987). P. Breathnach, 'Regional Government: The Missing Link in the National Spatial Strategy?' (Paper presented to the Regional Studies Association [Irish Branch] Conference *Ireland 2002: People, Place and Space*, Bunratty, 25–26 April 2002.

7. M. Porter, *The Competitive Advantage of Nations* (London 1990).

8. Department of Finance, *Ireland National Development Plan 2000–2006* (Dublin 1999).

9. Department of the Environment and Local Government, *The National Spatial Strategy 2002–2020: People, Places and Potential* (Dublin 2002), p. 10.

10. Department of the Environment and Local Government, *The National Spatial Strategy 2002–2020: People, Places and Potential* (Dublin 2002), p. 11.

11. Department of the Environment and Local Government, *The National Spatial Strategy 2002–2020: Indications for the Way Ahead* (Dublin 2001).

7. SYMBOLIC STREETSCAPES:
INTERROGATING MONUMENTAL SPACES OF DUBLIN
YVONNE WHELAN

1. C. Harris, 'Power, Modernity and Historical Geography', *Annals of the Association of American Geographers*, 81, 4 (1991), pp. 671–83, 678.

2. D. Cosgrove, 'Geography is Everywhere: Culture and Symbolism in Human Landscapes', in D. Gregory and R. Walford (eds), *New Horizons in Human Geography* (London 1989), p. 125.

3. D. Cosgrove, 'Iconography', in R.J. Johnston et al. (eds), *The Dictionary of Human Geography* (Oxford 1994), p. 269.

4. C.W.J. Withers, 'Place, Memory, Monument: Memorialising the Past in Contemporary Highland Scotland', *Ecumene*, 3 (1996), pp. 325–44, 327.

5. L. Sandercock, *Towards Cosmopolis* (New York 1988), p. 207.

6. *Dublin University Magazine* (March 1856), 321.

7. *The Nation*, 27 May 1843, 523.

8. *The Freeman's Journal*, 14 August 1882.

9. J.V. O'Brien, *Dear Dirty Dublin* (Berkeley/Los Angeles 1982), p, 35.

10. M.E. Daly, *Dublin: The Deposed Capital* (Cork 1985), p. 208.

11. *Ibid.*

12. It is significant, however, that Dublin Corporation was not always successful in its efforts to 'nationalize' the urban landscape. Plans to rename many of the city's streets in the decades before 1922 met with limited success. This is exemplified in the case of Sackville Street itself. Although a Dublin Corporation Act of 1890 provided clear authority for the authority to alter the names of streets in Dublin, it was not until after the achievement of political independence that the authority would formally effect the name change.

13. *The Freeman's Journal*, 26 April–5 May 1916.

14. *Irish Times*, 8 March 1966.

15. *Irish Times*, 9 March 1966.

16. Seanad Debates, 1969, cols. 915–916.

17. S. Bhreathnach-Lynch, 'Commemorating the Hero in Newly Independent Ireland: Expressions of Nationhood in Bronze and Stone', in L. McBride (ed.), *Images, Icons and the Irish Nationalist Imagination* (Dublin 1999), pp. 148–165, 148.

18. D. Fitzpatrick, 'Commemoration in the Irish Free State: A Chronicle of Embarrassment', in I. McBride (ed.), *History and Memory in Modern Ireland* (Cambridge 2001), pp. 184–204, 186.

19. D. Ley and J. Duncan, Epilogue in J. Duncan and D. Ley (eds), *Place/Culture/Representation* (London 1993), pp. 329–34, 329.

8. NO FRONTIERS, DIVERSITY WITHIN UNITY: BORDERS AND THE IDENTIFICATION WITH PLACE
JOSEPH BRADY

1. T. Packenham, *The Scramble for Africa* (London 1991).

2. J. Gillingham, *Coal, Steel, and the Rebirth of Europe, 1945–1955: The Germans and French from Ruhr Conflict to Economic Community* (Cambridge 1991).

3. B. Barber, *Jihad vs. McWorld: How Globalism and Tribalism are Reshaping the World* (New York 1996).

4. B. Bryson, *Down Under* (London 2000), p. 326.

5. Visit its impressive website at www.traffordcentre.co.uk.

6. M. Kneafesy and R. Cox, 'Gender and Irishness – How Irish Women in Coventry Make Home', *Irish Geography*, 35, 1 (2002), 6–15.

7. *Ibid.* 13.

8. http://www.euro.ecb.int/en/section/euro/specific.IT.html.

Acknowledgments

The late Michael Littleton of RTÉ, who was so closely associated with the Thomas Davis Lecture series over many years, was very supportive of the initial proposal that became *Engaging Spaces*. Ann Marie O'Callaghan of RTÉ commissioned the series and greatly encouraged its development so that it would be both broadly appealing and academically well grounded. The series producer, Martha McCarron, brought so much energy and professional commitment to our many contacts with her. She, along with her colleagues Tim Lehane and Seamus Hosey, showed the various contributors much about the art and skill of writing and speaking for radio.

The Lilliput Press, in particular Antony Farrell and Marsha Swan, took the submitted scripts, and, with a meticulous attention to detail, shaped this published work.

Joseph Brady (plates 27, 28, and 29), Michael Dee (plates 20 and 23), John Delaney (plate 13), Patrick Duffy (plates 4, 6 and 7) and Darren Kelly (plates 1 and 25) graciously provided photographs for publication. Plate 4 is taken from Theo McMahon, *Old Monaghan* (Monaghan 1994). Paul Murphy of St Patrick's College, Drumcondra, was, as ever, courteous and professional in his support – in spite of the short deadlines!

Professor Brendan Kennelly's foreword does speak for itself, although it would be even more enjoyable if one could hear it spoken in his own voice. His generosity in sharing his talent and his time is much appreciated.

My seven fellow contributors – geographers all – brought an infectious enthusiasm both to their broadcast and published scripts. In spite of many other demands in their work, they found the extra hours and days to push this project towards completion. I am very grateful to them all.

The Heritage Council and the Research Committee of St Patrick's College, Drumcondra, provided funding to assist this publication, and my indebtedness to them and Urban Institute Ireland is acknowledged.

Finally, I have engaged many spaces with four people whose patience allowed this project to happen – my wife, Norma, and our children, David, Marianne and James. You have made my journey through life-space so enjoyable. Thank you.

Notes on Contributors

Dr Joseph Brady, University College Dublin

Dr Mary Cawley, National University of Ireland at Galway

Professor Patrick Duffy, National University of Ireland at Maynooth

Professor Desmond Gillmor, Trinity College, Dublin

Jim Hourihane, St Patrick's College, Drumcondra, Dublin

Desmond McCafferty, Mary Immaculate College of Education at University of Limerick

Dr Ruth McManus, St Patrick's College, Drumcondra, Dublin

Dr Yvonne Whelan, Irish Academy for Cultural Studies, Derry

Dedication

This book is for Marlene, with great affection.

Titles by the same author:

Model for Murder

Take Time for Murder

No Medicine for Murder

One

The jumbo jet lifted smoothly from the runway and climbed sharply into a sky of scudding grey clouds. London's Heathrow and the surrounding area lay spread out below, rapidly dwindling, then disappearing as the plane was engulfed in the swirling mist.

Trisha Barrett looked away from the window and examined her fellow passengers; they sat dutifully upright, seat belts fastened, their expressions ranging from taut anxiety to bored indifference. The signs with the injunctions to 'Fasten seat belts' and 'No Smoking' went out and there was a concerted sigh of relief as belts were snapped off, seats adjusted. The flight attendants appeared with bright smiles and the welcome words, "Would you like a drink, madam?"

Trisha hesitated, she hardly ever drank alcohol, but this was an occasion, her first trans-atlantic flight, her first overseas assignment. She felt a reckless thrill as she said, "Thank you—um—a vodka and bitter lemon, please."

While she waited for the drink she thought back to the day when Jacqui Finson, the Fashion Editor of the magazine **YOU: TOMORROW**, called her into her office and said, "Trisha, how would you like a trip home?"

"*Home?* Are you giving me the sack?"

"Heavens no! Anything but. I meant would you like to go to Jamaica?"

"But - Jamaica's not home."

1

"Didn't your grandmother come from there?"

Trisha laughed, "Yes, but that was way back in the sixties. Both my parents were born here and so was I."

Jaqui regarded her thoughtfully, seemed about to say something, changed her mind and said lightly, "Just kidding - but would you like the trip?"

"*Would* I? But what for - *not* **FASHION-JAPAN...?**"

Jaqui grinned, "Yes, to cover the big Japanese showing and the midsummer edition of **YOU:TOMORROW.**"

"Oh Jaqui! Me! I can't believe it. Oh this is something I've dreamed of—I never thought it could possibly happen."

"Don't be too starry eyed, it's damned hard work."

"Yes I know, but it'll be worth every moment."

"Come to my office at nine tomorrow, I'll give you and the rest of the crew the details then."

Trisha's heart missed a beat.

The rest of the crew...

Would Jason be amongst them?

Would Carla?

Some of the excitement at the prospect of covering the show left her. If Jason and Carla were going to be included how would she be able to concentrate on her work, seeing them together, knowing that they would be invited to the inevitable parties and receptions as a pair—an item— Jason and Carla, when two months ago it had been 'Jason and Trisha'...she pulled up her runaway thoughts, she would have to accept the fact that Jason was out of her life—once she had thought that he would *always* be part of her future...

What had gone wrong?

Nothing had gone *wrong*, but Carla had joined the staff of **YOU: TOMORROW** - Carla with her long black hair, her wide grey eyes, her perfect figure and her low raspy voice. She didn't seem to make any conscious effort to attract men, but they were drawn to her as to a magnet—

2

Jason amongst them—and of all the admiring males in the office, it was Jason who attracted *her*, whom she singled out for her undivided attention. How could Trisha, with her short, curly reddish-brown hair and her strange amber eyes—eyes like a ginger cat, she had always bewailed—how could she with her lack of height and small figure, hope to compete with a glamorous woman like Carla? For all her twenty-one years, Trisha was often mistaken for a schoolgirl, with her size six clothing and the difficult to get two-and-a-half size shoes—she never could remember what the European equivalent was. Since she had gone to work at **YOU: TOMORROW**, she had learned to dress more maturely, and the brief time when it had been 'Jason and Trisha', she had blossomed lost the little girl image. He called her hair 'red-gold' and 'Titian', and vowed that her eyes haunted him. He was the first serious love in her life and she had floated on clouds of bemused delight—until Carla—then she became earthbound without warning. There began a series of broken dates—then no dates at all...

She tapped on Jaqui's door and in the outer office. Janet Morris, Jaqui's secretary said cheerfully, "Go right in Trisha, you're expected."

The inner office was fairly crowded and Trisha looked round, her heart racing again. She closed her eyes in relief, there was no perfectly coiffed shining black head present amongst the women, no brown haired head and broad shoulders above the rest of the men. Her heart resumed its normal pace and her voice was steady as she said, "Good morning Jaqui, sorry to have kept you waiting."

"You didn't, the others were early, some foul-up in the time given. You know everyone?"

Trisha glanced round again: Dolly Marks, Peter Bascoigne, Julia Towers, John Hastings, "Yes, except..."

"Except me - Hammond Verity."

A tall dark haired, dark eyed man unfolded from the windowsill, and she noted that he too, was head and shoulders above the rest. She gave him a tentative smile, "Hi, I'm Trisha Barrett."

"Yes, I know." She looked surprised and he grinned, "One couldn't work at **YOU: TOMORROW** for three weeks without being aware of you. Hullo Trisha Barrett."

Now what did *that* mean? Hopefully, a compliment, she could use a few. She didn't mention that until this moment, she had been quite unaware of him. She murmured in a neutral voice, "Hullo Hammond."

Right," Jaqui said briskly. "Let's get down to business: Dolly will cover swimwear, very important in that climate. Julia daywear and Trisha evening wear. Peter, men's wear, John and Hammond camera work..." she held up her hand as there was a murmur of protest, "I know that you generally have three camera men on these assignments, but you'll just have to manage." She paused, then picked up a paper from the pile in front of her. "You're booked for Kingston, Jamaica, on the 17th, the 7:30 flight."

"In the morning?" Dolly asked.

"Yes."

"That'll mean getting up in the middle of the night!"

"Do you good," Jaqui said unfeelingly. "I gather that quite often you get *in* in the middle of the night."

Dolly ignored the mild barb and asked, "The 17th, *this* month?"

"Yes."

"But today is the 15th."

"I'm well aware of that and I'm sorry about the rush, but all the arrangements have been made for weeks—the show was to have been covered by the other team, but they've been switched to Morocco."

The other team — Jason's team — he and Carla in romantic Morocco, Trisha thought bitterly, then turned her attention back to Jaqui, "...pick up your tickets here tomorrow, then you will be free to make your personal arrangements. Although it's freezing January here, it's sun, sea and sand where you're going—well, not in Kingston perhaps, but the second show is in Ocho Rios, so you may see a few famous faces amongst the tourists—so be sure and pack hot weather clothes—the allowance should cover the cost amply. There will be a lot of entertaining I gather."

Jaqui waved a hand in dismissal and they bunched out, Dolly calm through experience of many such assignments, whilst Julia and Trisha were filled with bubbling excitement.

"Your first such trip?" A deep voice asked at Trisha's side. She turned her head and looked up into Hammond Verity's dark eyes. My goodness, she thought, he is tall, even taller than Jason—oh, for heaven's sake, stop these comparisons, she told herself sharply. Even with high heels, the top of her head barely reached his shoulder. She became aware that he was smiling down at her and she flushed slightly under his amused gaze.

"I-I'm sorry. Yes, it is my first trip and as you can see, I'm sort of—flustered."

"I'd hoped," he said lightly, "That the flustering cause was me." Her flush deepened and he said, "Come and have a cup of coffee, as we are going to be working together over the next few weeks, we might as well get to know each other."

She hesitated, "I've got to clear my desk."

"Will that take long?"

"N'no—I've got an article to finish—it's all on Percy but I've got to edit the floppy discs before I can print."

"Percy? Floppy discs? Lady, you're talking technical jargon - that is pure Greek to me."

She laughed, "I doubt that, in this computer age. Percy is my personal portable computer—although portable is a moot point, I can't even lift him off my desk. I thought that everyone knew these days what a floppy disc was."

"Sorry, I'm into cameras, not computers." He looked down at her, his eyes teasing, "What about that cup of coffee? Keep Percy waiting for once."

"No, I can't do that."

"Then you must have dinner with me tonight. Where shall I pick you up?"

It wasn't an invitation; it was an order and Trisha, far from resenting his peremptory manner, replied, "What time?"

"Sevenish?"

"Fine. Make it here, then I can really clear my desk."

****

They dined at a West Indian restaurant in Bayswater, "To get the feeling of the coming trip, to set the tropical ambience," Hammond quipped. They had ackee and salt fish, curried goat and rice and peas, followed by mango ice cream, Blue Mountain coffee and Tia Maria — to Trisha it was a gourmet experience, until this new job she had eaten sparingly at fast food outlets or cooked at home.

"If this is a true sample of Jamaican cuisine, then I'm all for it."

"I would have thought that you were used to such food. You have Jamaican roots, don't you?" Hammond asked as he sipped his liqueur.

She looked surprised, "Yes, but sort of far back, I'm third generation 'Black British'."

He grinned, "With those eyes and hair it's hard to believe."

"You're the second person in two days to bring up my ancestry. How strange, years can go by without it's being mentioned and then suddenly, it's a current affair. How did you know about it?"

"Oh, I asked around, well Jaqui actually. I was curious."

"Why? I'm not *that* odd."

"Not odd—different to the usual Brit Miss. You have an aura of exoticism."

"Me? Exotic! You must be joking!"

He gave his rather lop sided grin, "Dead serious, you intrigued me as soon as I set my sights on you."

Trisha regarded him out of serious eyes. Was he teasing her? Having her on? For what purpose? "Hammond, if we are going to work together—we..." she stopped, what she had been about to say would have sounded stupid on their first date.

"We what?" he prompted. "Mustn't take each other too seriously?"

She flushed. "Something like that. I'm being silly—but—I shouldn't have come out tonight..."

"Too soon after Jason, eh?"

"How on earth do you know about Jason? You didn't join the staff until—until after it was all over."

"It's all around the office. Did you think that no one noticed the pieces of broken heart?"

"I'm sorry that I inflicted my private emotions on everyone," she said stiffly.

"It wasn't as bad as that. No, in these cases the only thing to do is to get out and forget..."

She gathered up her gloves and handbag, "So that's why you asked me out! For pity, over my—jilted state."

"No-no, you're quite wrong."

She stood up and said tightly, "Thank you for dinner, now if you will excuse me, good night."

She was gone before he could stop her and, by the time he paid the bill, shrugged himself into his camel coat and hurried out onto the street, she was nowhere in sight. He swore softly to himself under his breath, then set off to where he had parked his elderly, but much cherished, 1970 Jaguar. She was leaning against the bonnet, hugging herself against the freezing night air. He stopped in front of her, he didn't speak but looked down at her gravely.

"I'm sorry," she said in a small voice, "I was—very—rude, please forgive me."

"Did you mean what you said?" he demanded, "Do you honestly think that I asked you out, out of pity?"

"I don't know. I know I'm not attractive—I'm too small, too..."

"Don't be a little idiot. You are the most exquisite—Lord, you'll be a frozen miniature if you stay out in this wind much longer. Get into the car."

Once settled in the driver's seat, he turned on the heater and asked, "Where to?"

"It's not far, I share a garden flat further along the Bayswater Road."

"Where are you from?"

"I thought that you knew," she gave a small giggle, a reaction to her earlier outburst.

"I don't mean *then*, I mean now."

"I know, I'm sorry. I'm a country mouse, I was born in Kedington—a little country town near Cambridge."

"Parents still there?"

She didn't answer but her hands clenched and her lips folded. "I'm sorry, I shouldn't have asked."

"No, it's alright, it was a natural question, I have to learn to expect them. My parents—they—were both killed—in a pile-up in heavy fog on the M4—just over a year ago."

"I'm terribly sorry."

"It's alright. I'm getting over it. It happened so quickly, I tell myself that they knew nothing about it—like the astronauts back in '86. I—I think that's why I fell so heavily for Jason—he helped me through a difficult time."

He was silent as he steered the car through the mid-evening London traffic.

"Here we are," she said. He pulled up to a smooth halt at the curb. "Don't get out, it's so cold. Thank you again, and forgive my bad manners."

He leant across the hump of the gearbox, put one hand behind her head and gently kissed her unresisting lips. "Thank you," he said softly then laughed ruefully, "These Jags are the very devil for this sort of thing."

She gave a shaky laugh as he released her. He reached across and opened the door. He waited until her front door had closed before he drew away with a burst of quiet power.

She didn't see him the next day when she went to the office to collect her travel documents. She wasn't sure whether she was disappointed or relieved, and now, speeding across the Atlantic at six hundred miles an hour, she could see his dark head across the aisle at the other window seat. She felt a little miffed at his not having changed his seat to sit next to her. Had he really forgiven her for her outburst the other night—or was this his way of letting her know that he hadn't? Oh well, it was better this way, the assignment was going to take all her attention and energy, she didn't want the complication of even the slightest emotional involvement. The seat beside her was empty, the aisle seat was occupied by a buxomed West Indian woman, with sundry bags and packages at her feet. Then suddenly, her heart began to race as a well-known voice said, "Do forgive me for disturbing you madam." The woman got up with much difficulty and Jason slipped into the vacant seat.

"Hi Trish."

"Why—hullo. What are you doing here?" She gazed at him in disbelief.

"That's a charming welcome," he said dryly.

"But where did you spring from? We've been airborne for ages. I didn't see you at the airport?"

"Just having a chat with one of the crew," he said casually.

"I thought that you'd gone to Morocco?"

9

"Wangled the change."

"Why?"

He looked down at her - his dark blue eyes glinted with amusement. "Why do you think?"

"That you've been to Morocco and not to Jamaica?"

He laughed, "You don't consider yourself a good enough reason?"

She felt herself breathing a little faster, "No I don't."

"And yet you are - the sole reason."

"I can't believe that, not after the last couple of months."

"Because of Carla?"

"Of *course* because of Carla. How can you ask?"

"Oh that," he waved a hand airily. "Merely business."

"Business! All that togetherness *business*?"

"I assure you it is so. Carla's father is thinking of taking over **YOU: TOMORROW**—we need him, we need a shot in the arm. Prices of everything have escalated, paper, printing, distribution—you know that Trisha—we can't increase our prices more than marginally or we'll price ourselves out of the market."

"So what has Carla to do with it?"

"It was my job to make her persuade her old man to bail us out of a very sticky position."

She regarded him doubtfully, she desperately wanted to believe him: so near to him as she was now, so in range of the impossibly blue eyes, so close to the light sprinkle of grey at his temples—an added attraction in her eyes to his dark good looks— she was unable to think clearly, her mind, her body, her whole being were too conscious of his maleness. She took a deep breath to avoid a quiver in her voice as she asked after a long pause: "And did she?"

"Did who do what?"

"Did Carla persuade her father to buy the magazine?"

"It's practically in the bag."

"Why didn't you tell me? Why just drop me as you did?"

He didn't hesitate, "I thought that you knew, everyone else did."

She was silent - everyone else knew. So why hadn't anyone mentioned it to her? All she'd got were pitying looks behind her back and a forced bracing jollity to her face. Then she said, "So, won't this trip cancel out all your good work of the past few weeks? Carla may not spur 'daddy' on without your - encouragement." For the life of her she couldn't keep the note of sarcasm out of her voice.

For a moment, he looked uneasy and was saved from having to answer by the arrival of the meals' trolley, which stopped by their side. In the flurry of pulling down the shelves and placing the trays on them, with the drinks' trolley arriving immediately afterwards, the question was lost—although it hovered at the back of Trisha's mind.

"A drink madam? Sir?" The flight attendant asked in her cool, drama student type voice. Before Trisha could answer Jason said, "Champagne for us both."

"Yes sir."

As the glasses were placed before them and the small bottles deftly opened, she quietly protested, "Oh Jason, that's extravagant."

"Not a bit, we have to celebrate."

"Celebrate what?"

"Celebrate our first overseas assignment," he took an appreciative sip. "Mm. Good, very good. Tell me, is there any truth in the rumour that you are the heiress to a huge estate in Jamaica?"

She choked over the champagne and after she had regained her breath and sopped up the splashes from her silk blouse, she exclaimed in amazement, " An *heiress*? *Whatever* gave you that idea?"

"Not mine. It was all over the office."

Trisha looked at him sceptically, "I heard nothing—however did such a notion come about?"

"Remember the interview we did with Milton Carew—the Jamaican who's made a fortune in real estate in the north of England?" She nodded. "Well, he takes—or rather his wife takes—**YOU: TOMORROW**, she'd seen your name in the editorial list. She asked about you and when she heard that your family was originally from Jamaica, she said that perhaps you were one of *the* Barretts, and, as the last Barrett is an elderly lady with no family, you could possibly inherit the estate."

Trisha laughed, "I don't believe it, I just *don't* believe it."

"I admit, it does sound a bit romancy—Mills and Boonish. But are you?"

"Am I what?"

"One of *the* Barretts?"

"I didn't know until a moment ago that there were any 'the' Barretts."

"Oh well," he said easily. "Probably a highly exaggerated account, suitably embroidered for effect."

"Who did the interview?"

"Jennifer Grant."

She gave a peal of laughter, "Oh Jason, how could you have given that tale a moment's consideration? You know what Jennifer is—highly romantic and fantasizes even the grocery list."

"Yes. You're probably right. I should have thought of that myself. But her story, added to the enquiries about you..."

"Enquiries about me? From whom?"

"From Somerset House."

"Oh that, that was pure routine."

He opened his mouth to speak, decided against it, poured the rest of the champagne and said, "Drink up, we'll be landing shortly I should imagine."

She obediently drained her glass. The champagne had lulled her earlier doubts about Jason and she was filled with a quiet joy at being with him once again.

The captain's voice came over the intercom, preceded by a loud *ping* to get their attention, "Ladies and gentlemen, the island of Jamaica is in sight on your left. We shall be putting down at the Donald Sangster International Airport, Montego Bay, where all passengers will disembark and go through Health and Immigration. On-going passengers will re-emplane when called. The stopover will be about thirty minutes. The flight from Montego Bay to Kingston will take about twenty to twenty-five minutes, depending on head winds. We shall be touching down at the Norman Manley International Airport at about three-thirty. Thank you."

"Oh this is exciting," Trisha looked out of the window, anxious now to see the island where her grandmother had been born and grew up—and where her own deep roots were. She couldn't really accept that—England was her home, her roots were there, already she was feeling a sense of disorientation—she didn't like this new sensation. She looked down at the glittering deep blue sea and the island that was set like a green gem in the centre. "Oh Jason, Look—how absolutely beautiful!"

They were losing height and the island grew as each second passed. Below them, was a sea of unbelievable beauty, a patchwork of emerald, sapphire and aquamarine rippling in the afternoon sunlight like watered taffeta.

"I've never seen sea like that before, all those different colours, so sharply delineated."

"It's due to the different depths," Jason explained, "The lighter the colour the more shallow the water."

Above them was a sky of deep blue at the zenith shading to pale blue on the horizon. Huge white clouds, like sculptured mounds of detergent, drifted lazily - hardly seeming to move at all. They could see white houses nestled in the hills that rose behind the town and silver beaches fringed with palm trees and strange squat spreading trees that Trisha learned later were wild almond. Sunbathers and swimmers waved as the plane swooped over them. Small pleasure crafts, sped by a strong breeze, their gaily coloured sails taut, looked like toy boats on a vast pond, whilst others with roaring outboard motors had water skiers in tow, cutting wide V-shaped frothing wakes. To Trisha, fresh from an English winter, it was a fairy tale setting. The runway was in sight now, looming closer and snaking like a giant grey concrete ribbon. The plane touched down with scarcely a bump and raced along the tarmac until the reverse jets slowed the giant aircraft to a crawl.

As they stepped out of the plane, the heat hit them like a tangible object, engulfing them in a warm blanket. After the air-conditioned cabin, the contrast was overwhelming. Trisha felt her forehead and upper lip bead with sweat, "Whew! It's *hot!*"

"You'll get used to it in no time at all," Jason said in a comforting voice. "It's always a shock as you land."

The first class passengers had got off before the others and as Trisha watched the small knot of them walk across the tarmac in front of her she gave a gasp, "Jason—that girl in blue, she looks for all the world like Carla."

"Not surprising," he said easily, "She was travelling first class."

*T*he shock of Carla's presence took all the joy out of the flight. Trisha went through the formalities of Health and Immigration in silence. While the others exclaimed in wonder at the delights of the Bond shops, she sat on a bench in acute misery. Jason hadn't 'wangled' his inclusion on the team on her account. He had either been sent by Jaqui because they really needed another cameraman, or he was there because of Carla. But why lie and make her believe that she was the cause? It didn't make sense. When they re-boarded she shrank into her seat as far away from him as she could.

He glanced at her set expression, "What's the matter Trish? Heat getting at you?"

"How can you ask?" she burst out. "When *Carla* is on the plane!"

"Didn't I mention that she was?"

"You know perfectly well that you didn't. Why you bothered to conceal the fact I can't imagine, you couldn't have done so for long. What's she doing here anyway? I thought that she was going to Morocco with the other team?"

"I don't know where you got that idea, it was never on the cards. She's doing an article on some of the well known families in the island for the June and July issues—some of the old families who came over with Cromwell's

New Model Army." He reached over and took her hand, "Don't be upset love. She won't be with us - she'll be off and away all over the island." He bent down and kissed her on the mouth. His touch sent a thrill through her, as it always had done and, inspite of her disillusionment at his behaviour, she gave a shudder of ecstasy. The pressure of his mouth deepened, his tongue forced open still more, lips that had parted voluntarily, his probing tongue made her arch her back and give a small moan of pleasure.

He drew his mouth from hers at last and murmured, "It's been too long, God, how I've missed you."

She nodded, unable to speak. He still kept his arm round her as he leaned across her towards the window, "Now look down, we're going to fly east for a bit then turn and go right over the island from north to south."

"Oh! How lovely. How wild and untamed it looks." The sight momentarily banished all thoughts of Carla from her mind. Below them were mountains covered with close-packed trees. Deep vertical clefts, dark and mysterious, high valleys rich in pastureland—she could just make out grazing cows, brown and white, black and white, like toy animals viewed from that height. Clusters of little hut-like houses that clung to the mountainside proclaimed small villages, but there were vast tracts that appeared quite uninhabited. They flew along the high spine of the island for many miles, the higher mountains to their right, below them was the almost inaccessible area known as the Cockpit Country—where runaway slaves of the seventeenth century had their hideout. The plane veered to the south and then flew across the high peaks of the famed Blue Mountains. They weren't blue at that height but verdant with varying shades of green. Occasionally, bare patches of rock and eroded hillsides, sad tributes to forest fires and man-made erosion could be seen. As the plane flew further south over the hills of

16

upper St Andrew, they could see that the lower foothills were mostly populated by the opulent houses of the middle and upper classes, gracious homes surrounded by lush well tended gardens. In the little districts that dotted the foothills were village shops and clusters of small unpretentious houses of small rural communities.

Then, the land flattened out into a large plain and the sprawling city of Kingston and its spreading environs beneath them. To the west, across the harbour, was the township of Portmore, clear in the westering sunlight. They flew over the long and sanguine peninsula that enclosed the huge harbour, and came in to land at the Norman Manley International Airport which was sited just a few miles from the end of the man-made reclaimed narrow strip.

They had a long wait for their luggage as only some of the pieces had come in on an earlier flight, but when the remainder of the luggage did arrive, they cleared customs fairly easily as a member of the Tourist Board was waiting to greet them. They hired one of the tourist minibuses for the drive into Kingston. This was disappointing after the splendour they had seen from the air and drove back along the same narrow strip that they had flown over just an hour or so ago—the Palisadoes, it was called, although its official name had been changed to the Norman Manley Highway some years ago in honour of the former Prime Minister. It was narrow by international standards, broad by island standards, with a good surface, the tossing Caribbean Sea on one side, the still, grey-green waters on the other. Giant cacti, like great organ pipes, reared skyward in the sandy soil, and mangroves flourished, darkly tangled and mysterious. On the seaward side were one or two rusting hulks of foundered ships, presenting a derelict air of decay and neglect.

"Oh dear, this is all very squalid," Trisha exclaimed as the minibus wended its way along the Windward Road.

Rum shops and small stores lined the sides, unpaved and dirty, goats and chickens roamed freely amongst the dirty barefoot children. Sound systems blared the throbbing reggae beat above the sound of the traffic, which moved at an alarming pace along the congested roadway. The noise of the horns of buses, cars, and laden country buses was deafening and the driver wove his way through the maze of vehicles—some of which showed signs of damage: dented fenders and parti-coloured bodywork - mute testament to unintentional encounters. The slum area was soon left far behind as the bus made a right hand turn and the road led ever upward. Here the streets were unlittered, the houses grew bigger and were set in manicured gardens - the whole ambience changed for the better.

They reached the *BLACKBURN HOTEL* in New Kingston just as the brief tropic twilight deepened into night.

"Meet you in the Anancy Lounge for a drink before dinner? Jason said as they waited for the lift.

"I'm so tired," Trisha confessed, "I don't know if I'll have the energy to change and dress for dinner."

"You will. Take a shower and you'll get your second wind. 7:30 okay?"

She nodded. She had never been able to refuse him anything in the past. She couldn't now. "All right, 7:30."

He was right: the air-conditioned room, the shock of a needle-like cold shower, twenty minutes flat on her back with her eyes closed, revived her wonderfully and she went down to the dimly lit bar filled with a sense of well being. They had drinks under the huge figure of Anancy, *the Spider Man*, who leered down at them from the ceiling, in the centre of a large spider's web. The web motif was everywhere, on the place mats, the napkins and even on the glasses. Afterwards, they dined alone in a quiet corner of the Lignum Vitae Café. The rest of the group was nowhere to be seen. Trisha gave a deep sigh of contentment; this was like the old days...

"Penny for them?" His voice broke her reverie; she smiled at him across the candlelit table.

"I was just thinking that this is like the old days, you and me, alone in our own world."

"And that's how it will be from now on—you'll see."

She regarded him gravely. He sounded so sincere and confident. She wanted to believe him yet memories of his past treatment of her posed a big question—and she wasn't sure that she wanted to know the answer.

They rode up in the lift together and he left her at her door after holding her close for a long moment before kissing her goodnight. "You feel so right in my arms, I don't want to let you go."

It would have been so easy to say, *you don't have to, stay with me, love me as I'm sure only you can love.* But she eased out of his close embrace and said, "You have to I'm afraid. Good night Jason."

In the dim light of the corridor, she couldn't make out if his expression changed, but his voice was tender as he said, "Good night, my darling, sleep well."

She leant against the closed door after he had gone, her pulse racing after the bliss of his embrace, she recognised the urgency of his desire, barely held in check and every instinct told her to reach out and match it, but as always, something held her back.

Although she was tired to the point of exhaustion, she spent a restless night. The long journey, the excitement, the reunion with Jason and all the mixed emotions associated with the revival of their relationship, all had taken their toll and it wasn't until nearly dawn when at last she fell asleep.

She didn't wake until nearly 8:30 and, for a few minutes, gazed in wonderment at the ceiling of the strange room with an uneasy feeling that she would be terribly late for work—then she relaxed as she remembered where she was. No work today, today was for lazing and recovering from jetlag. She got out of bed and opened the curtains and the long French window and, as she stepped out onto the balcony, she gave a gasp of delight: the mountains over which they'd flown yesterday were revealed in all their towering rugged glory. "They really *are* blue," she exclaimed, "How simply marvellous." The shrill of the bedside telephone sent her back from the balcony, "Hullo?"

"Trisha? Jason." As if he had to tell her—the sound of his voice was engraved in her memory, even the distortion of the telephone line couldn't cloud recognition. "Are you still a slug-a-bed?"

"Just getting up—I hardly slept, and then of course, overslept. I'm still tired."

"Poor darling. Want to join me for breakfast?"

"Give me half-an-hour?"

"Right. The coffee shop on the mezzanine floor, The Blue Parrot."

After breakfast, Trisha went out to the pool deck and stretched out under a blue sunshade. She was still suffering from jetlag and decided to take it easy all morning. It was a new experience for her, up until now she had flown no further than to Italy or Spain. There was to be a reception that night hosted by the Jamaica Fashion Guild and the Jamaica Tourist Board, she needed to be fresh and rested for that.

"Mind if I join you?" A voice from above her asked.

She opened her eyes: outlined against the incredibly blue sky was Hammond Verity, clad in swim shorts with a beach towel draped over one shoulder. His dark hair was wet and droplets clung to the dark curling hair on his chest.

"Not at all. You look as if you'd been here for weeks."

He dropped onto the chaise beside her and flipped a

finger at his bronzed shoulders, "You mean this?"

"Mm-hm."

"I was in Venezuela a couple of months ago."

"Lucky you."

"Oh I don't know, one gets a bit fed up with hotel bedrooms after the first glamour of travel wears off."

She turned on her side to face him and propped herself up on one elbow, "It would take a lot of this to make me fed up. I find this fantastic! Just over twenty-four hours ago we were in snow and ice, muffled to the eyebrows in top coats, scarves and fur boots, now here we are: blue sky, a backdrop of glorious mountains, palm trees, swimming pool—the lot."

He grinned at her, "I find such enthusiasm infectious. I hope that you never lose it and become bored and blasé like—like so many of us."

"Do you have anyone in mind?"

He pursed his lips and gave a slight shrug, "Not really, but I've seen it happen so often, wild enthusiasm that all too rapidly dies to be replaced by cold cynicism."

"I must try to preserve my childlike naiveté," she said lightly.

"I did not say 'childlike'," he rolled over and faced her. "I'm not teasing you—I envy you. Don't change, little Trisha."

"What were you doing in Venezuela?" she asked after a pause.

"Free lancing. Took some pictures for the **NATIONAL GEOGRAPHIC,** covered a fashion show for **VOGUE** and another for **FLAIR.**"

"How super! And now you've settled down at **YOU: TOMORROW?**"

"I'll be there for a while," he said, then asked: "How about a swim?"

"Okay, it may wash away some of my cobwebs," she stood up and his eyes widened as he viewed her petite

21

figure. She flushed under his admiring gaze.

"Well," he drawled, "Who would have thought that under those layered winter clothes was such a gorgeous figure?"

"Stop it Hammond. You're embarrassing me."

He got up and looked down at her, "Forgive me, I wouldn't want to do that. I'm filled with delight and un-qualified admiration at such perfection."

She wrinkled her nose at him then dived into the pool at the deep end. For one so small, she had a good turn of speed and covered the length of the pool in a fast racing crawl. He caught up with her as she made the turn at the shallow end and companionably stayed beside her for a couple more lengths.

"Whew!" She flopped back onto the chaise, her red-gold hair in tight wet ringlets. She regarded him from behind huge dark designer sunglasses. "That was fun."

"The beauty of it is that one can swim every day all year round. Except of course when it rains—and believe me when it rains here it *rains!*"

"You've been here before?"

"I spent the first few years of my life here, and then for a spell when I was in my teens."

"Really?"

"My father was in the diplomatic service, my parents came here when I was only a few months old. He was first secretary for a few years then deputy high commis-sioner. He went from here to Bermuda as deputy then came back here as high commissioner."

"I'm impressed."

He grinned. "Don't be—commissioners, ambassadors, whatever—they're just people."

"To you perhaps, but to people like me they're very special people. Such a responsibility, isn't it? I mean a whole country judges another by its representatives."

"My, my - quite the philosopher," he laughed teasingly, then became serious, "But don't you see, what we're doing is representing our country from a different angle? We're under scrutiny from the local folk."

"I must mind my p's and q's then, mustn't I?"

"I imagine that you'd do that naturally," he said.

After that, they lazed for the most part in silence. Trisha felt a sense of companionship in Hammond's presence - a contentment that was far removed from the turbulence she always felt with Jason. This thought set her wondering as to what had happened to Jason, she hadn't seen him since breakfast. "Are you going into town?" he had asked and had seemed oddly relieved when she said, "No, not today. I'm going to rest off by the pool."

"You do that, but be careful of too much sun to begin with."

She laughed, "I have a built-in tan, remember?" She flipped a finger at her light coffee skin and he said, "Even so, be careful."

"Have lunch with me?" Hammond's question broke into her thoughts.

"That would be nice. Where?"

"Lignum Vitae Cafe?"

That would bring back memories of last night—and Jason. She paused - she'd got to stop this nonsense. She flashed him a brilliant smile. "Alright. In half-an-hour?"

Lunch was a quiet relaxed affair. He introduced her to yet more island delicacies: conch salad and a marvellous mélange of different fruit served in calabash gourds, sprinkled with freshly grated coconut and flavoured with one of the island's justly famous liqueurs.

Later that evening, Trisha looked at herself in a long mirror and was *almost* satisfied with her reflection. She'd been to the hotel's beauty parlour that afternoon and had the chlorine from the pool thoroughly shampooed out of her hair, and then had it set in a way quite unlike her usual style, which added years to her looks. She didn't normally indulge in such an extravagance as her hair was easy to manage and she usually washed it every other day and brushed it into a cascade of shining waves and curls. But tonight was special: she wore a black halter top with a fine gold swirling silk skirt, with diagonal black stripes. There was a wrap jacket to match but she decided that she didn't need it in the warm climate—then changed her mind and wore it slung nonchalantly over one shoulder. If only she were taller—even with her four-inch high heels on her Ferrangamo courts, she was—in her estimation—still too short.

"You'll just have to make the best of it," she told her reflection in the mirror, "Well, you just can't change it." She went downstairs, the reception was being held at the poolside, transformed for the occasion by dozens of lights set into the surrounding lawns on low poles. The chaises and umbrellas had given way to long tables, one set up as a bar, the other a buffet. Small tables and chairs were dotted about for those who preferred to sit to eat.

The area was crowded with stylishly dressed men and women of every complexion, ranging from the pink and white European visitors, through honey, light coffee to dark coffee islanders. From long blonde tresses to the attractive complicated cornrow braids, a style copied from African forebears and much more aesthetically pleasing than the once popular Afro. There was also a sprinkling of the newly fashionable close-cut hair for women, practically shaven in some cases, which showed off delicately formed skulls. The women were elegant, the men well tailored. Trisha was surprised, her ideas about Jamaica were based on the late Bob Marley or Peter Tosh, but there wasn't a 'lock' in sight. She joined the reception line which inched forward, as the hosts were not content with a brief handshake but chatted easily with each guest.

After she had shaken hands and exchanged a few words, she looked round for members of the group: Dolly was talking with much hand waving animation to a thick-set man with close-cut grizzled hair, who was wearing a grey kariba jacket. Most of the men were in conventional suits and ties, although a few sported brightly coloured shirt jackets, made fashionable a few years ago by a well-known public figure. Peter Gascoigne and Julia Towers were a little way apart from the main crowd, in deep conversation. Trisha idly wondered if they had something going for them, then dismissed the idea: Peter was reportedly happily married and Julia had been engaged for the last six months to a—also reportedly—fabulously wealthy banker. But then—these overseas trips could be like life on board ship, romance all the way, forgotten when once back on dry land.

There was no sign of the towering head and shoulders of either Jason or Hammond and she felt a stab of disappointment, then two hands dropped lightly on her shoulders from behind and a kiss was placed on the top of her head.

Jason!

A thrill shot through her and she turned quickly, her eyes flashing the message from her heart.

The look faded.

"Hammond!"

"You expected—hoped that it was someone else?"

"I—I—wasn't expecting anyone—to creep up—behind me," she stammered, embarrassed that she had been so obvious.

"It would have made me very happy to have been the cause of such a look of welcome," he said dryly as he removed his hands.

"Hammond—I'm sorry, I..."

"I've never known a girl who's sorry so often, a positive Pollyanna of sorrow." He regarded her gravely. "What we need is a drink and food. What are you doing standing all by yourself without sustenance of any sort?"

"I've only just arrived."

"Uh-huh. You've been standing here looking around for at least five minutes. Looking for Jason?"

"Why do you ask that?" her tone was too defensive and his dark eyes were hooded for a moment, then he looked up and asked, "Are things back on the old footing between you and Jason?"

"I don't think..."

"...Not that it's any of my business, but all the same I'm making it my business." He reached out and touched two glasses on a passing waiter's tray. "Scotch?"

"Yes, sir."

He picked them up and handed her one, "Bring two more in ten minutes."

The man grinned, white teeth in a dark face "Yes, sir."

"But I don't drink Scotch," Trisha made a faint protest.

"About time you started. We'll be over by the buffet," he told the waiter, "Come Trisha." He guided her with his free hand to the long buffet. A bewildering assortment of dishes was displayed. She looked at them in dismay:

"I don't know *what* to choose."

"Hold my glass and I'll choose for us both." He deftly piled two plates with the aid of a pair of tongs, extracted two napkins from a pile and secured two forks with dexterity. "Here we are, let's grab this table."

He put the plates down on a small table for two, held a chair for her then took his glass from her and took a deep swallow, "Come, drink up," he ordered.

She looked at him helplessly, "Hammond, you asked the waiter to bring two more in ten minutes, I can't possibly..."

"Oh yes, you can."

"But I don't normally drink anything strong."

"You did on the plane coming over, two vodka's and champagne."

"How did you...?"

"I was across the aisle, remember? Anyway, this is an occasion..."

She refrained from asking what was the occasion but looked down at her plate, "What's all this?"

He used his fork to point, "Escoveitched fish—very good, old island recipe. Salt fish and ackee—you had some in London, remember?" She nodded. "Avocado you do know, fried plantain you don't. Sweet and sour shrimps and sweet and sour baby ribs..."

"Baby?"

He laughed, "Not baby 'baby'—small, young—our hosts aren't cannibals I do assure you. Now *this*," he stabbed at a triangle that looked like fat toast, "is bammy. It's made from cassava flour, quite indigenous, the first inhabitants of the island—the Arawaks—they grew it, they cooked with cassava flour, in fact it was a staple food, together with fish—right, history lesson over. This last chap is called 'stamp and go'..."

She laughed, "Why?"

"I'm not really sure, something about eating by the wayside on a journey, it was so hot that it made you stamp, and then you went."

"You're having me on?"

"That is a possibility," he agreed lightly and she laughed. The culinary lesson had restored her former mood and she obediently drank the Scotch and sampled the food. "It's all super. Ow..." she choked and reached for her glass, "That's hot!"

"Now you know why it's called Stamp and Go!" he quipped.

The waiter appeared with their fresh drinks and she protested again, "You're turning me into an alcoholic."

"Nonsense, once in a while can do you no harm." He regarded her over the rim of his glass, "I asked you a question a little while ago."

She didn't ask him to repeat it but said, "I don't know, honestly. He—Jason—sat next to me on the plane..."

"I know."

"I didn't think you noticed."

"I not only noticed, that was my seat. Jason asked me to swap."

Her eyes opened wide in amazement, "Did you mind?" she asked involuntarily, then coloured at the boldness of her question.

"Of course I minded, but I thought that you'd rather be with Jason than with me. Why, I can't imagine," he grinned, then became serious. "Why do you let him treat you as he does?" She didn't answer and he went on, "Here he is now." He nodded towards the reception line which had thinned almost to the point of non-existence. Waiting together were Carla, looking stunning in a clinging red dress, and Jason, elegant in a ruffled dress shirt and a brocaded jacket. They were talking in low tones, their heads almost touching.

"Oh," Trisha's hand flew to her mouth and her eyes went wide, this time in anguish.

Hammond reached across and took both her hands in his. "They went to the north coast, right after breakfast. Carla wanted to arrange one of her interviews."

"You knew?"

"Saw them leave. Carla made a great point of letting me know."

"Why didn't you tell me?"

"And spoil your day? Anyway, I didn't want to tattle."

"Why not?" she asked bitterly. "All's fair in love and war, isn't it?"

Unexpectedly, he grinned, "Why yes, thank you for reminding me." Before she knew what he was doing, he pulled her hands to his chest, leant across the small table and kissed her. It wasn't the gentle kiss of the other night, which had been a feather light brush across her lips, but hard and demanding, crushing her mouth to his, as disturbing as Jason's had ever been and for a moment the world receded and there was no one else present in a maze of swooning delight.

He released her and the moment was lost. When she regained her breath she asked passionately, "Hammond, how could you? In front of all these people? Whatever will they think?"

"The men are wildly envious of me I imagine, the women—hopefully—envious of you," he grinned, quite unrepentant.

"May we join you?" A voice beside them asked. Trisha turned her head and Jason was standing there, his blue eyes coldly accusing.

Carla didn't conceal her amusement and asked, "Or are we interrupting this idyllic scene?"

Three

The next hour was a nightmare for Trisha. Jason had found two more chairs and the four of them were seated close together. He was coldly polite, Hammond was casually possessive and Carla continued to be openly amused.

Trisha had cast a quick look round, expecting that everyone would be staring at her, either in amusement or in surprised disapproval, but no one seemed to have noticed the incident—or were too well bred to appear to do so.

For the life of her, Trisha couldn't understand Jason's attitude: he'd spent the whole day with Carla, whose manner towards him left no doubt as to her feelings and intentions, and yet he was acting as if Trisha was the guilty party—and succeeded admirably in making her feel as if she was. She tried to appear natural, which resulted in her being nothing like her usual self: her voice was pitched too high, she laughed without reason and, yet, she was incapable of acting in any other way. In contrast to the svelte sophisticated Carla, she saw herself as a gauche schoolgirl. She wanted to run to the safety of her room, but remembered Hammond's words about being some kind of an ambassador and she felt that she couldn't with decency leave early and so give the impression that she wasn't enjoying the welcome party...

At least she could leave the table. She didn't have to

endure this unpleasantness. She got up. "Do excuse me but I want to have a word with Julia..."

"Julia left ten minutes ago," Hammond said as he too stood up. "But come, let us mingle, we've been too insular. 'Night Carla—Jason." He took her elbow and firmly guided her towards a knot of people who were grouped round a vivacious dark eyed, dark haired, dark skinned older woman.

"I wonder who that is?" Trisha murmured, curiosity overcoming her jumbled emotions.

"The lady holding court? Politician's wife? Stage star? Fashion designer—probably the latter, the place is swarming with others of that ilk. Let's find out, I see Peter Gascoigne amongst the worshippers."

They tacked themselves on to the fringe of the group, Peter caught sight of them and beckoned them to his side. "Hi you two, come and meet a fascinating lady. Miss Diedre Barrett, may I present two more members of our group from **YOU: TOMORROW**? Miss Trisha Barrett and Mr. Hammond Verity."

The fine dark eyes of Diedre Barrett came back to Trisha's after the introductions had been acknowledged. There was a strange wondering expression on her face as she asked, "Barrett, eh? With two tee's?" Trisha nodded. "How—interesting. It is an old island name. My particular branch has been here since Cromwell sent his New Model Army to capture the island. Miss Barrett, will it be possible for you to visit the north coast during your stay in Jamaica?"

"Oh yes, we go to Ocho Rios to cover the Japanese showing there and to photograph summer clothes for the July and August issues."

"Summer clothes in January," Diedre laughed. "Your summers can be colder than our deepest 'winter' months. How can you endure it? Here, it is endless summer - but it never gets boring. It must be fascinating working for a magazine."

"Yes it is. I love it."

"Yes, especially when it brings you to a place like this, but sometimes one gets sent to places one would rather give a miss," Hammond put in.

Diedre glanced at him, an experienced appraising look, liked what she saw and gave him one of her enchanting smiles, then flashed back to Trisha. "Where are you staying in Ocho Rios?"

"The Santa Gloria."

"You'll be comfortable there. Give me a ring when you've settled there. I live in Ocho Rios at an old house called **Pimento Hall**. You must come to lunch—I think that you will find it—interesting. Of course," she added hastily, "The luncheon invitation includes all of your group."

"Why thank you, how kind."

"Not at all, it will be my pleasure," Diedre smiled a gracious dismissal then drifted away on Peter's arm.

"I wonder what she meant by 'interesting'," Trisha said. "It seems an odd thing to say when inviting someone to lunch."

"What was interesting is what she did not say," Hammond said cryptically, then went on before she could comment, "It was patently apparent that the invitation was directed at you," he said thoughtfully, "The rest of us were simply an afterthought."

"You can't say 'patently apparent' it's tautologous." Trisha laughed, and then, before he could comment, she said, "It'll be interesting though to see an authentic old Jamaican house, I expect that's what she meant." She stifled a yawn, "Do you think that I can leave now? I'm so tired."

He glanced round, the numbers had thinned out considerably, "Yes, we'll both go."

"I wanted to leave earlier, but..."

"In the interests of representation and all that, eh?"

"How perceptive of you!"

"More than you know," he said shortly. He saw her to her door and said goodnight coolly, the earlier searing kiss might never have happened.

Despite the seesawing emotions that she had experienced over the last few days, she felt that sleep would come easily. She was just drifting off when the shrill ring of the phone by her bed brought her wide-awake.

"Hullo?"

"Trisha—I've got to see you."

"Not *now*?"

"Yes—now."

"No Jason—whatever it is must wait until the morning."

"I must see you *now*." His voice held an urgency she'd never heard before. Had he been drinking? She'd never known him drink too much—but then, what did she really know of him? A few short months of bliss, during which they hadn't touched on the past—hers or his—then Carla. The thought of Carla strengthened her incipient weakening.

"Trisha?"

"No Jason. Whatever it is can wait. Leave it until tomorrow."

"But..."

"No buts. I mean it Jason. Goodnight."

She put down the telephone without waiting for his reply. She was pleasantly surprised at her firmness. In the past, she would agree to anything he asked—well, not *anything*.

Now, sleep evaded her. She tossed and turned restlessly and, at last, in desperation she turned on the television, it quite often had a soporific effect on her. She would begin to watch a film, one that she had planned to see, and the next thing she woke up and had no idea what had passed between the title and the rolling credits. Perhaps that magic would work tonight. She clicked on the remote control. There wouldn't be much channel hopping for the island had only two television stations. *All rather primitive,* she thought, used to a dozen or more choices — plus the satellite dish. She was told later that most hotels had satellite dishes, but since the scrambling of many of the programmes from the States had become the norm, many had been dismantled.

It was an old black and white film she settled for, and she marvelled anew at the slimness of those early movie queens—women's bodies had changed their shape over the last forty years or so, she thought in surprise. The stilted more-English-than-the-English Hollywood voices were fast lulling her into oblivion when she heard a quiet knock at her door.

Who on earth would come calling at this hour?

Surely not Jason, after she had been so positive? *Yet, who else would?*

The handle began to turn and, as the door inched open, she cried out, "Who's there? What do you want?"

She was suddenly possessed of an irrational fear. She was quite powerless – even to reach out her hand for the telephone and summon help. The door opened wider and Dolly Marks' tousled head appeared round it.

"Trisha?"

The relief was overwhelming. "Dolly! What on earth— you frightened the life out of me."

Dolly came right into the room and Trisha switched on the bedside lamp and turned down the sound of the movie.

"Good Lord Trisha. You look as if you'd seen a ghost."

"I told you I was terrified, creeping in like that..."

"Who did you think it was on the other side of the door? One or other of your attentive swains?"

"What are you talking about?"

"If you indulge in public kissing—and I *do* mean *kissing*, wow! What a sizzler! —which produced such a look of fury on Jason's face..."

"Dolly, please, it's late, I'm tired. I do not care to discuss my love life—or lack of love life—at this or any other time. What do you want?" She knew that she sounded ungracious, but, at the best of times, Dolly tended to bring out the worst in her and this was quite definitely not the best of times.

"I've got a splitting headache—the local brew tastes divine, but oh dear, aspirin is my crying need at this moment."

"Aspirin no, but my own brand of painkiller, yes."

Trisha reached for a robe and slipped it on before she got out of bed.

"Do you always sleep naked?" Dolly asked, elaborately casual.

"Yes," Trisha said shortly. She padded into the bathroom and came back with a bottle of white tablets. "Here you are. One or two?"

"Just one, thanks." She poured a glass of water from a bedside flask and swallowed the tablet. "Why don't you use ordinary aspirin?"

"I'm allergic to aspirin. But anyway, I hardly ever take these—I only keep them for emergences, mostly other peoples. Well, goodnight, hope the headache clears up."

"Sorry to have disturbed you. I would've asked Julia—but it seemed that she had company—that's why I took so long to open your door." She shut the door behind her.

Trisha was now fully awake. She was sceptical for the reason for Dolly's visit—her barbed words as she left rather intimated that the visit had been for one purpose only—to see if either Jason or Hammond was there. *How humiliating.* Then, she remembered that Dolly had a reputation for meddling in other people's lives, and making snide remarks to which no one ever paid any attention—

she fervently hoped that that was so in this case. The television was still flickering, the actors mouthing their words. She turned up the sound, the programme had changed whilst Dolly had been there and she realised that it was a late night horror movie—definitely not to be watched after the fright she'd just had. She switched off the set and padded to the door and locked it.

"...Indulge in public kissing..." *Damn Hammond for putting me in such a position*—the demanding touch of his lips returned and despite her outrage, a responsive thrill had coursed through her body—and did again at the remembrance. *Was Jason really mad over that kiss?* The hope that he might be was comforting. Then, she remembered how he had gone off with Carla—all day—without a word. What sort of a game was he playing? He surely didn't think that she was so naive as to accept his explanation for his dancing attendance on Carla? And yet—wasn't that exactly what she was doing? Accepting all explanations, running back to him whenever he crooked a finger...oh, dear, she had hoped that this trip would be carefree and uninvolved, and here she was, only at the end of the second day and life was becoming more complicated with every passing hour.

Her thoughts went to the intriguing Diedre Barrett. They had never found out what she was—well, if she lived in an old house in the country, she probably didn't work at anything. She wasn't a young woman but it was difficult to pin an age to her. She had beautiful eyes, but no other claim to beauty. It was her supreme elegance and radiant vibrant vitality that drew all eyes—the men's with unconcealed admiration, the women's, in most cases, with unconcealed envy. What did she mean by the remark that Trisha might find it 'interesting' to visit her house for lunch? She puzzled over the remark and came to the conclusion that it had no significance—just one of those words tossed out on such an occasion—then suddenly there was daylight coming through the half-drawn curtains — sleep had crept upon her unaware.

She sprang out of bed — no lazing today — the Japanese fashion group was due to arrive — there was work to be done. The morning was spent in a conference of the group as to how they should approach the subject. They wanted a special angle: a fragile background to complement the collection, or a strong background to accentuate it? Something stark which would not distract from the clothes, or something that echoed the theme? Suggestions were tossed around, discussed and discarded until a definite policy was agreed upon.

The hotel was full, for, in addition to it being the height of the tourist season, there were similar magazine groups from Canada, the States, France and Germany. Conversation in the cafes and restaurants was like a modern Babel — or a miniature United Nations.

Trisha was relieved that once they got down to work both Jason and Hammond became impersonally professional; there was not even the vaguest reference by look, voice or deed to the highly charged emotions of the night before. Jason made no reference to his urgent telephone call and Trisha reluctantly accepted the unsavoury fact that he had been under the influence of drink. She was disappointed in him. She had an old fashioned aversion to heavy drinkers and the resultant change in personality, she didn't believe in the *in vino veritas* adage: truth was not revealed under the influence; rather the influence changed the *persona*...

"...what do you think Trisha?"

She looked up in surprise, the others had gone during her daydreaming, only Jason was left and apparently he had asked her a question. "I — er — sorry, what did you say?"

"I asked you if you would like to join us, some of us are going to meet the Japanese group."

"Oh yes, super. When are you leaving?"

"In about an hour—time for a quick bite before our transport arrives."

"Who's going?"

"Dolly, Hammond, Peter, you and myself."

"Not John and Julia?"

"No, it seems that they have other plans," he said dryly. Dolly's words came back to her '...went to see Julia, it seems she had company'...

"Oh dear," she said involuntarily. "Surely not."

"Surely not what?"

"I—um—I wasn't thinking—forget it."

"It's pretty clear what you *are* thinking—as we all are."

"But Jason—John's married."

"I know—and Julia is engaged. There's nothing we can do—except keep our mouths shut when we get home, we owe them that. Don't look so tragic. They're both adults and—these things happen on trips like this, you know, and not only on trips," he added.

"*I* don't know, but presumably you speak from experience," her voice held a tart note that sounded shrewish to her ears.

"No," he said mildly, "One doesn't have to experience something before one recognises that it's taking place."

"No, of course not. I'm sorry."

"Oh do stop apologising, darling," he said, paraphrasing Hammond.

She flushed a little at the endearment. He noticed her embarrassment and grinned. "You didn't used to mind my calling you 'darling'," he teased.

"It's not that I *mind*—it just seems—*hypocritical*—or the slack current usage of the term."

"Neither," he said emphatically, "I call you darling because you are very dear to me." He went on before she could reply, "About last night, I'm sorry if I upset you on the phone, but I was good and mad, I can tell you. Just what is between you and Hammond?" he demanded.

She looked at him with wide serious amber eyes, "No more than that which you *claim* is between you and Carla."

He got up and spread his hands, "Okay. I deserved that. Come on, I'll buy you lunch before we go off to the airport."

The 'buy you lunch' was a misnomer, for all their expenses were part of the trip. She gave a wry smile—well it was a nice gesture, but didn't hide the fact that he'd turned the conversation away from any more questioning...

Jason had hired a car for the drive to the airport, a 1999 Audi. It was air conditioned, which was a two-way blessing: it kept them cool and also cut out much of the noise of traffic that seemed to be an island feature: screeching tyres, blaring car radios and a gross overuse of horns. All this, in addition to the sound systems at bars and record shops along the way, added up to decibels that hurt the ears. They took the same route in reverse that they'd covered on the drive in. Trisha had learned that further along on the narrow strip beyond the airport was the town of Port Royal, which at one time had been an important city and had been known in pirate days as 'the wickedest city in the world'. It had been almost totally destroyed by an earthquake in 1692 and been rebuilt only to be razed by fire a few years later. Being the phoenix it was, it had risen once more after being nothing more than a sleepy fishing village. It was now in the process of being partially reconstructed in its original seventeenth architectural form as a tourist attraction, after the manner of Williamsburg.

Trisha sat in front with Jason, the other three in the back. He was a good driver but her heart was continually in her mouth: pedestrians wandered into the roadway, ignoring the sidewalks—some of which were unpaved, others were heaped with goods for sale. Children darted

across the road with alarming frequency, as did the goats —
who ambled unafraid and often showed more road sense
that the humans.

Jason took his left hand off the steering wheel and
patted her knee," Relax, you're as taut as a steel wire."

She gave a shaky laugh, "I don't know how you drive
with such confidence on these roads and the frightening
way the others drive."

He smiled, "It's not much different to London—I've
also driven in Italy and Singapore—your heart would
really do flips there."

"Remind me not to go there then."

When they reached the airport they found the place
crowded, the arrival and departure areas were packed.
Normally, they wouldn't have been allowed beyond a
certain point, but the Tourist Board had issued them with
special passes. The main entrance hall was cluttered with
boxes and packages, carrier bags and even bulging paper
bags. Children darted in and out, screaming with laughter, unchecked by their harassed parents.

"Let's make a way through this mob. Trisha, keep close
behind me or you'll be trampled," Jason said as he stopped
and looked up at the television monitor, "There's something wrong here, I'll ask over at the desk." They reached
the check-in counter. "Flight 236 from Miami, when do
you expect it. The monitor must be wrong."

"No sir, it's right, the flight has been delayed."

"But it shows that it won't arrive for another two
hours?"

The flight attendant gave a slight shrug, "I'm sorry
sir, there was a strong headwind over the Pacific and the
connecting flight from Los Angeles was subsequently
missed. May I suggest that you and your party wait in
the Horizon Lounge? Up the stairs, to your left, keep on
going after you reach the Waving Gallery."

"Thank you," Jason turned away from the counter.

"You heard? They nodded, not amused at having to spend all that time in the caucophony of milling humanity. "What would you like to do? Horizon Lounge?"

Trisha hesitated, "Could we—possibly—drive out to Port Royal? It's a bit further along. It's a very historic place."

"History isn't my bag," Dolly said flatly.

"Nor mine." Peter said.

"Oh never mind, it was just an idea," Trisha said. "I can always go another time."

"Better go while you've got the chance," Hammond urged. "I'm game."

"Right, so am I," Jason said briskly. "You two soak up the local brew, we three will imbibe a little culture."

Oh dear, Trisha thought, I had hoped that there would have been all of us, not just me and those two. "Look," she protested, "I don't want to drag you out there against your will."

"Not another word, Port Royal it is. Come on, let's fight our way out of this."

"Who are all these people anyway? They don't seem to be quite the type for international travel?" Peter remarked.

"How snobbish can you get," Hammond countered. "Probably 'informal importers/exporters'—known as 'higglers' in my day. They buy and sell in Miami, Haiti and Curacao—although Haiti's been a bit off limits what with all the brouhaha that's been going on there over the last couple of years—and believe me, some of these rather large ladies have made fortunes in the process. Come on you two, let's make tracks."

Trisha caught Dolly's cynical eye and hastily looked away. Why oh why had she suggested the expedition—it had seemed a good idea at the time, but had somehow backfired.

Jason swung the Audi right at the roundabout and

sped along the lonely road, bush and cactus on either side, more mangrove swamps and the slightly rank odour that accompanied them, not a dwelling in sight. They passed a lighthouse, looking as lonely and desolate as only such a building can look, then nothing until they reached the neat clean little town of Port Royal.

"Oh it's enchanting," Trisha exclaimed. "Look at that old fort. It's called Fort Charles, after Charles II—and come, let's walk on Lord Nelson's Quarterdeck." They climbed the wooden steps and Trisha read the plaque that stated: *In this place dwelt Horatio Nelson. You, who tread his footprints, remember his glory.* Isn't that something?"

The town held a unique fascination for them and after a while Hammond said: "It looks to me that if we want to do this place justice we must come back when we have more time, the church alone will take an hour or more." He gave a short laugh, "You know, I lived here for years and never came here except to take the boat to Lime Cay. The Maritime Museum will be worth a visit, there are lots of artifacts recovered from the sea—from the sunken city after the earthquake in 1692—and there's a whole mine of information still under twenty feet of water."

"You really are a mine of information on the subject yourself," Trisha said admiringly and Jason said shortly: "I think that we should get back—the plane may have picked up some speed and cut that two hour wait."

"What a hope," Hammond murmured. "At least let's have a cup of coffee before we start back."

They found a café that was little more than a stall and settled for cold beer and a piece of fried fish and bammy. "If I eat too much of this delicious island food, I'll need a new wardrobe when I get home."

"Isn't this home?" Hammond asked.

She gave a quick frown, why were people harping on that subject? First Jason - now Hammond. Her brow cleared as she slipped into the front seat, "Anyway, we've walked on Nelson's Quarterdeck, where the great man stood and watched for French invaders."

Jason slid the lever into 'drive' and grinned down at her, "Don't repeat that remark to cynical Dolly," he warned, "She'll probably deflate you with a 'Big deal! So what?' "

"I'm glad we came, thank you both."

"I enjoyed it. You Hammond?"

"So much so that I'm wondering if we couldn't fit in some of the shots for the Summer Special there. It has its own charm — sand sea and palm trees are a bit over worked and so are fast becoming under-rated,"

"Good idea. When we get back to the hotel I'll get on to Jaqui to get the go ahead to include Port Royal as a venue for shooting."

The two men chatted about the idea all the way back to the airport and Trisha sat silent, glad that their attention had been diverted from her—not for too long, she amended hastily—she grinned ruefully on the inside. When they showered her with attention, she wished they wouldn't and, yet, felt neglected when they didn't.

Four

Jason's hopes that the plane would have made up time were not realised. The arrival screen showed that in fact more time had been lost. In the end, the plane was nearly three hours late. The three 'culture vultures', as Dolly called them, joined her and Peter Gascoigne in the Horizon Lounge and Trisha tried to prolong the life of a vodka and orange juice for as long as she could.

"No really, no more," she protested when Peter wanted to re-order, "I don't drink very much and *never* at this time of day, it makes me woozy."

"Oh come on Trisha, be a sport..."

"Don't pressure her Peter, if she doesn't want any more then she doesn't," Hammond said firmly and she shot him a grateful look. He gave her a lazy intimate smile— which Jason observed. The small incident made him frown and he glanced from under knitted brows at Trisha and back at Hammond who gave him a bland smile, deepening Jason's frown and making Trisha acutely uncomfortable.

Dolly and Peter seemed to have heads made of cast iron and kept the barman busy. Trisha breathed an inward sigh of relief when the arrival of the plane was finally announced. They left the lounge and went down to the reception area. Blessedly, the milling crowd that had greeted them on their arrival earlier had thinned to a few

44

stragglers. There were no queues at the various check-out counters, the Waving Gallery was devoid of people but not of litter: empty drinks' cartons and paper bags were scattered everywhere, blowing from place to place in the stiff breeze, the customs area was deserted and there was an overall air of desolation.

"I hate airports," Trisha murmured as they made their way to the passenger exit gates. "They are either jam-packed and noisy, or deserted an cavern-like, there never seems to be a pleasant in-between."

"They hardly vary all over the world," Hammond said cheerfully. "It gets so that you hardly notice—and sometimes can't remember which country you're in."

"Well I hope that it gets to me sooner than later."

"The young are so impatient," he sighed.

"Wisdom from Methuselah!"

They had reached the Arrivals area and Hammond said, "There's a familiar face. Hi! Bruce!"

"Why! Hi there!" Bruce Ricketts from the Tourist Board greeted them warmly. They'd met him the night before and had been impressed with his bearing and enthusiasm for his job. "We're all here for the same reason? Good. Nice of you lot to join the welcoming party—I notice that none of the other groups had the same thoughtfulness. I've made all the arrangements — they'll be through Health and Immigration in no time. We'll all go to the VIP lounge while a couple of my folks deal with customs which, seeing the enormous number of cases, cartons and crates may take some time."

The desolation and desertion of the customs department was soon changed as the belated passengers poured in. They were all tired and short-tempered after the long delay and, despite the special treatment given to the visitors, there was much bustle and confusion. Trisha was glad when they reached the comparative quiet of the VIP lounge, although, even there, the noise level soon became pretty high, as introductions were made on both sides, drinks were dispensed all round—this time Trisha settled firmly for orange juice. There was a tangle of cables snaking over the floor as television crews from both the stations took shots, camcorders were much in evidence, and press reporters held tape recorders close to their mouths, whilst fax machines clattered every so often. A member of the Jamaica Fashion Guild conducted live interviews being recorded for later transmission. The television lights made a mockery of the air conditioning and the crowded room soon became uncomfortably warm.

All this, together with the unfamiliar high-pitched chatter of the exquisite Japanese models, the hearty laughter from the welcoming committee combined to give Trisha a headache and she made a silent vow never to participate in any similar function in the future.

"What's the matter love? You're looking fazed," Hammond whispered.

"It's all this confusion—I hate it."

"You'll get used to it—you'll *have* to, if you're going on with this job. It always gets hectic, the arrivals, the departures, the showing itself—one gets frantic that nothing will be ready on time—but it always is—and then you wonder why you worried—until the next time."

"Well, thanks for those comforting words!"

"To use an expression I loathe 'you're welcome'!" Hammond said lightly — then he became serious. "If you continue to look at me with those tiger eyes of yours, I'll forget myself again and kiss you in front of all these people—it may even get on the telly!" She moved hastily out of reach and he laughed softly, "Don't worry, I'll pick a quiet spot next time — where I can kiss you *properly*."

She felt her face flame, then saw that Jason was watching the exchange, tight lipped and hard eyed. He strolled over to them. "They want to interview us."

"What? Oh my goodness, I'm sure that I look a mess."

"You look, as always, perfectly gorgeous, doesn't she Jason?" Hammond asked with a wicked gleam.

"Yes," Jason said tensely. "Come on, they're waiting." He pushed his way through the crowd to where one of the television cameras was set up. A svelte dark woman greeted them, the interviewer, a well-known radio and television personality introduced herself before they went on camera. "Hi. My name is Alison Dugeld, just call me Alison." She was adept at putting people at ease and, after her initial nervousness, Trisha forgot that she was on camera and answered questions and elaborated answers about her work as if she had been under the fierce scrutiny of a battery of lenses, all her life. Then, the questions took on a personal tone:

"Miss Barrett, is this your first visit to Jamaica?"

"Yes it is."

"I hope that you are enjoying your stay?"

"I haven't had much time to, we only arrived the night before last, but I'm loving the heat—although at first I found it rather fierce—but I know I'm going to love it, the mountains are absolutely beautiful."

"I understand that you're going to the north coast? Whereabouts?"

"Ocho Rios, I'm looking forward to that, I've heard so much about it."

"I'm sure that you will enjoy it. Don't work too hard and miss our beaches. May I ask you a personal question?"

"Of course, but I may not care to answer it," Trisha said with a smile which took the sting out of her reply.

"That of course, is quite understood," Alison said smoothly. "Your name is one that has been in our island for many hundreds of years, do you have any connection with Jamaica?"

Trisha hesitated fractionally before saying, "My grandmother was Jamaican."

"Was she a Barrett?"

"Her name was Barrett."

"But was she born a Barrett?" Alison persisted with an odd intensity.

For some reason Trisha didn't like the turn the questions had taken and said evasively, "I shouldn't think so, I'm not really sure."

Dark brown eyes, rimmed with thick lashes under delicately made up lids, met her amber ones: Alison seemed about to pursue the trend, but all she said was, "Thank you Miss Barrett, now perhaps you could tell our viewers something about the purpose of your visit in connection with the Japanese Fashion Show?"

At last, it was over and off the air Alison whispered, "I'm sorry, I almost touched on forbidden ground, didn't I?"

"I don't quite know what you mean."

"My mistake. I was quite sure that I'd asked a question that you didn't want to answer."

Trisha wondered why Alison was being so persistent and became quite uncomfortable but was saved further embarrassment by Hammond saying, "It looks as if we can go now." He smiled at Alison and turned on the full battery of his charm, to which she responded rather archly and switched her attention from Trisha to him. "Hope we meet again soon," he murmured.

"Oh, I'm sure we will, I'll be covering the shows."

"I'll be looking forward to that. Goodbye. Come Trisha," he took Trisha's arm and steered her through the maze of cables. "You were super," he whispered. "In future, I'll be able to say when your name is on everyone's lips 'I was there, when a star was born'..."

"Oh Hammond, you are a clown!"

"Lost alas, to the Big Top."

Jason signalled them, "They're through customs, we can move out now." There was a hard edge to his voice and he regarded Hammond coldly, and then swept his gaze with equal coldness over Trisha. Hammond compounded his disapproval by raising an eyebrow and giving a short mocking laugh.

"'Move out? You've been seeing too many old war films, dear boy."

Jason scowled and for a moment Trisha saw him in a new light, as a petulant adolescent who was denied the candy he craved. She felt a sudden sense of loss mingled with relief that she had made the discovery—before it was too late...

Too late? Wasn't that anticipating events which were unlikely to take place?

There was more bustle and laughter as the visitors and their mass of luggage were loaded onto two tourist minibuses. The **YOU: TOMORROW** group got into the Audi and the entourage drove back in convoy to the city.

In deference to the comfort of the members of **FASHION: JAPAN**—as they were told was the official name of the group—a reception in their honour was not to be held until the following evening.

"When you've come half-way round the world," Jason said, "You don't want to chatter inanities at a cocktail party the first night out." He seemed to have recovered his good temper and Trisha wondered if she had imagined the flash of spoilt little boy attitude, and then decided that she hadn't. "Have dinner with me?" he murmured in a low voice, but not low enough, for Hammond said: "I'd planned to ask you both to have dinner with me. Perhaps Carla could join us?"

Trisha shot him a look of venom over her shoulder; he inclined his head and raised a cynical eyebrow.

Jason said smoothly, "Good idea—perhaps you could invite her." Trisha gave a sudden giggle, "Your serve Hammond, I think," she said.

As it turned out, Carla was not in the hotel and Jason

spent an hour and a half on the phone to Jaqui in London. Hammond's assistance was urgently sought by one of the Japanese cameramen, whose cameras and films had not arrived with the rest of the gear. In typical fashion, the airline was vague as to when they would arrive as it was not known just where along the route they had been misplaced and, so, Trisha spent the evening alone. She was relieved in a way, as she wasn't used to dual masculine attention—flattering though it was. She was glad for a little privacy and rang room service for a light supper, then made notes on her laptop about Port Royal. Perhaps she might be able to get an article about the old city from them, but she soon realised that she would need to make another visit to get some more information on the subject—how that could be fit into the tight schedule that lay ahead she had no idea.

She was just thinking of taking a shower and making an early night of when the telephone rang: "Hullo?"

"Trisha—Hammond. What are you doing?"

"I was just about to get ready for bed."

"What a splendid idea, like me to join you?" His tone was light and mocking, but there was an undercurrent that made her believe that he wasn't just being flippant.

"Certainly not," she said as lightly as she could, "'Fie, what a question's that, If thou wert near a lewd interpreter.'"

"Nerissa—no—Portia—*Merchant of Venice*—um—er—Act Four? No, Act Three *Scene* Four."

"Splendid, I'm impressed, not many people can spot that quotation."

"I only know it because we *did* the Merchant for A levels."

"All the same, very impressive."

"Why don't you join me in the Anancy Lounge and we'll swap a few more quotations—it's too early for bed—alone."

"Hammond! Will you stop being so outrageous?"

"Just kidding—or maybe just testing." She made no reply and he said, "Come on Trisha, we were going to have dinner together, remember?"

"Jason, you and I were going to have dinner together—and possibly Carla."

"So it didn't work out, I told you why for me. So what happened to Jason?"

"He got tied up on the phone to London and Carla wasn't around..."

"She is now," he began, and then stopped.

"She and Jason are together?" she asked in a tight voice.

"Er—yes."

She took a deep breath, "Alright, I'll be down in a few minutes."

The Anancy Lounge was dim and intimate. A combo played softly in the background, not loud enough to swamp conversation, just enough to set the mood and allow recognition of some old love songs. As Trisha entered, she paused just inside the doorway and looked around. Hammond unfolded his tall frame from a low chair and came towards her. "Shall we stay here or go out on the patio?"

"The patio—it's such a joy to be able to sit outside under the stars, with a tropical moon and all the little night creatures yakking away like mad."

"There are not many night creatures here in the big city, just you wait until we get to the north coast."

They talked companionably over their drinks and Trisha discovered that there was much more depth to him than he generally allowed to be revealed. He was knowledgeable on a variety of subjects and the time passed unnoticed, until she caught sight of her watch and exclaimed, "Gracious, it's late. I must go, tomorrow is too close for comfort." She stood up, "Thank you Hammond, I enjoyed this evening."

"The first of many I hope."

He saw her to her door and she felt a momentary qualm as she suddenly remembered his words at the airport about kissing her properly in a quiet spot, but he merely bent and brushed her forehead lightly with his lips.

The following day was hectic. There were misunderstandings due to the language barrier: the Japanese models all had a smattering of English and the administrative members of the group were proficient in varying degrees. Of course, the English group—as is the way of the English when it comes to foreign languages—had not one word of Japanese between them—if you discounted *wakarimasu* from those who had read Shogun more than once.

For the presentation of the collection, the ball room had been taken over, a stage and ramp installed, small rooms leading off were converted from offices to changing rooms, where a dozen racks of clothes, the cream of the leading Japanese designers, were hung, swathed in dust covers against prying eyes and jealously guarded by a small wiry security man.

The rehearsal, which had been arranged to start at ten am, didn't get under way until nearly noon, so that lunch went by almost unnoticed consisting of sandwiches and coffee consumed on the run.

Trisha's job was to make extensive notes of the evening wear which was her assignment, so that she could write up the descriptions and captions for the photographs which would eventually be chosen from amongst dozens of shots, for the June and July Issue of **YOU: TOMORROW**.

She also had to do interviews on tape with the models, the administrators, the designers, who were present, and with members of the Jamaica Fashion Guild. Fitting these in with all that was going on was not an easy job, as no one wanted to spare the time from the matter in hand to spend in being interviewed—although they all loved to see themselves in print.

Hammond and Jason were completely absorbed in photographing the models in close-up for details of cut and texture, accessories and accompanying make-up, and in depth to capture the overall picture.

Despite the distractions, Trisha worked fast. She was lost in admiration at the exquisite workmanship, the sumptuous fabrics and the unusual designs, which, although so far removed from the current trend favoured by Paris, Milan and Rome, were eminently *wearable*.

As for the models, she envied their exotic oriental beauty: their glossy black hair, cut and styled by a master hand: their flawless complexions enhanced by subtle delicate make-up and their perfect petite figures.

During a short break, Hammond echoed her thoughts, "These girls are marvelously photogenic. Their skin tones and texture are gifts from the gods of the camera. Do you realise that although the modern Japanese girl has changed drastically from those of forty years or so ago, they still retain a mysterious allure that is as different as cod's roe is to caviar to the western acceptance and concept of beauty?"

She sipped her coffee, "Yes, they've changed, just like we in the west have changed. Have you watched any old thirties or forties movies recently?"

He shook his head, "What about them?"

"The *shape* of women's bodies has changed. In those days they were all very slim, with incredibly tiny waists which made their shoulders look broad—Lauren Bacall is a case in point. You only see figures like that now on the aging movie queens who have kept their weight down and star in the soaps."

He thought for a moment then laughed, "You're right—up to a point. You've generalised of course, but, if I

remember rightly, your waist would not look amiss in a forties movie."

She put down her coffee mug and said firmly,
"Hammond, please no more remarks like that. I must keep
my mind—all my concentration—on my work. This is my
first overseas assignment and I must make it a success—my
whole future in **YOU: TOMORROW** may depend on how
I handle it."

He looked down at her, a strange expression in his dark
eyes, "There are other futures possible besides making a success as a fashion writer," he said cryptically, then asked,
"Have you laid down your ground rules to Jason?"

She flushed, "Not—yet."

"I warn you, that unless you do—and it is obvious from
his reactions that you have—I shall ignore them as applied
to me."

"Is that—a threat?"

"No, a friendly warning—or should I say—a promise?"

"It seems to me that that remark borders on ignoring
the 'ground rules' as you call them, at the outset. But it doesn't
look as if I'll need to lay down any for Jason, not after the
way he's been behaving."

"Carla?"

"Yes," she said, "The ubiquitous Carla."

He covered her hand with one of his, she glanced down
at it, it completely enveloped her small one. Despite her earlier words, she made no attempt to withdraw it. "Never mind,
love," he said softly, "You've always got me."

Since the previous evening spent so amicably in the
Anancy Lounge, their relationship had undergone a subtle
change. She wasn't quite sure where it would lead to, but
she was happy to go along with it—up to a point. She was
still hurt and angry with Jason who hadn't bothered to en-
quire last night after he was through with his call to Jaqui,
whether she had dined alone or not at all, but had ignored
her and teamed up again with Carla. She thrust the memo-

ries away as she and Hammond finished their brief lunch and returned to work. The rehearsal went on until after five-thirty. The reception for the Japanese group was slated for six-thirty—although the locals wouldn't arrive until much later, six-thirty Jamaica-time could very easily become eight o'clock real time—so that there was barely time to shower and dress to be ready for the beginning of the reception.

The poolside scene was even more animated than that of two nights ago and Trisha found herself caught in a group of Tourist Board and Jamaica Fashion Guild members. The attractive Japanese models were monopolised by the susceptible Jamaican males, and whilst they didn't understand the local inflexion and lilt, they smiled and nodded, happily aware that they were being admired and desired.

Trisha was ready to drop by the time it was polite or her to leave. She had successfully avoided both Jason and Hammond all the evening, Hammond because he was respecting her edict—he had raised his glass and a quizzical eyebrow to her from across the pool—and Jason because he was once again by Carla's side. The sight made Trisha want to lash out in frustration at the nearest inanimate object, but she kept the smile on her face and interest in her voice as she listened to and joined in the conversation that flowed around her.

The quietness of her room was bliss after the endless chatter that had gone on at the reception and she slipped thankfully out of her high-heeled pumps and the figure hugging dress that she had worn. She brushed her hair with unnecessary vigour and admonished her reflection in the mirror, "You're a fool, Patricia Barrett, you yearn after a man who picks you up and drops you when he pleases, who pays attention to another woman right under your nose, and is blatant about it because he knows that you will run to his side at the crook of a finger. Yet, you spurn the man who is very attracted to you—and, admit it—that you find very attractive. In the end, you wind up with a dull evening listening to a boring dissertation about the island's problems. You..." she stopped abruptly as there came a knock on her door. Not Dolly again—she'd had enough of Dolly in the past few days to last a lifetime...

She put down the hairbrush and tightened the belt of her thin terry robe. She went to the door and called: "Who is it?"

"Jason—may I come in?"

Despite her good intentions, her heart missed a beat then began to race, "What do you want?"

"I want to talk to you—which I can't do very well like this."

She hesitated: this was plain idiocy—it made a mockery of her ruling to Hammond.

Her hand hovered over the press button lock, then depressed it and turned the handle. Jason was still fully dressed in the pale blue dress shirt and light blue pants, the navy corduroy jacket that he'd worn earlier was slung over one shoulder.

He glanced down at her, unsmiling, "Aren't you going to ask me in?"

She stood aside and he stepped into the room and closed the door firmly behind him.

Her heart was still racing, but she managed to keep her voice light, "Well, what do you want to talk about? Won't you sit down?" she added formally and waved her hand to two armchairs by the French windows which led onto the balcony.

"No thank you, I won't be long. What do you mean by avoiding me all day?" Before waiting for her to answer, he went on, "You spend the morning whispering to Hammond and the evening flirting outrageously with some of the local blades."

All other emotions were blotted out in a slowly mounting anger, "Have you quite finished?" her tone was icy. "I spent the morning and afternoon working damn hard—as you very well know. Hammond and I are on the same assignment—not by choice but by Jacqui's decree—as you also know very well. My 'outrageous flirting' was nothing more nor less than an attempt to be alert and polite when in fact I was deadly bored. *And,"* she was now getting into her stride, *"You* spent the evening *glued* to Carla's side."

"You could have joined us."

She looked at him in amazement, *"Joined* you? And break up your romantic duet?"

"I've told you, there is nothing romantic in our association, which is merely one to encourage her to persuade her father—but you know all this, I've explained it all before."

"And who instigated the association?"

"Jaqui—at the editorial board's suggestion."

"You make it sound very convincing, but your attentiveness towards Carla has nothing of a business approach, however much you protest otherwise and as for her attitude towards you—to say that it's predatory is putting it mildly," she ended with as much sarcasm as she could summon.

"Nonsense, I would have thought that you'd realise that I've got to make it convincing—after all there's a few million pounds at stake."

She was still shaking with rage and, without thinking, she burst out, "So what does that make you? The 90's version of a 30's lounger lizard?"

A ringing slap stung her cheek, she gazed at him in disbelief, then she was in his arms and his lips were on hers. He drew away sufficiently to murmur, "Oh my darling, forgive me—how could I ever hit you—but that you should say—should think..." his lips came down hard on hers again, bruising, fiercely demanding, urgently probing tongue to responsive tongue, then her arms were round his neck, his hands caressed her body through the thin robe, until she lost all sense of time and place in the mounting desire that consumed them both.

Five

The next day, the preparations for the evening showing were confined to the visiting fashion group, so the **YOU: TOMORROW** team was free to rest up for the rush later. Most of the team's work was done, additional notes and shots might be taken at the actual showing, but most of the work for the special edition had been done at the rehearsal.

Jason and Hammond would cover the audience—which was expected to be very prestigious and fashion conscious—for the glossy pages of the sister magazine **THEM: TODAY**. After that, they were free until they went to Ocho Rios by road two days later.

The models who would show the British designs of summer wear were not due in the island until the end of the week, which would give the camera crew time to select suitable spots for back drops.

Trisha ordered breakfast through Room Service and, when it arrived, she had the waiter place the tray on the table on the balcony. Her room was on the twelfth floor and the traffic on the busy main road was far enough below her for the roar and hum of the assorted vehicles and the incessant sounding of horns to be just a background to her jumbled thoughts and emotions. She barely touched the wedge of golden pawpaw, toyed with a piece of toast and finally settled for coffee.

How could she go downstairs and face Jason? He had

made it very plain what he thought of her, how could she *ever* face him again?

She shut her eyes against the memory of last night, but the action only served to bring the scene more sharply into focus...

Their embraces had become more demanding and explicit, they had sunk down onto the bed and had both risen to the heights of ecstasy that cried out for fulfillment, when at the last moment she had pushed her hands against his chest in sudden panic, "No—no Jason—please—I can't..."

'Don't worry my darling, let me really love you—we'll make such beautiful love together..."

"No—I said NO!"

The look of naked passion in his eyes gradually faded to disbelief and then changed to scornful anger. He stood up and said bitingly, "So that is what you are! There's a name for girls like you, but I won't sully your *maidenly* ears with it. You lead a man on until a point is reached, and then..."

She looked at him, her eyes tragic. Her voice quivered as she said in a low voice, "I'm sorry, I truly..." she began, but he cut in with a savage: "Don't make it worse with your infernal apologies." He glared at her and took one step towards her, she shrank back in sudden fear at the look in his eyes. He gave a bitter laugh, "Don't worry, I won't take you by force. I only accept what is given freely." He turned on his heel and strode to the door, which he opened and shut without a sound.

I would have banged it, she thought irrelevantly, then realised that he didn't want to advertise his presence—especially in the face of rejection. The enormity of what she had done began to seep into her consciousness and she turned her face into the pillow and wept...

Now, she put down her coffee cup and ran her fingers through her hair. *How had she got into this mess?* She asked herself in despair. *You would have been in a worse mess if you'd let Jason stay,* an inner voice cautioned. *But would I?* She countered. *I might have been blissfully happy and filled with contentment, not in this state of confusion, embarrassment and self-condemnation.*

She got up from the table and looked unseeingly at the soaring mass of the mountain range that had given her such joy two days ago. How was she going to get through the day? How was she going to be able to cope with the evening when so much depended on it? She gave herself a mental shake and said aloud, "For goodness' sake girl, pull yourself together, you're acting as if you'd committed a crime. All you've done is rejected advances that you objected to..."

Objected to?

Was all that moaning and clutching hands, uninhibited response to kisses, objection? No my girl, you were just plain scared and now you're not big enough to admit it. All those warnings about AIDS and promiscuity have certainly got through to you. The fears that Jason had slept around—as office gossip had it—were the main factor of your sudden rejection. Adding to which you're blowing the whole incident up out of proportion. Nobody knows of it except Jason—and he won't speak of it, that's for sure...

She showered under a stinging stream of warm water, then switched to the coldest until she gasped. She returned to the balcony and dried her hair in the stiff breeze and styled it with vigorous brush strokes—the action reminded her that she was doing just that when Jason knocked at her door. This thought brought again a flood of mixed emotions: remorse and relief, self blame and self praise, shame at her behaviour and pride that she had stopped the downhill race in time—a flood of feeling threatened to engulf her once more...

With effort, she took hold of herself: *You are being hopelessly self indulgent and self pitying, the trouble is that you are so inexperienced in these matters that you have no idea how to avoid such a situation, or to handle it properly when it arises. In this day and age it is laughable—and pitiable, the normal twelve to fourteen old knows more about these sexual matters than you do. Grow up, girl, learn to live in the real world, get out of your snug little cocoon of fantasy...*

She decided that she would dress, go downstairs, call a cab and go back to Port Royal, perhaps, there in soaking up the peaceful past, she could forget for a few hours the turbulent present. She shut the thought away that all she was doing was running away from the present...She put on dark glasses, picked up her bag, checked that she had enough cash without having to stop at the desk and cash a traveller's cheque and went swiftly along the corridor to the lifts.

Downstairs, the registration area was crowded and busy, as was the lobby, which was packed with arriving and departing guests. Designer luggage stood cheek by jowl with old-fashioned battered hide cases. Bellboys stacked and unpacked trolleys with expertise, taxis drew up and sped away from the curb outside the glass doors with regularity, depositing new guests and picking up old ones.

She wended her way through the throng, hoping to get outside and into a cab without meeting anyone of the team, when she heard her name called. She kept going as if she hadn't heard. A hand grasped her elbow and slowed her pace. She turned in trepidation and felt relief when she saw that it was Hammond.

"Hey, hey, hey," he said, "why all the rush? And what happened to you at breakfast?" He looked down at her and frowned. "Are you alright?"

She drew a deep breath, "I'm fine. I had breakfast on my balcony. Please Hammond, I'm in a hurry."

"Where are you off to?"

"I'm going to Port Royal." She could have bitten her tongue out. Why hadn't she said that she had an emergency dental appointment or something? He said quickly: "Good, I wanted to pay a second visit myself. I'll join you."

She opened her mouth to protest, then remembered how he had demonstrated at their first meeting a calm assumption that anything that he wanted to do was alright with her, and closed it again.

He hailed a taxi and helped her in. She was silent during the half hour or so it took to get to their destination. He glanced sideways at her a few times and seemed about to speak, but her set expression and anguished eyes kept him silent. There was comparatively little traffic on the road at that hour and they made good time out to the narrow strip of ground that led to the airport and so to Port Royal. Overhead, the sky was a brilliant blue with drifting white clouds. On the harbour's side, the waters were still and dark, barely rippling, but on the seaward side, the Caribbean Ocean was dancing in the sunlight, frothing white horses crested each wavelet, dashing onto the beach leaving a line of foam before receding and repeating the whole process. Hammond was barely conscious of the scene. His whole attention was centred on Trisha as hers was turned inwards.

The little town was even more enchanting than they remembered and, gradually, Trisha's inner turmoil faded and was replaced by curiosity. She soon realised from their elderly guide's account of the events which had taken place there, that what she had termed the 'peaceful past' had been much more physically turbulent than her mental and emotional present.

They gazed in awe at the massive silver tankard which had been Sir Henry Morgan's, the Welsh pirate who later became the governor of the island, a pillar of respectability and the scourge of any remaining pirates. Hammond took shots of possible sites for the summer issue. "We'll come back after we've finished on the north coast. Jason got the go ahead from Jaqui," he said as they sipped ice-cold lager beer and tucked into a lobster salad at a small seafood cafe. "Well, you look more like yourself, this old town has done you good." He reached across the table and covered her hands with his, "Like to tell me about it love?"

She looked down, her eyes suddenly filled with tears. It was tempting to confide in him, to pour out her misery—but what if—what if the scene of last night was repeated with Hammond as the principal actor? His understanding and sympathy might very well lead them into a like position. She drew her hands away and said coolly, "No thank you, it's nothing that I can't handle. Shall we go?"

For a moment, he looked as if she had struck him. He said in a tone that matched hers, "Why not?"

The drive back to the hotel was accomplished in silence. Hammond was obviously hurt and bewildered by her attitude, and she was plunged again into misery. She knew that she had behaved atrociously to both Jason and Hammond and would thoroughly deserve it if they treated her in a cool, distant professional manner from now on.

What was the *matter* with her? Other girls accepted attention from men without getting uptight and defensive—*other* girls, she told herself, had no compunction about sleeping with men to whom they were attracted. In the permissive society to which she belonged, Trisha was the odd girl out. Even with the advent of AIDS, most of her women friends shrugged it off with 'it couldn't happen to me' attitude. So why was she different? Perhaps it had something to do with the fact that she had come strongly under the influence of her maternal grandmother, whom she adored. Gran' had the values of an earlier age and had instilled them into Trisha without making those values seem dated or fusty. God knows, Trisha thought, I've seen too many of my friends sleep around and after the first flush of a new relationship, know nothing but a life of disappointed frustration. I don't want that for myself. Now that the fear of AIDS was gaining momentum, perhaps the old fashioned values would return—but for a very different reason...Hammond's voice brought her out of her reverie.

"Here we are," he paused, "Trisha?"

"Yes?" she met his eyes then looked away.

"Look love, I'm sorry that I offended you by asking what was wrong. I had hoped that we were on a closer footing than apparently we are. Whatever's bothering you, put it behind you for tonight. As you reminded me yesterday, this is your first big show, your future at **YOU: TOMORROW** may depend on how you handle it. Make an effort Trisha. You've got to learn early in this game that personal problems *must* be subjugated to public life."

His voice was so kind, not censorious as she felt that he had every right to be, that the ready tears came to her eyes, "I'm sor..." He put a finger on her lips, "No, don't say it." As they entered the hotel, he touched her arm briefly, "All right?"

She nodded. "Yes, thank you Hammond, you've helped so much and—I'm such a fool..."

He nodded, "You are indeed," he said, then added in a different tone, "I'm always here when you need me."

"Even when...?" she stopped, not wanting to go deeper into the earlier events, but he nodded again and said, "Even when."

She spent the afternoon studying the notes that she had made at the rehearsal the day before then planned the final write-up. Then, she turned her attention to the interviews she had done so far, the others would have to be done on the north coast. She had the ability to get total recall months later of a person or a place by reading the notes she had taken on site.

She managed to banish most of her disturbing thoughts by doing her *Hatha Yoga Asanas*. The physical rhythmic movements refreshed her body and mind so that by the time she came to dress for the evening she was in command of herself, and felt that she could face whatever presented itself—or more probably, *who*ever presented *him*self.

For the event, she had brought a sleek dress from the French House of Girot, in dull amber jersey, with touches of black at the left shoulder and right hip. With it, she wore an amber and jet necklace, a legacy from her grandmother—once rather despised as being hopelessly old fashioned, now come full circle and revered as ultra high fashion. She felt a thrill of excited anticipation as she made her way to the ballroom, set with rows of gilt-backed, velvet covered chairs. Champagne would be served during the showing and a late buffet afterwards— again by the pool.

Although it was early, everyone from **YOU: TOMORROW** was present and a few of the invited guests were drifting in. Trisha glanced round at the sound of Carla's unmistakable ringing laugh. She was as usual absolutely stunning in a one-shouldered white jersey gown, which was a marvellous foil for her high piled black hair and perfect figure. As always, she had the effect of making Trisha feel insignificant, which was partially dispelled by Hammond's low whistle of approval as he handed her a glass of champagne.

"Wow! You look like a million dollars. If you were in the show tonight, you'd walk away with top honours."

"Against those exotic Orientals? You've got to be kidding."

"Dead serious, I do assure you. You have your own particular brand of exoticism—as I think I mentioned before."

Despite the compliments, his manner was easy and impersonal. There were no heavy undertones of meaning— the events of the morning might never have happened.

Against her will, she found herself searching the room for a glimpse of Jason, then felt a surge of relief when she saw him busy with his camera at the far end of the room.

The room was beginning to fill up now, a distinguished gathering of diplomats from most of the foreign embassies, a big contingent from the Japanese Embassy, members of parliament and the senate, prominent business men and women and many representatives from the arts. The final flurry occurred when the Governor-General entered with his party: there were presentations, flashes of bulbs as newsmen recorded the moment for the late TV news, the next morning's papers and the overseas press.

Trisha sipped her champagne and turned to Hammond, "Isn't this exciting?"

He nodded, "For you, yes. For me..." he shrugged, "When you've seen as many of these junkets as I have, I hope that you'll still get a thrill out of it."

"Don't you feel anything any more?"

He considered the question, "Yes and no—there is a sameness that tends to pall—but it's a challenge to record each one from a fresh angle."

"Yes, I see what you mean—at least, I think I do."

"What is really exciting is when a new star is born, a new model takes the world of fashion by storm, and you've taken the first shots of her—you're in. You're home and dry."

"Has that ever happened to you?"

He grinned, "I feel it in my bones that that little Yodoko is going to zoom to the top overnight—*this* night—if I'm any judge. I said the same about Kimberley Mais—and look what's happened to her, if only I'd been there when *that* happened. Come, we'd best take our places, the show is about to start."

The actual showing was vastly different from the rehearsal: the girls were the same, the clothes were the same, but there was an added magical sparkle that had been absent earlier. The applause was spontaneous, the catego-

ries were introduced by Fujiki, an enchanting petite bru-
nette with perfect command of English, even down to a
few local idioms.

"You see," Hammond murmured as he lowered his
camera, "Small is beautiful. That girl has certainly done
her homework."

"A-one on the ambassadorial front, eh?"

"You betcha! Wow! Look at *this!*"

This was a one piece swim-skin—as the latest swim
wear had been dubbed—cut with such cunning that it
was daring and revealing, at the same time being well
within the bounds of decency and good taste. It was worn
by Yodoko, and by the storm of applause that greeted
her, Trisha felt that Hammond's predictions might well
be on the way to becoming reality.

Each category was outstanding in concept, execution
and presentation. The showing ended with all the models, both male and female, on stage and down the ramp,
with the audience on its feet, giving thunderous physical
and vocal applause.

Trisha was buoyed up by the whole glittering evening
and even after she was back in her room, the problems
that had beset her earlier were hardly given a second
thought.

The next day was almost anticlimactic—the pressure
was off, the elaborate receptions were over, none of the
Japanese group was visible as they packed up for the move
to the north coast. Trisha was looking forward to the time
to be spent in Ocho Rios, she'd heard so much about it,
the fabled play place of the rich and famous. She went
down to the pool for a swim before lunch but was driven
indoors by the heat which was unbearable—even in the
shade of the big umbrellas slotted through the centres of the
tables that dotted the pool deck. That night, she dined alone
in her room. Even though she had regained control of her
emotions, she didn't want to lose it by being in close contact

with Jason—especially if he was still in Carla's company. As for Hammond—he had treated her on the night of the show as if nothing had happened to cause a rift between them, but when she met him in the lift the next morning on the way down to the coffee shop for breakfast, he had given her a formal 'Good morning', unsmiling, his eyes inscrutable. What had happened to the burgeoning friendship between them? Had he learned what had happened—or rather, what hadn't happened—between her and Jason? If so, then how, only Jason could have told him—did men talk to each other of such things? She had no idea—she realised that she had no idea about too many things. If she had confided in him out at Port Royal, the friendship might have blossomed into something more permanent, but she had slammed the door in his face and was now paying the penalty. Had his seeming forgiveness of her behaviour been a cover because of the showing that night...questions, questions, but never any answers...

Trisha was glad when the time came to pack up and move over to the north coast. The drive across the main mountain range opened up new vistas of delight for her. The first part of the journey was on a fairly wide flat road that soon became a dual carriageway that bypassed Spanish Town, the old capital, first of the Spaniards who had moved from the original island capital, Seville in St Ann, and then of the English—later the British. After that, the road became a single highway again and ran along a deep gorge with a broad river at the bottom on the right, then across a rather dangerous looking flat bridge—appropriately called the Flat Bridge—dangerous because there were no railings, merely a series of low concrete bumps, and the green water seemed very close, practically lapping the underside of the bridge. Then, the river was on the left, gurgling and tumbling over great grey river stones. Across the other side, the hill rose steeply, covered in scrub and close-packed trees, hung with tangling lianas and wild orchids.

"It's very jungly over there," Trisha said, but Hammond shook his head,

"It looks so but it's only heavy bush. Actually, the railway tunnel is bored through that hill."

"Really? It must be rather scary..."

"Not anymore. The railway fell into disuse for years—more's the pity."

"Look at the great chunks of rock on this side of the road. Some of them look as if they're just balanced and could crash down with the faintest breath of wind."

"Do they ever?" Dolly asked the driver.

"Do what do what ma'am?"

"Do those great rocks all up the hillside ever come crashing down?"

"Sometimes," the driver said laconically, then caught sight in his rear view mirror Dolly and Trisha's wide eyed concern, and added, "Not to worry ma'am, it mostly only happens after very heavy rain, when the earth's soft—or sometimes after a long period of drought, when the earth gets powdery."

Nobody dared to ask what was the present condition, and their fears were in no way allayed when they passed a sign stating BEWARE OF FALLING ROCKS. They were all thankful when they left the gorge and were back on the open highway. The road started to climb in earnest when they reached the bottom of the mountain known as Mount Diablo, then became very steep with continuous hairpin bends. There was nothing between them and the valley below other than a low dry-packed wall—which had been broached in places, mute testimony to careless driving, emphasised by a rusting car far down the hillside. Small houses clung to the hillsides, or clustered in the valleys far below—little isolated districts whose inhabitants lived lives vastly removed from urban life. Hillocks of yam plants made brighter patches of green amongst the general greenery, as they marched down the hills in terraced rows.

"Oh look," Trisha exclaimed, "Down there, in that meadow — lovely brown cows munching away under that enormous tree. Look, there's a clump of bamboo by the pond. It's all so incredibly lush and beautiful."

"You really are a town mouse, aren't you?" Hammond said indulgently, "That 'enormous tree' is a ceiba — otherwise known as a cotton tree."

"Cotton? I thought cotton grew on low bushes, I've seen people picking it in old pictures about slavery in the South."

"Not the cotton one uses for sheets, but silk cotton."

"Kapok?"

"Probably, I really don't know, but I do know that duppies live in cotton trees."

"*Duppies?*"

"Ghosts, spirits of the dead. It's an old African superstition."

"You believe that?"

He grinned, "It may be safer to believe than disbelieve."

They soon began to descend, spiraling down in a succession of deep corners, past small towns of one street, little settlements of a cluster of houses and one shop, and sellers on the roadside in collections of thatch roofed stalls, piled high with pineapples and grapefruit and strange fruit that Trisha had no idea of what they were. They came to another gorge: this one had once been a river bed but now it was a narrow road, steep and slippery from the leaves that fell from the tree and fern covered hillside that rose on either side, so high that only a thin wash of sunlight could penetrate.

"Ooh." Trisha breathed, "I wouldn't like to be here after dark, it's jolly spooky."

"With owls and bats and other crawlies that come out at night," Hammond put in with a grin.

"*Don't*," she shuddered, then asked the driver, "Mr Henson, are there any wild animals here?"

"No ma'am. 'cept a few crocodiles, an' they're far from here on the other side o' the island — an' there's not many o' them left. We on'y has mongoose on this side. They do say though that there are coneys in the Hellshire Hills."

"Mongoose? What do they look like?"

"Well, ma'am, its hard to say..."

"They're rather like an English weasel," Hammond put in. "Long and thinnish, with a long skinny tail and dull brown fur."

"How big?"

"Hmm. About seven to ten inches long plus a six to eight inch tail. They're quite cute, especially when they sit up on their hind legs and look around to see what's what."

"And coneys?"

"Similar to a rabbit but much bigger, very shy—very much in danger of becoming extinct."

"Just that Mr Henson? Crocodiles, mongoose and coneys?"

"Well, there's a lot of different kinds of lizards..."

"And the bird life is prodigious as well as rare butterflies," Hammond added, "And that covers the local fauna," he said with a laugh. "If you want monkeys, go to Trinidad, if you want big cats, go to the South American mainland."

Trisha couldn't resist a glance at Jason, who sat obliquely across from her. He turned his head at the same time, their eyes met and held, she flushed scarlet and couldn't drag her eyes from his. He deliberately turned his head away and began an animated conversation with Carla who sat beside him. Unnecessarily close, Trisha thought, the seats were wide enough for three. She pressed her lips together and hoped that she wasn't going to cry. All the joy of the discovery of the wild countryside had gone out of her day and she felt the old familiar misery seeping back.

Hammond had noted the incident. He began to speak in a low voice about the history of the island and its various peoples and in her growing fascination for the subject she managed to regain control.

The minibus swung out of the darkness of the gorge into

bright sunshine and soon the glittering sea was before them patchworked in brilliant colours.

Six

"It's another world," Trisha breathed later that evening. The whole team was sitting on a flagged patio that overlooked the white sands and the rippling sea beyond. The air was soft and scented with jasmine and wild vanilla. Between the patio and the beach was a garden that descended in a series of terraces, thickly planted with every shade of hibiscus, their delicate blooms nodding in the gentle breeze, already curling in death as the night approached—their lifespan lasted only from dawn to dusk. Clumps of brilliant bougainvillea spilled their red, purple, pink or white flowers in cascades. Palms and giant ferns were studded amongst the shrubs and the whole had a wild unplanned casual beauty like nothing she had ever known.

The sun sank in a glorious welter of red and gold, great green rays fanned out and spanned the western sky, the pale blue dome above them deepened rapidly, then the colours disappeared as if wiped away by a giant duster as the first stars winked out in a navy blue sky.

"That was quick." Trisha exclaimed. "One moment day—the next, night."

"That's the way it is in the tropics," Hammond said, "One moment sunshine and blue skies, the next moonlight..."

A waiter arrived to take their orders for drinks. Trisha refused and Hammond urged, "Come on Trisha, relax for once, this calls for a celebration, join me in a Planter's

Punch."

"What are we celebrating?"

He waved a hand, "All this beauty, exotic tropical island, your first assignment and—being here together," he added in a voice so low that only she could hear. She caught her breath at his tone of utter sincerity and was glad of the near darkness which hid her expression.

On each table were squat candles, set deep in coloured glass bowls that gave off a soft glow, and down the terraced steps that led to the beach, torches had been set in the ground, gas flames flaring and dancing in the breeze.

"Trisha?"

"Yes, alright, I'd love a Planters Punch."

"To celebrate? All that we have to celebrate?"

She hesitated, then said recklessly, "Yes, why not? Let's drink to celebrate."

"For all the reasons I gave?"

The pause before she nodded was minimal.

His hand sought hers under cover of the table and after the first tense reluctance she let it lay enveloped in his.

The drinks were expertly mixed and potent, laughter from other groups along the patio became more uninhibited as guests imbibed the various concoctions for which the hotel was famous. The waiter announced that dinner was now being served, either in the dining room or on the larger patio. As they rose Hammond glanced at Trisha, his eyebrows raised. She interpreted the unspoken message and nodded. By tacit consent, they dined alone on the other patio. Barbecues were placed at intervals and the succulent aroma of sizzling steaks, lobster or chicken wafted across to them, whetting their appetites, titillating their taste buds. Waiters deftly flambéed dishes at the diners' elbows. There was an aura of good living that was at odds with the starving millions in other parts of the world. Trisha murmured as much to Hammond, who replied, "Don't be misled by all this, there's hunger, poverty and squalor here too. It's just that we visitors are not shown such places—the ghettos, as the people call them. Not that the people are kept there by outside force or edict, but they are forced to stay there by economic reasons, they're so poor they just can't move away."

She put down her fork. The food was suddenly repugnant to her, "It's not fair is it?"

"Of course it isn't—but my dear girl, agonising over it won't help matters."

"I'm not—it's just—I mean, what we're doing here—showing off gorgeous clothes, photographing them for people who've never been hungry in their lives, and probably won't be, ever. They spend as much on one of our magazines as some people spend in a week to feed a family." She broke off in confusion at his cynical half smile. "Well? That's so isn't it?"

He put down his knife and fork, "What's got into you? Suddenly wanting to right the wrongs of the world?"

"I'm sor..." she caught his eye and gave a slight shrug. "It won't happen again."

Whether she meant that she wouldn't express her concern for the welfare of the world's under privileged or for apologising for so doing wasn't quite clear. He refilled their glasses with dry white wine, and then tapped the bottle. "Very good this—made here." He took an appreciative sip, and added, "I hear a reggae band, shall we go dancing when you've finished your coffee?

The question made her pause, dancing meant close contact, which could lead to...for the second time that evening she said recklessly, "Why not?"

She slowly sipped her coffee, "It's very good isn't it?"

"Ought to be, one of the finest coffees in the world. Blue Mountain coffee—some say *the* finest. It grows high up in the Blue Mountains—surprisingly!" he laughed.

"How high are these mountains?"

"The highest peak is well over seven thousand feet—not all that high when you think of other famous ranges, but for a small island, pretty impressive. Come, let's go—or my feet will dance off all by themselves."

The reggae music pulsed as the drums throbbed out the heavy rhythm. It issued an invitation to dance with the whole of one's body and to throw inhibitions to the wind. The combination of the Planter's Punch before dinner, the wine, the music and the whole ambience of the scene, combined to make Trisha shed her scruples and, when a combo that played old-time ballads replaced the reggae band, she melted into Hammond's arms with no resistance or reserve. They danced well together, for all his height and her lack of it. She felt right in his arms— hadn't she felt 'right' in Jason's arms? She told herself that this wasn't the time to ask such questions, that was yesterday, this was now—tomorrow could take care of itself. The melody came to an end and they just stood there, his arms still holding her, her body still curved into his. His eyes were very tender in the dim light, then the rippling notes of a piano introduced the haunting Portuguese rhythm of a favourite of many years back, *The Shadow of Your Smile*, and once more they moved off to the beat, bodies attuned, responding with every step to the sensuous tempo. He bent and kissed the top of her head that barely reached to his shoulder: the soft scent of the red-gold curls acted like an aphrodisiac and an overwhelming desire swept through his loins. His arm tightened and his breath became ragged as he murmured against her hair, "Let's go down to the beach."

She nodded, knowing that she was being foolish, but she was in a reckless mood, foreign to her nature, unable—unwilling—to act otherwise.

They wended their way through the other dancers and out onto the patio, then through the fragrant garden down the terraced steps. There were night sounds all around them now that they had left the hotel behind them. She stopped. "Listen! What's that?"

"Tree frogs," he replied promptly. "So small they're no bigger than your thumbnail. The lower notes are crickets and *that* is a croaking lizard," as a harsh strident sound came from nearby—too near for her comfort, she gave a start of alarm and he put his arm round her, "They won't hurt you, all perfectly harmless. All the little night creatures you wanted to hear back at the Blackburn, all 'yakking away like mad' as you put it."

He turned her towards him and tightened his hold.

She made a halfhearted attempt to draw away but he crushed her to him and bent his head and kissed her, all the pent-up desire was in his mouth as he forced hers open. She surrendered to the urgency of his demanding probing tongue and began to respond in a manner in which she had not believed she was capable. Her response to Jason the other night was tame compared to this. They were both breathless, panting with mounting passion, when they finally broke away. He looked down at her, she couldn't read the expression in his eyes, but his voice was rough as he said, "What have you done to me? Turned my whole world upside down, turned the old cynical worldly-wise Hammond into a soft hearted schoolboy, drooling over his first love." He sounded angry and she tilted back her head and looked at him in amazement.

"What do you mean?"

He shook his head, "Nothing—I'm talking nonsense."

"I don't understand?"

"There's nothing to understand." The moment of passion had passed, he released her and they continued on their way down to the beach, hands not touching and conscious that a milestone of some sort had been reached. On the beach, they paused, "Oh, isn't it beautiful?" she breathed.

"Like a perfect black and white print."

She laughed softly, "Do you see everything in terms of your work?"

"Mostly, I believe that most creative artists do—don't you in your writing?"

"Well yes, I suppose so."

"Look at the sea—rippling silver, the white sands stark in the moonlight, huge rocks, black against the sand, shadows clear-cut. Just look at that moon. You'll never see anything quite like that again."

They gazed up at the dark blue sky, a limitless dome studded with huge brilliant stars. The moon, barely on the wane, swung almost above their heads, bathing the whole scene in a wash of silver light so bright that colours could easily be distinguished.

"Remember what we toasted in celebration?" he asked softly, his former unexplained sudden anger was gone and might never have been. She nodded, wary again. "This is another celebration."

He turned her to face him and looked down at her, her features strangely paled by the moonlight, her eyes veiled with a desire that she couldn't hide. His kiss was savagely demanding and, once again, she felt a searing passion rise to match his when the magic was broken by a woman's low seductive laugh. They drew apart as they saw Carla and Jason coming towards them, hands linked and swaying in unison with each step. They stopped abruptly when they recognised the recently entwined bodies as those of Trisha and Hammond.

"Well," Carla's laugh was now mocking, "*Well* met by moonlight—to misquote Titania..."

The surprise of discovery made Trisha say sharply, "Correction—to misquote *Oberon*..."

Carla's eyes snapped, "For heaven's sake, what difference does it make?"

"Apparently nothing to you—to others, alot."

"Now, now, girls," Hammond said easily as he moved

further away from Trisha, "This setting is too beautiful for squabbles."

Jason hadn't said a word but the smile had left his face and he dropped Carla's hand when he saw Trisha and Hammond in a close embrace. What he didn't realise was that Trisha had made an involuntary move to break away at the first sound of Carla's laughter, but Hammond's firm hold about her waist prevented her from doing so. Now, he said in a tight voice, "Come Carla, let us leave these two—love birds—to continue to bill and coo. We are so patently in the way. Good night to you both," he added curtly.

"'Night," Hammond called to their receding backs.

Trisha said nothing, the moment of their discovery had been like a bucket of icy water doused over her aroused emotions and fevered body.

"Trisha?"

"I'm very tired, I must get to bed. I haven't been sleeping too well these last few nights."

He moved close again, "I can assure you a good night's sleep."

His meaning was clear and she felt the blood rush to her face. "No—please let me go."

"You were only too ready to say 'yes' before we were interrupted," he said roughly and pulled her close to him.

"Please let me go, I should never have—I feel—so *ashamed*."

He released her so abruptly that she staggered.

"Ashamed? What's the matter with you Trisha?" he demanded. "You lead a man to a certain point with unspoken promises—and then you step back and say 'no'. I cannot understand you. You're like a Victorian Miss transported from another age."

His words were a paraphrase of Jason's, and the scene with Jason flashed through her mind, what had he thought when he came upon them so unexpectedly, in as a compromising position as the one that they had been in a few nights ago—once more she had landed herself in a situation that she couldn't—or wouldn't—handle.

"I'm so sor..." she began, then broke off and turned and half ran up the cut stone steps and entered the lobby by a side entrance, bypassing the brightly lit lobby and the Smuggler's Cove Patio Bar.

Once in her room, she tossed off her clothes and stood under a warm shower until all self-disgust and shame were washed away. She towelled off briskly, then slipped between the cool sheets and lay gazing up at the ceiling.

What *was* the matter with her, she asked herself in despair. She had never considered herself a ditherer— she had always been certain of her course of action, but since Jason had come into her life—no, since *Carla* had come into *Jason's* life—she had been full of indecision and uncertainty. She didn't know what or who she wanted. She fled from Jason's attempt to make love to her, yet was filled with jealousy when she saw him with Carla. She responded to Hammond—*how would that episode have ended if there had been no interruption?* Her face flamed again as she acknowledged the inevitable outcome: Hammond had raised her to such a height of unbridled desire, that she would have done anything to have assuaged it—and probably would have given in to that desire if Jason and Carla had not arrived on the scene—instead she had hurt him by saying that she felt ashamed...would she have gone the whole way if it had come to that or would she have drawn back at the last minute as she had done with Jason? She couldn't answer any of the questions that clamoured in her mind, and her thoughts went round and round like a mouse on a wheel...

The tossing nights had so become the norm that she was prepared for yet another. To her surprise, she opened her eyes to sunlight streaming through the billowing white curtains.

She felt marvellous, the events of the night before shrank to their proper perspective and she was able to think rationally, able to admit that her behaviour had been less than adult. As she stood under a cold needle-spray shower, she admonished herself scornfully, "You are an utter fool Trisha. You've blown up the events of the past few days so that you can't think straight.

So Jason wanted to go to bed with you—instead of being flattered, you act the outraged Victorian-type Miss. You act insanely jealous of what he swears is pure business—although how he can justify strolling on the beach in the moonlight holding hands as business, I'll never understand. You rebound onto Hammond and when he wants to go to bed with you, you become all Victorian again. Why are you so special? Probably every other girl you know lost her virginity years ago—yet you cling to yours in the darndest old fashioned way—but would you if you loved someone? Really loved? "I don't know," she said aloud as she stepped out of the shower and wrapped a king-size bath towel round her body and a smaller one round her dripping hair. Maybe that was the answer, maybe what she thought was love for Jason, wasn't the real thing. If not, what was it?

She went out onto the balcony and drank in the scene—an incredibly fine white sand beach, stretching for what seemed miles on either side as far as she could see, dotted with wind-angled palms, their fronds resembling huge feather dusters, and the strangely squat flat-topped wild almond trees with their broad fleshy leaves. On the beach below, her hotel room were scattered white *chaise lounge* under brilliant blue umbrellas. Attendants were placing brightly coloured cushions on the chairs and checking piles of beach towels: others were raking the sands to level them and remove any litter left by untidy guests. She glanced at her watch—only a little after six and all this activity in progress...

At this time of day, it was quiet and peaceful, only the soft susurrus of the lazy wavelets as they broke on the white sand, then left a gleaming wet dark strand as they receded: the sound of a distant seabird, or the nearer trill of a Jamaican nightingale—Mockingbird—as it practised a few notes before breaking into full throated glorious song. Beyond the dark line of the reef that lay a hundred or more metres out from the shore, the ocean was gently rippling, no white horses crested the slight waves.

Near at hand, she could hear the muted chink of china as breakfast trays were prepared...

The peace was shattered by the high stut-stut-stut of an outboard motor as a thirty-foot cabin cruiser roared into view. It moved through the calm sea and left a white churning wake that fanned out in an ever widening V, then, as it disappeared from her view, the diminishing roar was left to attest to its passing, the slow ripples regained ascendence.

Trisha dragged her gaze from the fascinating scene and realised that while she had been absorbed. She had removed the towel from her head and the early morning sun and breeze had completed the drying process. She dressed and brushed her shining red-gold hair into a froth of curls on top of her head—she had discovered that hair on the nape quickly became wet and clinging in the heat of the day.

As the lift carried her down to the lobby and the coffee shop, some of her newly discovered confidence threatened to leave her; the old doubts and uncertainties were in danger of returning. She squared her slight shoulders and tilted her chin as she strode purposefully towards the louder chink of china and the fragrant aroma of coffee and freshly baked bread that proclaimed her destination. She pushed through the glass doors and stepped into air-conditioned coolness—even at that early hour the day was heating up. It was difficult to visualise the freezing

London she had left, a January that had been one of the coldest on record—and now this. She had been told that next month, February, was generally the coolest, dryest month—well, she wouldn't be able to put it to the test, she would be back in bleak London and all this would be just a memory. She couldn't imagine how fierce the heat would be in August—why try to? she asked herself, you'll never know. After this assignment, it was unlikely that she would come this way again...her thoughts were jolted by a quiet voice at her elbow: "A table for one ma'am?"

She gave a quick glance round the coffee shop, there didn't appear to be any of the other members of the team present, they were probably in the other coffee shop on the mezzanine floor, that was why she had chosen this one, she didn't feel like company yet. She smiled at the waiter, "Thank you, yes, just for one."

"This way please."

He led the way with a sinuous feline tread so often manifested by the islanders—large felines, she thought, not tame domestic ones—to a table set for two by a large window that overlooked the swimming pool. "It is self service, ma'am." he prompted, "Except for coffee."

"Yes, thank you again, this is fine."

She hung her jacket over the back of one of the chairs and made her way to the self-service buffet table. There was a bewildering variety from which to choose, such an abundance of food that her appetite for eggs and bacon, sausages and scrambled eggs or waffles dripping with syrup, deserted her and she chose a wedge of pawpaw, a fat yellow banana and a thin slice of muskmelon. When she returned to her table, there was a steaming pot of coffee there and a basket of assorted croissants, rolls and Danish pastry. The assortment of fruit was delicious, a melange of flavours and textures, the coffee was such as she had tasted no where else in the world—but then, she told herself with a rueful smile, she hadn't been to many parts of the world. The local daily papers had been left folded beside her plate, a freshly picked yellow hibiscus floated in a bowl in the centre of the table, to her left she could see sun bronzed bodies lazing by the pool, adding yet another patina of colour. It was all so exotic, so removed from her usual daily life—and it would all be over in another week, just another memory to cherish—she pushed away the intrusive thought that there were too many memories that she would rather forget.

She took another sip of coffee and weakened over a fresh croissant which she spread with one of the tart local preserves. Then, she opened one of the papers. She was glad to see that the showing in Kingston had been given good coverage and she skimmed over it. Her eyes were riveted by a full-length picture of herself, with a close-up head and shoulders inset. Underneath, the caption read:

TRISHA (PATRICIA TOPAZE) BARRETT,
a fashion writer with the YOU: TOMORROW team,
has strong Jamaican connections.
This reporter tried in vain to ascertain the truth of
the rumour that Miss Barrett is a direct descendent
of Colonel Hersey Barrett, who came to the island with
Cromwell's New Model Army in 1655. Miss Barrett
was not available for questioning.

Trisha slapped the paper down in sudden irritation. *What nonsense was this?* No one had approached her! Now who would have given out that she was 'not available'? How this stupid rumour had come into being she had no idea—then the memory of something Jason had said on the plane came back, "Tell me," his voice had been almost elaborately casual. "Is there any truth in the rumour that you are the heiress to a huge estate in Jamaica?" What nonsense, if there'd been any truth in it, her grandmother would most certainly have told her...who was the writer of the article? It was unsigned...that woman, Alison something or other, the one who had interviewed her on television, she hinted at some connection...and how in the *world* had they got hold of that *stupid* middle name? Topaze! What romantic impulse had prompted her mother to give her such a pretentious name? She'd asked her grandmother on many occasions, about the name and her forebears in Jamaica, but she always became vague when the subject was mentioned. Who could have dug up any information about her and given it to the press? Jason? For spite? Hammond—ditto? Let's hope that the rest of the group are not reading the local rag, she thought crossly. She took comfort in the thought that it was most unlikely that they would...

"May I join you?"

Trisha was brought back to the moment by the question. She looked up in surprise at Carla, exquisitely groomed as always. The usual mocking expression that was such a feature on her face was absent for once and her large grey eyes were friendly and guileless.

"Be my guest, I've practically finished anyhow," she sounded ungracious but the words and tone were out before she could stop them. She folded the newspaper, then her hand tightened on it as Carla reached across.

"May I? I always find so much amusement in these local efforts, so insular, ignoring the wider issues..."

"That may be true of some—but not this one, it's one of the oldest newspapers in the world, over one hundred and sixty years no less. I think that you'll be pleasantly surprised at the contents." She made to rise, still keeping a firm hold on the paper but Carla put out a restraining hand, "Don't go yet, join me in another cup of coffee. I wanted to say how sorry I am that we—Jason and myself—disturbed your little idyll with Hammond—he's a lovely man, I'm sure that you'll be very happy with..."

"But—there's nothing between us, it was—just—an incident."

Carla's eyes narrowed, "Hammond isn't a person to go in for 'incidents'—and quite frankly, I didn't think you were—in spite of Jason..."

Trisha seized on the first sentence, "Oh? I didn't know that you knew Hammond before he joined the staff?"

"Not really 'know'," Carla said in an offhand manner, "I'd seen him around town—press conferences, social bashes, that sort of thing. I'm sorry that you're not serious about him—I was congratulating myself that you were one danger out of the way..."

"Danger? I don't understand?"

"You will, when my engagement to Jason is announced."

Seven

Trisha was left speechless my Carla's words, who, after a long moment of silence, asked with a return of the mocking gleam in her eyes, "Aren't you going to wish me happiness?"

Trisha found her voice with difficulty, "Of course—give my congratulations to Jason..."

"Not a word of this—to anyone," Carla said hastily. "We can't make the announcement until my father has made his bid—and it's been accepted—for **YOU: TO-MORROW.**"

"Why not?"

"We—er—don't want anyone screaming 'nepotism'."

"I don't see that it matters one way or the other—they'll scream it anyway." Some of the shock was wearing off and Trisha didn't bother to mask her feelings towards Carla, even if her father was to become the new owner and her future with the magazine was jeopardised by her attitude towards his daughter. "They will, you know."

Carla said coldly, "All the same, we'd appreciate it if you didn't mention it."

"Then why," Trisha demanded, "did you make such a point of telling me?"

Carla was saved an explanation by the arrival of the waiter with her coffee and Trisha took the opportunity to gather up her purse, her jacket and hurriedly left the table and went blindly from the coffee shop, still gripping the paper. Her self-esteem was hurt more than her emotions. She had been made a fool of by Jason's actions: but why had he acted as he had? What did he hope to gain by letting her think that she was number one in his life, when all the time he was paying court to Carla? How long did he think that he could pull the wool over her eyes? She was thinking in clichés but couldn't help herself—how could he have lied and *lied* to her? He'd sworn over and over again that the relationship between himself and Carla was one of business only—and now *this*—he was lost to her forever—alright, so she too was to blame, if she hadn't been such a little fool he may not have gone back to Carla—gone back? Had he indeed ever left her? How gullible and naive she had been, a schoolgirl would have seen through him from the start, but Trisha—dear sweet stupid trusting Trisha—she gets fooled time after time...such accusations and questions went round and round in her head like a carousel, always moving, getting nowhere.

There was not even the panacea of work to blunt the hurt, for the **YOU: TOMORROW** models would not be arriving until much later that evening, so today was her own. She was sorry now that she had put all her notes on her lap computer—that would have taken her mind off herself and her self-pitying jag. She had to fill in the time somehow—a brochure on the lobby counter caught her eye as she passed through on the way to the lifts and she picked it up and leafed though it, *Ah! Yes! I'll go to the Crafts Market and the Gallery.* She'd heard that both produced some excellent pieces...as she entered her room the telephone by her bed was ringing. Her heart stopped for a moment—if it was Jason how should she treat him? If it was Hammond—but surely not either of them, not after the way they had parted—it was neither, it was an unfamiliar woman's voice:

"Miss Barrett?"

"Speaking."

"This is Diedre Barrett."

For a moment Trisha's mind was blank, then recollection came flooding back—of course, the enchanting lady of mystery, "Oh Miss Barrett, how kind of you to call."

"*You* were going to call me," there was the faintest note of reproach in the strong almost husky voice.

"I'm terribly sorry, I did mean to—but—things have been—well, difficult..."

"I'm so sorry. To do with the show? The hotel? Is there anything I can do to smooth things over?"

"Oh no—it's nothing like that—work-wise everything is smooth—it's just..."

"Your personal life getting out of hand?" Diedre asked. "I'm not surprised, you are very attractive. I expect the men swarm like bees—it gets difficult to juggle them successfully. Am I right?"

Trisha gave a rueful laugh, "Too right, I'm afraid."

"My dear, you're very young—*things loom* at your age. It'll pass, everything will fall into place. Now, I rang you to ask you to come over, look around the house and property, have lunch and so forth—how does that strike you?"

It was the reprieve that Trisha needed, "Marvellous! What time—and how do I get there?"

"I'll send a car for you—in about half-an-hour?"

"Perfect. Thank you—thank you so much Miss Barrett."

"Don't make me feel as old as I am—it's Mrs. but Diedre will do very nicely. See you." The telephone clicked off at the other end and Trisha sat looking down at the receiver for a long moment before she set it back on the rest. Nothing had been said this time about the rest of the team being invited to lunch—maybe it was all for the best, she felt a vast relief at not having to stay in or near the hotel, where she would be on tenterhooks that she might run into either Jason or Hammond.

Half-an-hour, Diedre had said, now what to wear? She settled for a green and white candy striped shirtdress, which would take her through the day and into the evening if necessary. She examined her reflection in the bathroom mirror as she brushed her hair and was appalled at what she saw: pale cheeks, dark rings under eyes that had lost their sparkle and a new droop to her full mouth—the legacy of turbulent emotions and sleepless nights—oh well, a price had to paid for all that turmoil—she turned from the mirror as once again the telephone shrilled.

She hesitated before picking it up. "Hullo?"

"Miss Barrett?"

"Yes, speaking."

"Front desk: your transport has arrived."

"I'll be right down. Thank you."

Heavens, half-an-hour gone already. She had to wait for the lift—or elevator, as they called it here, funny, the local vocabulary was very Americanised—not really surprising though, they were so much closer to the States than to Britain...

The red light moved slowly down then stopped with a soft *ping!* The doors opened and Trisha stepped in. She was glad to see two other occupants, she hated being in a lift by herself—just another of her silly ways.

In the lobby, she paused and looked around, a man in a white shirt and a black bow-tie came forward, he took off his peaked chauffeur's cap, "Good morning ma'am, Miss Barrett?" His dark eyes widened a little as he faced her, then the cool professional mask came down.

"Yes, good morning. You are...?"

"I'm Martin ma'am, Miss Diedre's driver. This way please ma'am."

Trisha examined curiously as she followed him to the hotel exit. He was slim and dark, probably in his fifties. He had a soft polite manner, in no way obsequious, rather a self-confident pride. He seemed like a Jamaican counterpart of that almost vanished breed, a family retainer—which she discovered later, he was, for he had served the Barretts from the time he was a young boy, as his father and grandfather had done before him.

Parked in the driveway under the *porte-cochere* was a splendid silver-grey Rolls Royce—of uncertain vintage but in superb condition. Trisha felt like Cinderella as Martin held the door for her. She noticed the curious glances of some incoming tourists and was rather overwhelmed by the splendour and felt like a film star—all that was needed now was a thirty's type mink coat trailing over one shoulder, or nonchalantly dragged along the ground, she told herself with an inward giggle. Suddenly, her mood lifted as she was transported into another world of wealth and understated luxury.

The interior of the car was as impressive as the exterior, white hide upholstery and thick dark grey plush carpeting. Martin closed the passenger door with a soft click and settled himself into the driver's seat, quite impervious to the admiring comments of the bystanders. Trisha could hear only the faintest purr of the engine as they glided away from the curb. They turned left out of the driveway into the main road that ran along the coastline, past a cluster of high rise towers, through the famous town of Ocho Rios, with its bustle of shops, craft stalls, wayside artists displaying their wares, where visitors bargained amicably with the vendors: past boutiques and restaurants and a few old fashioned hotels that had more charm and character than the concrete and steel towers. The narrow main street was congested with country buses, taxis, private cars, cyclists, donkey carts and pedestrians all vying for position.

Martin inched through patiently, only touching the horn when imminent danger threatened—a jaywalker, a goat or one of the innumerable chickens that dashed across the road, apparently welcoming an early death. He swung the car off the main road onto an unsurfaced narrow road, hardly qualified for the name, which climbed sharply with many twists and turns. The coast fell away abruptly beneath them, the hotels and the houses dwindled in size and Trisha could see the whole lovely curving coast with its blinding white beaches and the impossibly blue sea meeting the horizon in a grey blur: she caught her breath audibly at the sight and Martin's dark eyes met hers briefly in the rearview mirror.

"I'm driving too fast for you ma'am?"

"Oh no, you're a marvellous driver—it's just that it's all so beautiful..."

A smile touched his lips, "Your first time in the island ma'am?"

"Yes."

He gave a short nod. "It generally affects people like that ma'am, the first time, but I expect you'll get used to it."

"What a pity to do that—to lose the wonder of it all."

Again, the dark eyes met hers, they held a slightly puzzled expression, "Not everyone does—Miss Diedre, she never has and she's woken up to that view for the past—well, since she was a little girl. Seems you might be like her."

They turned off the bumpy narrow road into a broad, white, smoothly rolled driveway through a pair of massive iron gates flanked by two stone columns. Trisha barely had time to note the name carved into them--*Pimento Hill*. The driveway had a broad strip of neatly clipped grass down the centre, on either side of which was crushed white limestone that gave off a cloud of fine dust as the Rolls' wheels propelled it powerfully upwards. The approach to the house seemed endless and Trisha was somewhat awestruck at the grandeur of the world that she was entering. She gave another gasp of pleased surprise when the house came into view and Martin said, "*Pimento Hall* is one of the greatest great-houses left..."

"*Pimento Hall?* I thought that it said *Pimento Hill* on the gate posts?"

"*That's right ma'am.* The property call *Pimento Hill,* the house *Pimento Hall,* but mos' people jus' say *Pimento Hill.*"

"I see. Sorry to interrupt, do go on."

"The house date from 1660 an' belong to the first Barrett—but Miss Diedre'll tell you all 'bout it. She love the house."

Trisha was struck anew by the man's speech and quiet way. Her idea of Jamaican men had been influenced by the pop singers with their 'locks' and the second and third generation British West Indian youths who featured in the bloody riots in Liverpool and elsewhere, highlighted and often blown out of proportion by the television coverage that such events received. She had no idea of the hardworking middle class Caribbean blacks who had been accepted into society and were well integrated. She was amazed at the island's prosperous middle class who lived a lifestyle that might well be the envy of their counterparts in Britain and, as for the handful of the wealthy upper class—many of whom had been to Oxford or Cambridge—or even Harvard and Wellesley, that was a further revelation. The trip had opened her eyes and had given her an awareness of the island and its people, that otherwise she would never have known.

The Rolls slid to a stop at the foot of a graceful stone double stairway with railings of intricate wrought iron. Trisha stepped out of the car and looked up at the house, filled with a sense of wonderment. The lower walls were of cut-stone, the upper of hardwood. The roof was shingled with cedar, the rich colour weathered to a soft ash over the years, with here and there a patch of cinnamon brown where repairs had been made.

"Miss Diedre is on the landing Miss Barrett," Martin's

voice broke in on her bemused fascinated absorption.

"Oh, I'm so sorry, how rude of me. Thank you so much Mr—er..."

"Just Martin ma'am, it's been a pleasure," he said with a half smile.

Trisha nodded and went lightly up the stone steps to where Diedre waited. "I'm sorry that I kept you waiting, I was lost in admiration of your lovely house."

"I'm glad you like it, it means a great deal to me."

"So Martin said, he also said that it is one of the oldest great-houses in existence."

Diedre nodded, "And *the* oldest in constant use. It was built by my Great-great—give or take a few greats and possibly grands—grandfather. But come—it's hot in the sun, I promise you a history lesson later— that is, if you're interested?"

"Oh I am! I find it all absolutely fascinating."

They stepped into the house through eight-foot high heavy mahogany double doors, Trisha was blinded for the moment after going from bright sunlight into the cool gloom of the square entrance hall. As her eyes adjusted to the changed light she saw that a flight of steps went down to the ground floor, again of mahogany and highly polished—the thought went fleetingly through her mind that such a gloss on stairs could be potentially danger-ous. The floor under her feet was mahogany, almost black with over three hundred years of polishing, the boards were fifteen inches or more wide...

She looked up as Diedre, who was regarding her with an indulgent smile and another unreadable expression behind her dark eyes, murmured, "You are really enamoured, aren't you?"

Trisha laughed, "I'm completely bowled over, I couldn't have imagined this in my wildest dreams—and yet—this must sound awfully silly—I feel as if—almost as if, I'd come home."

Diedre's expression changed as she said after a momentary pause, "That's the nicest compliment I've had in a long time. Come this way my dear, we'll have coffee on the side verandah." She led the way through a side door and Trisha saw that a wide verandah ran along the side of the house and apparently continued round the corner. "Does the verandah go all round the house?"

"Yes, but on the bedroom side it's partitioned off so that each bedroom has its own private verandah."

Trisha looked about her with avid interest, the verandah on that side of the house was about twenty feet wide and fifty or more feet long, it was dotted with tables and chairs, swinging settees and plant stands. Piles of magazines, newspapers and books proclaimed that a lot of living was done there. Baskets of ferns of a dozen varieties hung from the raftered ceiling, spilling their bright green fronds to almost head height, creating a cool aura of natural decoration. Potted plants stood on benches against the railing, African violets of every conceivable colour were the only ones that Trisha recognised. The furniture was of bamboo, with bright cushions, the tables bamboo with glass tops. It all blended so perfectly with the surroundings and the ambience of the house that subconsciously Trisha made mental notes for an article for the summer issue. Beyond the verandah and below, the grounds of *Pimento Hill* sloped gently down in terraced beauty.

They settled themselves into a swinging settee and Martin wheeled along a laden trolley, having switched roles from chauffeur to butler. Trisha raised her eyes at the feast before them—'have coffee' Diedre had said—this looked more like a banquet. In addition to a huge silver coffee pot were plates of wafer thin cassava cakes, bridge rolls, croissant, various cheeses, dishes of preserves and a bowl of fruit. Diedre caught her expression and laughed: "We keep to the old old ways here—this meal is called 'second breakfast'. The custom goes back to slavery days when the planters were up and out long before dawn with just a light meal inside them, then they came back as the sun drove them in, to enjoy a heavier meal. They ate no more until dinner at about five. In those days, second breakfast was really substantial—of a dozen or more dishes, meats, fowl and fish, all washed down with sangaree or white rum. I keep to a modified version as I have coffee and fruit at five each morning, as I find that I work better before the rest of the household is up and about." She glanced at Trisha's small frame and smiled, "I won't inflict the island's customs on you—but I do advise you to try one of these cassava cakes, they are light —in fact, that is their true name—Cassava Lace cakes."

Trisha bit into one, it was meltingly crisp and quite unlike anything that she had tasted in her life, "Umm, delicious."

"It has a bigger relative, quite thick and solid, called a Bammy."

"Ah, now that I do know, I had some at the buffet the other evening."

"I'm glad that they serve you Jamaican dishes now, a few years ago the hotels served nothing but steaks, fried chicken, hamburgers and hot dogs." Diedre stirred her coffee and said softly, "You said on the phone that you were having problems. I know that it's none of my business, but talk about it if it'll help. You're far from home with not a shoulder to lean on. I won't be upset if you choose not to."

To her amazement, Trisha found that she did want to talk to Diedre, she, who had never been able to confide in her mother, who had never had a sister or a close enough girl friend to extend and exchange confidences—to do so was alien to her nature, but Diedre had such a warm, sympathetic, undemanding way about her, that before she knew it she was pouring out all the intricacies of her love life.

"You must think that I'm very stupid in this day and age to be so—so prudish."

"Not at all," Diedre murmured. "I don't believe in all this hopping into bed as a matter of course—especially in view of the AIDS epidemic—but I do believe that if you really loved one of your young men, you wouldn't have hesitated."

"But if it's not love, what *did* I—*do* I—feel?"

"Just good—or bad, considering your point of view— old fashioned lust, my dear," Diedre said dryly. "The night, the moon, soft music and an admiring male, all guaranteed to turn even the most level headed girl's head. Added to which, you probably *want* to fall in love, the fact that you've got this far in life—how old are you? twenty-two? twenty-three?"

"Twenty-two—well, almost twenty-two—in about ten more months."

Diedre laughed, then went on, "Yes, well, the fact that you are in your twenties and haven't had a raging love affair is probably unconsciously urging you on. And you make the very common, very natural mistake of believing that admiring and liking a person is the real thing. It happens to the man too, he admires a girl's figure and her face, they may have many things in common, then the combination of soft music, a glittering dome of stars and a full moon, conspire to make him declare feelings— and possibly intentions—that he'd regret having made in the bright light of day."

Trisha looked at the older woman in amazement, "It's almost as if you were *there*," she said.

Diedre laughed ruefully, "It's the road most of us travel, it's only in romantic novels or the 'soaps' that it's love at first sight, that one's destined mate is the first love. Well, not always, I've known one or two, but it's rare. Not that that stops people hoping and believing that it might happen to them."

"Then how do you *know* when it's not lust but love?"

Diedre laughed again, "You'll know, oh yes indeed, you'll know."

Trisha's eyes strayed to Diedre's left hand, it was laden with rings but she couldn't see a wedding ring. "There isn't one," Diedre said, reading the glance. "There was, many years ago—but it didn't work out." There was a short silence, and then she said briskly, "Now tell me about yourself, your work, your life in London—you can leave out the love life, we've covered that."

Trisha smiled, she was amazed that she had poured out her heart to this comparative stranger—no, not comparative, she'd only met her once before, and briefly at that—and yet she felt no embarrassment, just a vast relief that she had been able to talk about it and get it in perspective. She explained her role on the staff of **YOU: TOMORROW,** the excitement of an overseas assignment, the team work that went into compiling a feature such as they were doing now.

"It's exciting, I love to write—so far I've been restricted to captions and one or two interviews. I wonder—could I do a feature on *you*? Just on spec that Jaqui might use it..."

"Jaqui?"

"My editor, Jaqueline Finson..."

"I'm sorry, I never give interviews. If I gave one to you, I'd have the pack down on me, not to mention the paparazzi. And of what interest to your reader's did you think I'd be?"

Trisha looked deflated, "I—er—just though that you must have led—I mean, do lead—and exciting life."

Diedre gave her low chuckling laugh, "Exciting? In an old great-house on top of a hill miles from anybody? A sort of lady farmer?"

"Is that what you are? You don't look it."

Diedre laughed again, "I'm teasing you—I do export pimento berries and grow exotic ferns, caladiums and orchids for export, but my real work is—come, let me show you." She got up just as Martin returned to wheel away the trolley.

"Mr. Nigel phoned, Miss Diedre, he said he'd be home for dinner."

"Oh good. Trisha, you must stay for dinner."

"But I couldn't possibly impose..."

"No imposition at all, I want you to meet Nigel."

"Nigel?"

"My son, he lives here—more or less," she added cryptically. "Martin, if you want me, we'll be in Percy's room."

"Very good ma'am."

Who on earth is Percy? Trisha wondered, *Another son?*

Once again, Diedre read her thoughts, "You'll see," she smiled.

They re-entered the house through French doors further along the verandah and Trisha noted that the floor of the room was striped in many different coloured woods. She stopped and looked down in amazement.

"Lovely, isn't it?" Diedre asked. "The original floor of this room, there's black ebony, golden yucca, veined lignum vitae, mahogany, cedar, green mahoe and blue mahoe—the colours of the mahoes are sadly faded over the years but they are still beautiful." She walked briskly through the long room which appeared to be a drawing room, Trisha glimpsed Queen Anne sofas and Sheraton type chairs—Sheraton *type*, she thought, I bet that they're the real thing—but Diedre's pace was too brisk for her to get more than a fleeting impression. They left the room and went down a corridor that was as wide as a room with doors opening off each side. Diedre opened one of these and Trisha stepped from the past into the present: on one side of the room was a large computer table on which sat a PC/2, a printer and a second monitor. Next to that was a desk graced by an electric typewriter, across from that was a large desk piled with what appeared to be

manuscripts, next to that a metal filing cabinet, on top of
which were two telephones, one a modern machine with a
battery of buttons, the other an old fashioned up-right. An
answering machine and a fax machine sat jowl by jowl. The
rest of the wall space was lined from floor to ceiling with
bookshelves tightly packed.

Trisha looked round in amazement, Diedre laughed
at her expression, "*This*," she put her hand on the computer, "This is Percy, and all this," she waved her hand
round the room, "Is known to one and all as 'Percy's
room'."

"How very strange," Trisha exclaimed, "I have a computer in my office in London and—you're not going to
believe this—I call him Percy, too."

"Well, it's sort of logical isn't it? Personal Portable Computer—although how they can call them portable, have
you ever tried to porter them anywhere?"

"No. I wondered who or what Percy was..."

"Who my dear, who. He has quite a personality, he
beeps madly at me if I make a mistake, and flashes up
scathing messages on his screen."

Trisha laughed ruefully, "So does my Percy, I find
myself apologising to him."

"Don't we all?"

"But why do you need a computer—and all this? You
said 'your real work'?"

In answer, Diedre waved a hand to one of the shelves
that were packed with hardbacks and paperbacks. Trisha
looked puzzled then bent to read the spines, each one
had the same author's name: D.T. Barrett.

"*You're* D.T. Barrett?"

Diedre nodded, pleased at the reaction, "Have you
heard of me?"

"*Heard* of you! You're one of my favourite writers—
but I thought D.T.Barrett was a *man!*"

"Should I be flattered? Yes, I think so. There's something

so derogatory when one is dismissed as a 'woman' writer."

"Surely not these days?"

"Even in these days. It always infuriates me when a critic writes condescendingly that such and such is a *'woman's'* book."

Trisha regarded the older woman with awe, "To *meet* you—just like this, I'm overwhelmed."

"Don't be, I'm no different now than I was to the Diedre you've been talking to all the morning." She gave slight frown, "You didn't really know who I was?"

"Oh no. I hadn't a clue."

"When you suggested an interview, I thought that you might."

"No, I just thought that you'd be a marvellous person to interview—now of course more than ever, but I do see your point—you'd be swamped. When we first saw you at the reception at the Blackburn, we wondered who—or rather what—you were."

"And what did you decide?"

"Let me see: politician's wife..."

"...heaven forbid!"

"Famous actress..."

"...oh, I could live with that!"

"Writer—yes, Hammond actually said that, then said that you were probably one of the many dress designers who were present."

"Well, he wasn't far wrong on that last point, I do design all my own clothes..." there was a discreet tap on the door, "Come."

The door opened and Martin announced: "Lunch is served Miss Diedre."

"Good gracious, how the time flies. Thank you Martin, we'll be right there."

Eight

Lunch was a light affair, served in the breakfast room, which looked out onto yet another spectacular view. On the breeze was wafted the spicy aroma of pimento berries drying on the huge concrete barbecues. This was yet another new world for Trisha: the old house with its white painted 'tray' ceilings—so-called because they were like inverted trays—the beautiful furniture, genuine Queen Anne sofas and Sheraton chairs, as Diedre confirmed. There were chairs known as 'Spanish chairs' or 'Planter's Chairs' which were made from one continuous piece of leather for the back and seat, set in a mahogany frame, the head rest fanned out high and wide, elegant and unbelievably comfortable. There were solid mahogany tables and chairs, consoles and sideboards: china buffets laden with fragile bone china and heavy silver teapots and coffee urns: the whole produced an atmosphere of complete luxury and continuity.

The soft footed Martin served the table—and Diedre herself was so elegant and strangely exotic, with her perfect coffee coloured skin, large dark hazel eyes fringed with the sweeping black lashes that every Jamaican woman looked upon as a birthright...

"You're very quiet my dear. Is everything to your liking?"

"Oh, yes, everything is super—too super, it rather overwhelms me."

Diedre smiled, "I like enthusiasm, so many young people are so bored with life—which must *make* life boring! Now, here we still keep to the old ways and have a siesta between lunch and tea, which, incidentally, will be brought to you in the bedroom that I've put at your disposal. Perhaps between tea and dinner you would entertain yourself? I work during those hours. You are free to wander about the house as much as you like—don't be afraid to open shut doors—and of course, explore the grounds."

"That sounds wonderful."

Trisha was taken to her room by Doreta, a young black girl who regarded her with wide, rather awed eyes. Trisha was a little puzzled by this, for, after all, the child—she was little more—must see a number of strangers at the Barrett house. She said warmly, "Thank you Doreta, what a lovely room."

"Yes ma'am. Me will bring you tea later ma'am—if it please you?"

"That will be very nice. Thank you again."

Doreta gave a sketch of an old fashioned bob and with a last wondering look at Trisha went quietly from the room. Left alone, Trisha looked about her in wonderment, she had stepped even further back into the past: dominating the centre of the room was a high four-poster with pineapple carving on the posts and a massive headboard, also intricately carved with large and small pineapples. There was a frothing white mosquito net draped from the tester and folded across the foot of the bed was a white crocheted bedspread. Trisha touched it with careful fingers: it was exquisitely worked, again repeating the pineapple motif. There was an antique marble-topped washstand with an enormous china ewer and washbasin which she viewed with deep suspicion. *How am I ever going to pick that up and pour out any water?* She asked herself, then gave a sigh of relief as she espied through an open doorway that a modern bathroom had been added—all Tiffany marble and gold plated taps, no less.

She decided that, she too, would take a leaf from the past and take a siesta. She fell asleep almost as soon as her head touched the pillow and awoke to hear the soft voiced Doreta saying, "Miss Trisha, ma'am, is you tea me bring."

For a moment, Trisha wondered where she was, the high white tray ceiling above her head, the high bed, the faint fragrance of khus khus from the big hanging press and above all, the dark face at her elbow, carrying a tray that seemed too big for her slight body.

"Oh my goodness, thank you Doreta, I thought I was dreaming." She struggled to a sitting position and Doreta carefully placed the tray across her lap. "Mhmmm, this looks delicious."

"Yes ma'am, de cake dem, is fresh bake."

"Did *you* bake it?"

Doreta lost her unexplainable awe of Trisha and giggled, "Not so ma'am—is me mudder. She cook to Miss D'dre."

"Your mother? How many people work here?"

"Well, is me mudder an' fader..."

"Your father too?"

"'im is call Martin..."

"Oh, it's a family affair."

"Ma'am?"

"Never mind, go on."

"Me big sister do de wash an' me two brudder work eena de yard—an' me cousin 'elp dem."

Trisha was having a little difficulty in following the local speech with its rising Welsh-like lilt, but she got the general idea. While Doreta was talking she had poured tea from a gleaming silver teapot and had tasted a forkful of cake, feather light, topped with fluffy coconut icing. "Mhmmm! Delicious! I would soon put on weight if I had much of this."

"Yes ma'am, it will mek yu fat," Doreta said as if that

were a virtue to be aimed at, "Me will tell me mudder you like de cake."

"Tell her that it is the most delicious cake I have ever eaten, much much nicer than I've ever had before, either homemade or bought from a pastry shop."

"Fe true ma'am? Better dan fram foreign?"

This last stumped Trisha for a moment, then she got it and laughed, "Indeed, much better than foreign."

Doreta gave a giggle of pleasure, "Me mudder be well please ma'am. Miss D'dre say when you hear de firs' gong, she askin' you to go to de drawin' room."

"Which is the drawing room?"

"De one wid de stripe floor, dem."

"About what time does the first gong sound?"

Doreta wrinkled her smooth brow; evidently time was not important in this tropical Eden. "Is when Miss D'dre take har drink before dinner."

"I see, thank you very much."

Doreta closed the door softly behind her, as Trisha poured a second cup of tea she thought again: This is a different world, *seven* servants, in this day and age—but then it's an enormous house and the grounds seem vast. She glanced at her watch—4:30. She must have slept for *hours*. That long outpouring to which she had subjected Diedre had done her so much good. She swung her feet over the side of the high bed and slid to the floor, which again she noted, was made from broad planks of mahogany, with patchwork scatter rugs. She washed her face, gave a quick flip of powder over her nose, brushed her hair and decided that she would take advantage of Diedre's offer and explore the house. She soon discovered that it was a house of many steps, two down here, three up there, a short flight down, a long flight up and it seemed as if there were dozens of rooms. She was loath to go into rooms where the doors were shut--despite Diedre's suggestion that she should—but revelled in those that were open. The whole place was like a treasure chest, "Like a museum," she said aloud. But no, it didn't feel like a museum, but more like a home that had always been lived in and lovingly cared for all through the years that lay between the first occupants way back in the seventeenth century and those of today.

She realised that the house was built into the hillside, so that some floors were only one storey high while others were three. She ventured down the stairs that she had noted in the entrance hall. They were so highly polished that she feared that she might slip, so took off her sandals and went down in bare feet. She reached the bottom safely and saw that a pair of massive mahogany doors, twin to those above, opened onto a broad flagged terrace that ran under the landing. The doors had been left open—to Trisha, city-wise, although country bred, where break-ins, robbery and muggings were the norm, this seemed very strange and singularly trusting—then she remembered the length of the driveway and the size of the property—there were no casual passersbys to see an open door. She went round the stone outside double stairway and noted that a spanking new Jaguar XJS V12 convertible was parked in front of them. She glanced at its sleek lines curiously, there had been quite a stir when it had first come on the market, bristling with advanced electronic devices. If she remembered rightly, it cost an absolute packet: whoever owned this super-car had quite a bit of money. *Another visitor? Or the son Nigel?* She idly wondered, then wandered off to explore the grounds. They were cultivated for the width of about an acre or so around the house, with terraced flower beds and neatly clipped grass walk ways, but further afield the grass was long and lush—she noticed cow pats and fervently hoped that the cows responsible were now far away—she had a town mouse fear of the creatures, for all that she'd grown up in a small country town. There was so much to see but it was still quite hot and she decided to return to the house and have a shower before 'first gong'. When she reached the stone stairway the elegant Jaguar was gone, she felt a slight disappointment, now she would never know who owned it.

Back in her room she looked ruefully down at her dress, she'd worn it all day and now wished that she'd brought something to change—oh, well, it couldn't be helped, it had stood up well and looked fresh enough.

She luxuriated in the shower, the water was like silk—rainwater from the big tank she had espied high up on the hill at the back of the house, she assumed. As she sat on the verandah that opened off 'her' room and dried her hair in the sun, she realised with a small sense of surprise that she hadn't thought of Jason or Hammond since she had confided in Diedre. All the agonising, the indecision had gone—forever? Probably not, tomorrow she'd be back, see-sawing between them—but would she, she'd hurt them both—no, not hurt so much as insulted them—it wasn't likely that they'd risk the same treatment a second time. Then, she remembered that Jason had recovered sufficiently to propose marriage to Carla. Was Diedre right and she wasn't in love with either of them—one or the other—or both? She didn't really believe that one could be in love with two people at once—although some of her girl friends had sworn that it was not only possible but, in actual fact, they had experienced it themselves. Now, in her new found wisdom, she was highly sceptical of that...These speculations had been made in a calm objective manner, with none of the former accompanying turmoil that had been the case just a few short hours ago and she gave a small smile of satisfaction, it seemed that she was back in the driver's seat and quite capable of determining where she wanted to go.

Her hair was dry and the sun had almost gone, leaving a welter of red and gold tinted clouds. She never became tired of watching the fabulously unbelievably beautiful sunsets and marvelled each time at their variety and splendour. It was quite dark when she finally returned to the bedroom to finish dressing. She was just in time, for as she flicked a brush through her hair, and added lipstick to her full curving lips, she heard the faint boom of a gong. She surveyed her reflection, she had no need of mascara as her long curling lashes framed eyes that had smudged shadows naturally and her golden skin gleamed like matte silk, "You're jolly lucky, Trisha Barrett," she told herself, "And don't you forget it."

She found her way through the intricacies of corridors and steps and arrived at the drawing room door just as Diedre did from the opposite direction.

"Hullo my dear. Oh you do look rested, I'm so glad."

"I am, I slept like a top—dreadful, in the middle of the afternoon."

"No, no, you need a rest in the heat of the day, it helps you to acclimatise to the change in temperature."

"Well, I don't really need to do that. I've only a week left, then it's back to sleet and snow. Ugh!"

Diedre seemed about to say something—then changed her mind. The drawing room was softly lit by standard and table lamps, which threw shadows on the off-white walls. Filmy white curtains fluttered in the soft evening breeze that brought with it the ever-present spice scent of pimento, mixed with jasmine, wild vanilla and citrus blossoms. From the garden came the continuous sound of tree frogs and crickets, which Trisha had come to love—one more aspect of the island that she would miss when she left.

Martin wheeled in a drinks trolley and Diedre asked, "Would you like a drink here or on the verandah?"

"On the verandah please, it's so wonderful to be *able* to sit outdoors in January!"

"It may be chilly..."

"*Chilly?* It's in the high eighties!"

"Not here, we're always about ten degrees cooler in

the day than down in the town and at night the temperature drops dramatically, especially at this time of the year."

Trisha giggled, "They'll never believe all this at the office."

"All this?"

"This fantastic house, the lovely grounds, being driven here in a Rolls—and meeting D.T. Barrett, especially that."

Diedre smiled, "I doubt that it will interest them."

"Of course it will, I'll be the envy of the office. You are very popular—but you must know that?"

"Sometimes one wonders if anyone reads what one has laboured over—until the royalty statements come in, and a bag of fan mail."

"I've never met anybody who had fan mail before. What do they write about?"

"Oh all sorts of things, some of them funny, some touching. I answer them all but it's a bit of a bind sometimes—not the answering, just finding time to do so."

"You don't have a secretary?"

"No, I haven't found anyone I could bear to have around..." Diedre stopped, Trisha couldn't make out her expression in the dim light but had a strong impression that she had been about to add something and wondered why she had decided against doing so.

"What may I pour you ma'am?" Martin asked at her elbow.

"Oh I don't know. I'm not awfully up in drinks," Trisha said apologetically.

"Have a Martin Special—if you have no particular preference." Diedre advised.

"What's a Martin's Special?"

"Light rum, pineapple juice, a dash of lime and some secret ingredient that he won't divulge."

Martin gave his half smile and Trisha exclaimed, "Sounds super."

They settled into comfortably cushioned cane chairs and Diedre asked, "You like your job at the magazine?"

"Yes, it's lots of fun. If I make a good job of this assignment I'll go on other overseas trips."

"Your Martin Special, Miss Trisha," Martin placed a glass beside her on a small table, placed another beside Diedre then melted silently back into the house.

"Martin has accepted you my dear—'Miss Trisha' is the greatest compliment."

"Really? Doreta called me the same."

"Old island custom—sadly dying out."

Trisha took a sip. "Lovely," she said then asked tentatively, "Did—did your work go well this afternoon—or don't you like to talk about it?"

"Bless you child, I don't mind. Yes, it went well, in spite of the fact that I'm approaching the most difficult part—the ending."

"The ending?"

"Yes—for me. Other people find the beginning the problem, no one writes the same way..."

"I wish I could write."

"But you do..."

"No, I mean like you—books."

"Then make a start! You'll never get anywhere by just wishing or hoping."

Before Trisha could reply, there was the sound of approaching footsteps from inside the house and a man stepped onto the verandah.

"Sorry I'm late Dee. I was here earlier this afternoon but was called away as Rosabelle chose this afternoon to foal. I had to stay with her to settle her down for a while." He bent and brushed Diedre's forehead with his lips. Trisha couldn't make out his features in the gloom of the verandah but his voice was pleasing, warm and low.

"Nigel, I want you to meet Miss Barrett, otherwise known as Trisha. Trisha—my son Nigel."

"My apologies, I didn't see you in this light. How do you do?"

His hand enveloped hers and she felt a tremor run up her arm then continue down into her stomach. He sat down in a chair beside her and in the faint shaft of light from one of the drawing room lamps she saw that he was of a fairer complexion than his mother, cafe au lait as opposed to coffee with a dash. He had black hair that curled on the nape of his neck, heavy dark brows and what appeared to be black eyes, but were probably dark brown. He had a high-bridged aquiline nose and a stubborn chin and beautifully shaped mobile lips. She could sense the almost animal magnetism he exuded and wondered if he knew the effect he created...she forced herself to concentrate on what he was saying rather than on *him*.

"...my mother tells me that this is your first visit to the island?"

"Yes, I'm loving every moment of it—well, of the island."

"Why the qualification?"

"None of your business," Diedre said quickly.

"Sorry, I wasn't being nosey, just..."

"It's quite alright," Trisha said, then surprising herself, added," If I didn't subconsciously want that question asked, I shouldn't have made the qualification."

Diedre laughed, "My, my, quite the Freudian student, aren't we?"

Nigel got up, "Let me get you another drink? What's your poison?"

"A Martin Special."

"You could do worse."

He stood in the full shaft of light from the drawing room and she saw that he was very tall, well over six feet she judged. She gave a small inward sigh, tall men always dwarfed her, even a man of five foot six was tall by comparison...

"Thank you," she took the proffered glass, their fingers brushed and again the tremor shot through her.

"Dee?"

"Thank you darling, a small whisky."

When they were settled once more, Nigel said, "I gather that you're out here in connection with the fashion shindig at the Santa Gloria?"

"Really, Nigel, what a description," Diedre protested.

"No, no, it's very apt. At times, that's what it seems like and then it gets sorted out and—presto! We've got a show. You must come and see it."

"*Unhuh*! Not my bag."

"What is your bag?"

"I'm just a farmer—fashionable clothes and skinny models are way out of my ambit."

You don't *look* like a farmer or *sound* like one, Trisha thought, more like a lawyer or a doctor or...

She sensed that Diedre was watching her and glanced across at her, it was difficult to read the expression in her fine dark eyes, but there was a small enigmatic smile about her lips.

Just then, the gong sounded and Diedre stood up, "Dinner—if you haven't finished your drinks feel free to bring them with you."

Trisha rose and followed Diedre into the house and through to the dining room. Nigel followed and she was very conscious of him looming behind her.

"This is known as the small dining room," Diedre said. "The dining room proper is cavernous for the three of us."

Small it certainly was not in Trisha's eyes. It had a table that could seat ten easily, a heavy mahogany buffet against one wall and a breakfront china cabinet against another, lurked like large beasts of prey just beyond the reach of light from the cluster of candles in the middle of the table. By the flickering flames, Trisha saw Nigel Barrett properly: he wasn't good looking in the conventional sense, his brows were too heavy, his nose too beaky, his eyes hooded and deep-set, but it was a strong face, a face to remember, a face that spoke of character—a face to haunt your dreams, the thought arose unbidden, and Trisha dropped her eyes, afraid that they might reveal her thoughts.

He saw Trisha. He inhaled sharply and widened his eyes.

"*Nigel!*" Diedre's voice held an almost warning tone, he dragged his gaze from Trisha's face reluctantly. "Dee?"

"Later."

Trisha was intrigued over this peculiar exchange between mother and son. Whatever did it mean? Maybe Nigel always reacted strongly when he met a new girl—although she couldn't believe that, for his easy sophisticated man of the world manner belied it. Maybe it was just that they had such a good rapport that they could carry on a truncated conversation that made sense to them but to no one else. Whatever it was, it was no concern of hers. She would probably never see these two people again after tonight—unless Nigel changed his mind and attended the showing.

Soup was served, and ever so often, his eyes would fasten on her face with a look of wonder, which by the end of the meal he had schooled to a cool impersonality.

"Shall we have coffee and liqueur in the drawing room?" Diedre asked and without waiting for a reply, led the way.

There was a grand piano in one corner and Diedre said, "Play something for us, Nigel..."

An expression of relief touched his face for a moment then was gone. Trisha felt a faint wash of indignation, so he would rather play the piano than talk to her—not that he'd talked much at dinner, it had been left to Diedre to carry the conversation, which she had done with admirable ease. His manner was at variance with that which he had displayed on the verandah, there he had talked fluently on many subjects, it was only after...

Only after he had seen me in the light that he was silenced. How very odd. Now if it had been Carla with whom he had been confronted, one could understand it. Her thoughts were diverted as the first notes of a superbly tuned piano turned the night to magic. He was a fine pianist and Trisha was enchanted, her brief flash of annoyance drowned in the glorious rippling notes. What was that he was playing? It was tantalizingly familiar — then it came to her — the theme from *Dangerous Moonlight* — an old nineteen forties film she seen recently on a late show.

"That was beautiful, how marvelously you play."

"Thank you, but you must really thank Dee. She used to make me practise for hours — a real task-master."

"Nonsense," Diedre said placidly, "You were a strange child and loved to practise."

Nigel stood and shut the piano. "Dee?"

Diedre put down her coffee, "Yes, I think so."

Nigel looked down at Trisha, his expression inscrutable, "Would you come with us? We have something to show you."

Trisha looked from one to the other in amazement — a tremor of apprehension ran down her spine. *What mystery was about to be revealed?* That there was one she had no doubt, Nigel's whole attitude proclaimed it. She tried to think of a light retort but both Diedre and Nigel were so serious that she abandoned the effort and just nodded. Diedre led the way with Nigel striding beside Trisha. She felt very small, even with her three-inch heels, she didn't reach to his shoulder. Diedre walked quickly, her heels tapping on the wooden floor.

Trisha felt a rising tide of — excitement? Apprehension? She wondered wildly what was going to happen — after all, she hardly knew these people. Diedre she had met once before, briefly. Nigel less than three hours ago, what did she know of them?

No one knew where she was or who she was with...

She stopped and gave a little gasp...

Nigel turned and looked down into her wide fear-filled eyes, his own softened to an unbelievable gentleness.

"Don't be alarmed. Trisha, I'm sorry, we've been acting oddly and now you're scared stiff—please don't look like that."

"What's the matter?" Diedre called, she had her hand on the knob of a closed door. "Do you have the key Nigel?"

"Right here. I'm afraid we've frightened little Trisha."

"Oh my poor child, I'm so sorry—come, you'll soon be reassured."

Nigel produced a key from his pocket. The lock turned creakily as if seldom used, the door swung open and he put a hand in and pressed a switch.

Trisha saw that it was a portrait gallery, as lights sprang up over paintings that covered three of the four walls.

"The family gallery," Nigel said with a smile.

Trisha felt a vast relief. How silly she had been, but why had they acted as they had? So secretively, so solemnly as if something of great portent was to be revealed. She glanced round, "Are these all your ancestors?"

"Yes, right back to the first Barrett, who was one of those regicides who decided that Charles the first should lose his head—not an ancestor to be proud of, but we got a bit better as we went along. But come." He took Trisha's hand and led her to the end of the room. He pressed another switch and the full-length portrait of an eighteenth century lady was flooded with light.

Trisha stood perfectly still—her heart began to race violently as her eyes grew huge with shock. She looked in bewilderment from Diedre to Nigel who were both smiling broadly at her reaction...

Looking down at her was a portrait of herself.

115

Nine

It was the next morning. Trisha sat silent and withdrawn beside Nigel as he drove her in the luxurious new Jaguar XJS back to the hotel. She was too bemused to take more than a glancing interest in the car, despite the fact that she had been so intrigued with it the day before. The events of the last evening had shaken her to the core, for in spite of the many hints that had come her way over the past few weeks regarding the possibility that she might be an heiress, she had never given the slightest credence to what she had dismissed as a stupid rumour. Now that it was a proven fact, she was still unable to assimilate it all.

After the amazing revelation of the portrait, Trisha had been so agitated that Diedre declared, "You're staying the night. Nigel can take you back early tomorrow."

"But I should be there *now*--the models will have arrived from London and I should..."

"Nonsense," Diedre said briskly, "There are enough people in your group to take care of them."

"But..."

"No buts—as a cousin or aunt many times removed I feel that I can order you about. I will telephone the hotel—who shall I ask for?"

Trisha gave in," I think the best thing is to ring the desk and ask them to tell any one member of the team **YOU: TOMORROW** that they can reach that I'm staying

116

over and will be back tomorrow morning. There's sure to be someone around. Don't you think that's the best thing?'

"Yes, that should do it." Diedre smiled kindly at Trisha's dazed expression." Poor child, you don't know what it's all about. Nigel, ring for Martin to bring champagne—the Heidsieck-Brut, the '76—I feel we need to celebrate, as well as steady our nerves. While you're doing that, I'll make that phone call."

Trisha lay back in the deep chair and listened to Diedre's husky voice in the other room and nearer at hand Nigel's low voiced instructions to Martin. So much had happened since she'd got up that morning: her introduction to an ambience and a way of life that she'd only read about but had never imagined she would experience; finding that she was the guest in the house of a world famous author; her disconcerting meeting with Nigel—who had an effect on her, the like of which she'd never known—culminating in seeing a portrait of what seemed to be in every detail—except for the clothes—as one of herself. She felt as if she was living in a dream world—but one from which she couldn't shake herself awake. She was strangely disoriented, filled with a sense of unreality.

Diedre returned and said, "That's all settled, I spoke to a desk clerk who sounded intelligent, but is probably moronic, but he promised to put notes in various pigeonholes. Okay?"

Trisha gave a shaky smile, "Thank you."

"Pour the champagne Nigel and we'll try to explain the complexities of the situation as well as we can."

Nigel handed her a glass and regarded her gravely, "This will put you back on track."

She nodded, unwilling for some reason to meet his eyes. She sipped the sparkling wine and listened to Diedre's lilting husky voice, whilst Nigel lounged on a settee, his expression inscrutable.

"This house as it stands today, was altered slightly from

the original and added to by Nigel Barret, way back in the mid-eighteenth century. He was a direct descendent of the Barrett who fought with Cromwell's New Model Army and helped in the capture of Jamaica—that is a complicated story, we won't go into that, for it's not really germane to *our* story. Anyway, Nigel had a brother who lived in England, who married a girl called Topaze—no one ever knew her surname. She was—er—well, a lady who earned the title of The Golden Harlot..." Trisha gave a little gasp and Diedre smiled. "She married Justin—Nigel's brother—who was killed in a duel—it is said that the duel was over Topaze, but there are so many legends surrounding her name that one can never be sure of the facts. Anyway, Justin in his will left all he possessed to his wife—but when she arrived in Jamaica to claim her inheritance she discovered that Nigel was in possession and refused to accept Topaze as the rightful heir. When her claim was upheld in the courts, Nigel disagreed and said he would fight it, but the situation was resolved by Nigel and Topaze marrying—*but* by the terms of Justin's will Topaze was to retain possession even if she did marry again. Further, she was to will the estate to *female* descendents on condition that they did the same.' Diedre paused and Trisha frowned, where was all this leading to, she asked herself. At the back of her mind, she knew the answer: the questions and hints over the past two weeks, the newspaper article—was that only today? It seemed weeks ago...

Diedre was speaking again, "Your grandmother was my aunt, who inherited *Pimento Hill*, under the still extant terms..."

"How did you know about my grandmother?" She knew the answer even as she asked the question—the enquiries made about her in London, which had led to all those stupid rumours about her being an heiress...

She sat up straight, "The portrait? That was Topaze?"

"Yes, she was your great-great-whatever-grandmother—it might well be a portrait of you. The likeness is uncanny—and then of course, your middle name, which again under the terms of the will, was to be passed down to each female. I am Diedre Topaze, believe it or not! When I saw you in Kingston I was amazed—and you see how Nigel reacted when he saw you tonight..."

"It was as if the portrait, which I've known and admired all my life, had suddenly become flesh and blood," Nigel put in. "I tell you, it gave me a jolt."

"Does this mean," Trisha began in a wondering voice, "That..."

"That you are the last of the Barrett heiresses, yes."

"But why did my grandmother never tell me any of this?"

"We can only guess at that, probably because she didn't think that the terms of such an old will would be honoured today, especially as she had migrated so long ago."

"But how—I mean, how did the women down the years, keep the name of Barrett?"

Diedre glanced briefly at Nigel before she said, "Quite simply, they married a Barrett. There are a number of branches to choose from so there is no fear of interbreeding."

Trisha felt her face flame and she carefully avoided meeting Nigel's eyes. She put down her glass with a hand that trembled slightly and stood up. "This has all been a great shock and difficult to take in. I would like to go to bed, if you will excuse me. I doubt though, if I'll sleep..." she remembered Hammond's words '...I can ensure you a good night's sleep...' and she felt her face flush again at the implication. Against her will she looked at Nigel. He regarded her with a quizzical smile and she had the uncanny conviction that he had read her mind, but all he said was: "It'll all seem more rational in the morning. Good night Trisha."

"Good night Nigel—Diedre."

Diedre got up, "Of course, it's been a shock and we didn't make it any easier for you. You wouldn't have believed us if we'd just told you, we needed the evidence of the portrait. I'll see you to your room."

"Please don't bother. I'm sure that I can find my way."

She found her way with surprising ease and discovered that the bed had been carefully turned down, a white lace nightgown laid out on the pillow, a pink robe was over the back of a bamboo rocker, the mosquito net tucked in, leaving an opening for her to slip under. There were fresh towels in the bathroom and ice water in a flask on the bedside table. She felt pampered, yet, at the same time, troubled by many questions to which she wondered if there were any answers. She was as bewildered as if indeed she had stepped back into the past and her recent life at modern hotels, her job, the people that she knew, were all part of an elaborate dream.

Surprisingly, despite her chaotic thoughts, she *did* sleep dreamlessly and woke just before dawn. She pulled on the terry robe—it was sizes too big—and stepped out onto the enclosed verandah outside her room. It was gloriously cool, sleepy birds were waking with little chirps and tentative trills before bursting into full-scale song. The sea looked flat and quite still from that height; away to the east the mountains were black silhouettes against a pale apricot sky, then their outline was rimmed with bronze as the sun crept higher. Below her, the garden was quiet and deserted, dew lay heavily on the emerald grass and frosted the leaves of shrubs and blossoms of plants to which she could put no name. The magical beauty of it almost made her forget the added complexities of her life—although this latest revelation made her earlier worries fade to insignificance.

There was a tap at her door. She glanced at her watch, not yet six, who on earth..."Who is it?" she called with a slight tremor in her voice.

"Is me ma'am, Doreta. Miss Trisha, is you coffee me bring."

"Oh thank you, how lovely. Do come in."

Doreta placed the tray on a low table on the verandah then scuttled out, still a bit in awe of Trisha...why? The answer came in a flash of understanding, of course, the portrait—the whole staff must have seen the portrait and recognised her exact likeness to it and wondered who she was. They must also know of the peculiar inheritance clause in the Barrett wills and had probably speculated about her status in the family. Oh dear, yesterday she thought that she had troubles, they paled to nothing now. She stirred the coffee and bit into a banana.

Why should she think that she had troubles?

She should be dancing for joy. She had discovered that she was heir to all this—she looked out at the rolling hillside, the lush vegetation and so much more that she hadn't yet seen, and this beautiful old house filled with furniture worth a fortune—so why did she have such a feeling of apprehension?

She finished her coffee and went to have a quick shower, suddenly impatient to get out of this house and away from the strangers who had, without warning, become so enmeshed in her life.

Now, as she sat beside Nigel, she tried to force her thoughts away from the past twenty four hours and concentrate on the coming show, there was a lot of work to do over the next few days...

Nigel, too, was silent. He drove with panache and confidence, keeping a steady speed down hill and round the deep hair-pin bends, then, when they reached the main road and the traffic began to build, he threaded his way with consummate ease past smoke-belching diesel trucks, reckless loud-horned mini-buses, darting barefoot children, idling jay-walking pedestrians, bleating goats and squawking chickens.

For once, Trisha's heart wasn't in her mouth at every looming peril, her hands were limp in her lap, not gripping the edge of her seat as she so often did, neither did her feet reach involuntarily for the controls as each new obstacle appeared. Was it because she was so pre-occupied with what she had learnt the night before, or was it because she had complete confidence in Nigel's driving?

They reached the hotel and he pulled up under the *porte-cochere*, he was out of his seat and had her door open before it had registered that the journey was over. He looked down at her gravely, "Don't worry Trisha. You've taken this all rather strangely, most girls would have been wild with excitement—but then, you're not most girls, are you?"

She looked up at him. She was seeing him for the first time full faced in daylight. His eyes were so dark a brown that they were almost black—she remembered suddenly how tender they had become when she got scared last night. He was older than she had first thought; there was the faintest touch of silver amongst the black hair at his temples. She looked away and said, "I suppose I am acting oddly, but I haven't taken it all in yet and it seems to me that there are many questions screaming for answers."

"Which I am sure can be answered satisfactorily. Whenever you're ready to ask, just say so."

"I doubt if there will be time. I've a busy time ahead and we leave in a week's time, had you forgotten?"

"I don't think that I ever knew. But Trisha..."

"Thank you Nigel, for driving me back. Goodbye." She held out her hand in a formal gesture, he took it in both his and she felt again the electric shock that his touch produced. She lifted her head and their eyes met in a long questioning look. Then he said, "It's not goodbye, Trisha you know that."

She didn't answer, but walked quickly from the car and through the swinging doors before he could say another word. He looked thoughtful as he re-entered the Jaguar and failed to see the hostile look from a tall dark haired man or the look of admiration from a girl with long black hair and widely spaced grey eyes as they returned to the hotel from the tennis courts.

As Trisha entered her room, the telephone was ringing. "Hullo?"

"Thank God you're back."

"Hammond?"

"Yes, where have you been? I've been ringing your room..."

"I don't see why..."

"Don't you? You go off early yesterday morning without a word—fail to turn up when the models arrived and were seen returning from wherever with some handsome local gent in a spanking new snazzy car."

"Have you finished?" she asked coldly.

"No, I haven't," he was explosive, she cut in:

"Well I have. I owe you no explanation of where I was or who I was with. It so happens that messages were left at the desk last night, giving my whereabouts."

"I received no message."

"That is hardly my fault."

There was silence from the other end. He said in a tight voice, "I trust that you remember that we have a rehearsal today, a show to go on tomorrow night and that we have to start shooting the feature the day after?"

"Of course I remember—why do you think I'm here? Thank you for calling, goodbye."

She put down the receiver and stood looking down at the silent instrument. Hammond—he'd sounded distressed enough and she'd slapped him down, but what else could she do after the humiliating scene when they'd parted the other night? She sighed sharply. There was work to do—the affairs of her heart must be put on hold for the time being.

As she changed, she forced her mind away from her personal problems and concentrated on the Japanese Collection that was to take place the following night. It was going to be quite different from the Kingston showing, which meant a whole new set of photographs, a whole new set of captions and descriptions, new interviews from different angles of the models and the designers, the seamstresses—there was an awesome amount of work to be done, but it was a good thing, it would keep her mind off her own worries. She decided to have another cup of coffee and a Danish before going to the rehearsal—it seemed ages since she'd drunk coffee on the verandah at *Pimento Hill*—no, no thoughts of that nature: that was the past, all she had to do was to concentrate on the present, to take each hour, each day, one at a time. She paused momentarily as she entered the coffee shop and saw Jason, Carla, Hammond and Dolly seated at a table for four. They waved her over.

"The wanderer returns," Jason said grimly.

She gave him a surprised look, "I wonder that you noticed I'd gone," she said lightly.

"But of course he did," Carla said sharply. "*And* when you came in this morning," she added spitefully. "Tell me darling, who was that simply divine man you were with— or don't you know?"

Trisha tensed, if she said who he was there'd be a barrage of questions—she couldn't face that, not yet. "I don't know exactly, he was staying at *Pimento Hall*—Diedre Barrett's place—you remember, we met her in Kingston last week? He offered to drive me back. Now, if you'll excuse me..." she moved quickly away to a vacant window seat, her heart thudding. How could she put it all behind her and concentrate on the matter in hand if they kept on and on? She was near to tears and looked up with swimming eyes as Hammond slid into the seat opposite.

"Look love," the utter kindness in his voice made the tears brim over, "Are you in some sort of trouble?"

She shook her head, "No—at least—I don't think so. I'm surprised that you care..."

"Of course I care," he said gruffly.

"Even—after the other night?"

"Perhaps more so after the other night."

She regarded him gravely, "I'm sorry that I was so rude on the phone just now."

"That's alright—I was possessive," he grinned ruefully, "But that's only because I was worried."

"Hammond, I am—I mean I have found myself in a—strange situation. I would like to talk about it, but not now, I'm trying to put it at the back of my mind, until all our work is done."

He regarded her with a slight frown, "One question—and then I'll respect your wish?"

She nodded, "One question—which I may not be able to answer."

"Does it have anything to do with your visit to the Barretts yesterday?"

She hesitated. "Yes—and no. Put it this way, if I hadn't gone to *Pimento Hill*, it wouldn't have changed the situation. That's it Hammond, no more."

"Alright, but remember, I'm here if you need me." He got up, "What can I get you from the counter?"

"Oh I forgot, it's self-service! I've been so waited on..." she bit her lip, "Coffee and Danish please."

He nodded, ignoring the implication of the broken sentence and loped off to the self-service counter.

****

Gradually, as the morning wore on, the vagaries of the world of fashion took precedence over everything else. One of the Japanese models had a tantrum and everything stopped whilst the Directrice straightened things out. The quick outburst in high-pitched Japanese was followed by a hiccupping storm of weeping.

"What she needs is you have her elegant little bottom slapped." Hammond grinned.

"Would you like to volunteer for the job?" Trisha asked lightly.

"I can think of less pleasant occupations—and more pleasant ones," he added. His tone matched hers but there was an undercurrent which brought a faint flush to her cheeks.

The cause of the tantrum was removed—nothing more than a shoe strap that was an eighth of an inch too loose— and the rehearsal resumed its multi-troubled fraught way. Lunch was a sandwich and local brew eaten, once more, on the run.

"I don't think beer at this time of day is a good idea," Trisha said. "It'll make me sleepy."

"No time for that my girl," Hammond said briskly. "Hopefully we'll be through by five and you can snatch a nice little nap then."

His hopes were not realised for it was after seven when the co-ordinator declared his satisfaction with the outcome of the day's work. Trisha gathered together her voluminous notes, while Hammond gathered up his extensive gear.

"Whew! I'm bushed," she said.

"Meet me in the *Smuggler's Cove Bar* and we'll have a quiet drink before dinner?"

She hesitated a moment, the memory of champagne after dinner had intruded—she pushed it firmly away. "I'd love to. I'll no doubt revive after a cold shower and the knowledge that today is behind us." That was a funny way of putting it, she thought, but he made no comment and they went in companionable silence towards the lifts.

It was a pleasant evening. They had a couple of drinks on the patio under a canopy of stars, then went to dinner in the informal dining room, *The Golden Ducat.* They talked about the day's work and the following night's showing.

There were no undercurrents—they behaved only as good friends, the sexual overtone completely absent. Trisha welcomed the change and became relaxed and unguarded so was all the more caught off balance when Hammond asked in a casual voice, "When are you going to let me make love to you?"

She drew in her breath in exasperation, "Oh Hammond, why spoil the evening? It was so pleasant—until now."

"I'm flattered that you view the prospect with such repugnance..."

"I don't—you misunderstand me. It's just that—that I've got a lot on my plate—and—I want to get this assignment finished—before—I indulge my private life."

His hand closed over hers, "Is that a sort—of promise?"

"I didn't mean it to be."

"Trisha, you must know that I'm very much in love with you."

She withdrew her hand with difficulty, "No, I didn't know."

"So you think that I want to go to bed with you for sheer lust?"

"It happens all the time, doesn't it?"

"Yes, but not to me." He looked at her sharply and said in a wondering tone, "You've changed since this trip began—you've changed in the last twenty-four hours. What happened to you out at *Pimento Hill*, what passed between you and Nigel Barrett?"

Her eyes narrowed, "How did you know about Nigel Barrett?"

"Because you told me—us—when you came into the coffee shop this morning. You said that Nigel Barrett was *staying* at *Pimento Hill*, which is an odd way of putting it, seeing that he *lives* there."

"You seem very well informed," she said in a cool

voice.

For a moment, his eyes became guarded then he laughed and said easily, "I *lived* here, remember? The Barretts are a household word."

She regarded him appraisingly, the easy friendly atmosphere was gone, the storm warnings were out—why? What had been said to trigger such a reaction? "Hammond," she said carefully, "Do you think that we can keep away from personalities until after our work here is done? I did ask this morning, please respect my wishes."

"If that's the way you want it—but I warn you, once work is behind us, I shall bring all my big guns to bear. I hear music, would you like to dance?"

"No thank you, I'm terribly tired, I'll see you in the morning." Memories of dancing with him were very close to the surface. She couldn't risk a recurrence of those events—though perhaps, she thought with an inward wry grin—that was just what he had in mind.

She slept well for the first part of the night and then was plagued by dreams, dreams of *Pimento Hall* where she stepped back in time and *was* Topaze Barrett, so happily married to Nigel—who was the image of the present day Nigel. They were dancing, their hands touched and she felt an exquisite thrill course through her body, then his face changed and became Hammond's, the thrill of ecstasy became one of fear and she tried to run away but her feet were clamped to the floor, the face changed once more to Jason's, he was looking at her sadly and said, "Don't do it Topaze. What do you know of this man?"

"What do you care? You're going to marry Carla."

"No, you've got it wrong, I'm going to marry you."

She wanted to cry out, "But I don't want to marry you, not now Jason..." but the words wouldn't come, however much she struggled to utter them...

She woke up, the dream dissolving as she asked herself, *What did it mean?* Who was Jason warning her about?

Hammond or Nigel?

She sat up in bed and pushed the damp tendrils of hair off her forehead. How stupid she was—it was only a dream, triggered by her involvement with two men—one couldn't say three men, for although Nigel was in the dream they had only had one short meeting—well, two if you counted one evening and the drive the next morning—fragments of the dream stayed with her in her half awake state, then she slept again until just after dawn. The dream had faded by then, but as she stepped under the shower she remembered what had nagged at the back of her mind last night: Hammond had said that she had told them that Nigel Barrett had driven her back—she hadn't, when Carla asked, "Who was that divine man you were with" she had said, "I'm not quite sure," or something to that effect. So, how had Hammond known? The question returned to plague her on and off during the morning, until the pressure of work drove it from her mind.

****

The showing of the Japanese Collection was drawing to a close, it had been a great success, attended by all manner of celebrities, either holidaying on the north coast or having flown down from North America or up from Kingston for the purpose. There was to be a reception afterwards. Trisha wished that she could skip it, but it would look bad to do so. Amongst the crowd, she glimpsed Diedre's neat figure and beautifully coiffed head. Sitting next to her was Nigel, supremely elegant in a finely tailored black jacket and tie. So, he had changed his mind and had come to the show—I wonder what triggered the change? She gazed at his profile as if seeing it for the first time and, at that moment, he turned his head and their eyes met. She felt weak at the knees and lost all sense of time or place—she felt as if she was drowning in the black depths of his eyes, then he broke the spell with a smile and a wave of his hand. She returned the gesture and looked away to find Hammond regarding her with a curiously hard gaze. "Your feelings are showing, my dear," he said in a voice she'd never heard before.

"I—I don't know what you mean."

"No? You don't look at me like that—nor Jason."

"Jason? I have no right to look at Jason—he's going to marry Carla."

The words were out before she could stop them, how awful! Carla had asked her...

"Marry Carla? You're talking through your hat!"

"I'm not, she told me so herself, but she asked me not to say anything until after the deal had been clinched between her father and the magazine..."

"You really are an innocent. That's one of the oldest gambits in the world, designed specifically to scare off the competition."

"But why? It would come out in the end..."

"Not if she maneuvered Jason to her way of thinking—here he is, ask him yourself."

"I can't do that," she hissed.

"It went well, didn't it?" Jason asked as he joined them. He looked at Trisha and gave her the lazy smile that used to turn her legs to water, now the spell was broken—there was no sweet memory of his crushing kisses, no sudden racing of the pulse. She felt faintly surprised then enormously relieved. He sensed the change and gave a small frown as he said, "I see that your friends from *Pimento Hall* are here, giving the old feudal tone to the event, I suppose?"

"Don't be ridiculous, just because they are an old family, doesn't make them any less—of the people."

"Oh, I am sure not, though I doubt if they'd agree with you. This is a rare occasion for Nigel Barrett to grace an event like this. He is noted for keeping himself to his august self."

"That sounds very petty Jason. And anyway, how do you know so much about the Barretts? You haven't lived here as well, have you?"

For a moment, he was disconcerted, then he met Hammond's eyes, which held an ironic gleam as he asked, "Yes Jason, how do you know so much about them?"

"I don't know—read about them in a magazine, some article of an interview Diedre Barrett gave."

Trisha went quite still. The storm warnings were out again in full blast.

Why had Jason lied?

Diedre had stated clearly that she never gave interviews...what on earth could be the point of such a lie?

A burst of clapping cut short her speculations, the audience rose, still applauding enthusiastically, then it was all over and the patrons were drifting out onto the moonlit washed patio. Trisha stood at the edge of the patio and gazed at the colourful scene as the guests mingled and discussed the showing: nothing really registered. She was still puzzling over the fact that Jason had deliberately lied to her—as had Hammond earlier. *Was it coincidence? It must be so...*

She gave a start as a voice behind her asked, "Have you quite recovered from the shock we gave you the other night?"

She turned and looked up at Nigel, who was looking down at her as he had done in her dream. Her heart almost stopped, then raced in a manner that made her breathless.

Ten

His nearness threw her into turmoil, "You startled me!"

"I'm sorry, but you knew I was here, you didn't think I would leave without seeking you out?"

"I was—somewhat—preoccupied."

"And didn't think of me at all—I'm shattered, the fatal charm of the Barretts must be losing it's potency."

She laughed, "I hadn't heard of the 'fatal charm'. Do all the Barretts have it?"

"Of course—you included." He was holding two glasses of champagne and handed her one. "I asked you a question."

"Yes, I'm sorry. About the other evening, I don't know..."

"You seem to have done—you look marvellous."

"Thank you. What made you change your mind and come here tonight?"

"I was curious. I wanted to see you—at work."

"I wasn't really working tonight, all that was done at the rehearsal, the actual show is more of a gel. What did you think of it?"

"As I said, not my bag, but it was very well done—and well received."

She sipped her champagne, "I thought that your—Diedre, was with you?"

"She was but she was tired and went home. She sent

you her love. When are you coming to *Pimento Hall* again?"

"I don't know. We're leaving the island soon and still have a lot of work to do."

"It's waiting for you..."

"What do you mean?"

"*Pimento Hill*—it will be yours—didn't that fact penetrate?"

"Not really. It's all rather dreamlike. But even if it is true, it will be years and years, Diedre is still a young—well, youngish—woman."

"Dee is a very sick woman."

"She can't be, she's so vibrant, so..."

"I'm afraid that it's true. Look, let's get away from this mob. There's a table under that almond tree."

He put his hand under her elbow to guide her and as in her dream she experienced the same piercing sweetness at his touch. He signalled a passing waiter, "Evans, would you bring a bottle of Bollinger Brut Special Cuvee? We'll be over there."

"Yes Mr. Barrett, right away."

"Do you know all the waiters by name?"

"Most of them in this part of the world, I've lived here all my life you know."

She could feel the fine white sand seeping under her evening sandals and when they were seated she kicked them off.

Nigel noted the action and grinned, "Shoes off! What next? Bonnets over the windmill or hair down?"

She smiled, then became serious as she surveyed him in the moonlight, dappled by the broad flat almond leaves, "About Diedre?"

He looked down into his glass for a moment, then looked up and said gravely, "Yes, I'm afraid that it's just a question of time. She's being very brave about it. She does as much work as she can and leads as normal a life as is possible. She's accepted the inevitable."

Trisha felt the tears spring and her voice shook as she murmured, "I can't believe it. How terrible."

"Don't feel like that—she doesn't. She's had a very good life—and when she goes, it'll be quick and pain-less."

She looked at him curiously—he seemed so calm and dispassionate. He caught her expression and said softly, "I care—very much—but I've known about it for some months now. I grieved at first, but like Dee I've come to terms with it and learned to hide my grief so as not to upset her."

Trisha was silent, no one would guess from the lovely calm manner, the gaiety and wit...she felt an inexpress-ible sadness, as if the news had been about a dearly loved relative.

The waiter arrived with the champagne in an ice bucket. After two glasses had been poured and the bottle returned to the bucket, Nigel said, "It is stated amongst wine buffs that this is to be savoured amongst good friends on very special occasions."

She looked at him wordlessly, he lifted his glass to her and asked softly, "This is a very special occasion for me, how about you?"

"It's an occasion that I shall always remember," she said evasively.

"That's a crumb." His tone became solemn again as he went on, "Because of Dee's illness we instigated in-quiries about you..."

"It was *you* in London?"

"Yes me—personally. I'm sorry, it wasn't snooping re-ally—we just wanted to find out what manner of person was going to inherit *Pimento Hill*."

"Yet you made no effort to contact me in London?"

"No, I thought it would be better to meet—on your future home ground..."

"I don't understand?"

"You don't think that it was by chance that you were sent here?"

"I'd hoped it was because it was thought that I was good enough to handle the assignment," she said stiffly.

"Oh but you are, I just speeded up the process a little."

"You speeded...what are you saying?"

"I had a little talk with your editor..."

"What right have you to meddle in my career..." she began hotly, but his hand came down on hers and his voice was low and caressing as he murmured, "You said yourself that there were questions to be asked, don't get mad until you have all the answers."

"*My* questions—to your face. You were asking questions behind my back."

"I'm sorry if that upsets you, but we considered that under the peculiar circumstances it was the way to go about the matter."

"I'm sorry to be so touchy but your enquiries set off a spate of speculation and started all sorts of rumours, culminating in that newspaper article. I still don't know who the writer is."

He shook his head, "Neither do I, but most of the journalists would know the terms of the will and would speculate about anyone with the name of Topaze Barrett."

"How did they get hold of that name? I never use it."

"Passport? A few enquiries at the airport?"

"That must be it."

"You know, when I saw you the other evening I was flabbergasted—there was not just a *resemblance* to the portrait, it was as if the first Topaze had returned."

Unthinkingly she asked, "Are *you* like the *first* Nigel?" then coloured at the question and was glad of the dim setting which hid her confusion.

Nigel gave a light laugh. "Oh no, he was tall, dark and very good looking."

Her eyes widened, "It seems as if someone is fishing for

compliments."

He laughed again. "There is a portrait of him too, in the gallery, you can judge for yourself. So, when are you coming back?"

"I've told you, I just don't know, we have three day's heavy shooting and are booked back on the thirtieth."

"Don't go back at all. Stay here—and marry me."

The words took her breath away. She choked slightly on the champagne, then said in a dazed voice, "Marry you? But I don't know you!"

"That can easily be remedied..."

"I can't..."

"Why not? You're not committed to either of those two who were with you?"

"No... no! Of course not."

"Then why not?"

"Nigel," she gestured helplessly. "I don't know you—you don't know me—and—this may sound silly in these times—but I will want to love the man I marry."

"I'm glad that you feel that way, I don't think it's silly at all." He leant across the table and kissed her lips, a hard demanding probing kiss that left her weak and helpless. "It wouldn't be too hard to love me, would it?"

She gathered her wits as best she could, "I wouldn't want it to be one sided," she managed to get out.

"It wouldn't be," he said softly.

"You don't know me," she repeated. She slipped her feet back into her sandals and stood up. "I must go, I'm terribly tired. Thanks so much for the cham..."

He had also risen and stood very close to her; she could feel the magnetism that she had sensed at their first meeting, enveloping her in waves, dulling her senses to all but his presence. She broke the spell with an effort and said:

"Good night, Nigel, give my love to Diedre."

"I wish that you would give it to me—but not in that way, not as a social gesture."

She ignored the first part of his remark and answered the second, "It wasn't a social gesture. I—I feel as if I'd known her for years—there was an instant bond..."

"Which I assure you was mutual. So it wouldn't be beyond the realms of possibility to have such an instant bond between us?" She didn't answer and he went on, "You say that I don't know you, but I do, as a small boy I used to go to the gallery and gaze and gaze at your face..."

"No, not my face!" She burst out. "The first Topaze, we look alike, but from what little I've heard of her, that is as far as it goes."

He grinned, "She was quite a gal, through no fault of her own I understand. In those days, girls were forced into selling their bodies, but even before she married Nigel she became eminently respectable and died a pillar of the church and an object of veneration by the old and young alike."

"You seem to know a great deal about her?"

"There are some old letters and a sort of journal, you'll love browsing through them."

She felt herself being drawn to him as if by a magnet and she resisted with all her might. She couldn't commit herself—either way—it had all happened so fast that she was out of her emotional depth.

"Trisha?"

"No more tonight, I—cannot take any more emotional buffets. Good night Nigel,"

He put out a hand and took her wrist, lightly encircling it; she sensed the hidden strength and a tremor shook her. If he noticed, he gave no indication of so doing. "Trisha, if you do decide to go, come to *Pimento Hill* before you leave. I want to show you the original will, so that you may be assured of the authenticity of all that we have told you."

"The original will? Surely that has no validity now?"

"Diedre will show you her mother's and hers, which have

complied with Topaze's wishes—or rather, with Justin's wishes—and continued the tradition."

There was the unspoken rider that there was another tradition—that the heiress always kept her name by marrying a Barrett. She knew that he was thinking along those lines and she was determined that she would make no mention of it.

"Please Nigel, it has been quite a day."

He kissed the back of her hand—it was a gesture that she had seen done in old movies and she had always squirmed with embarrassment—she thought it sloppy sentimentality in its most extreme form, but it didn't seem so when Nigel did it, it seemed an expression of tenderness and—reverence—which was putting it rather strongly but she could think of nothing more adequate.

"Good night," she whispered, then went quickly through the powdery sand to the dew wet grass and so to the patio and up to her room.

She went out onto the balcony and leant on the rail and gazed down into the shadowed garden. It was late— after one—the hotel was quiet, no music, no chattering guests or laughter, no clink of glasses or clatter of crockery, only the soft susurrus of the ever-restless sea, the sound of a light breeze in the rustling palm fronds. Further afield, she could hear the distant barking of night-marauding dogs and the occasional muted roar of a late motorist on the highway.

The memory of the peace and quiet of *Pimento Hill* returned and she experienced again the feeling she had when she had first set foot in the house, that she had returned home—she didn't know then that she was descended from a former mistress of the estate, so it was not hindsight. She knew nothing of her antecedents except that her grandmother was a Barrett and came from Jamaica—she straightened—her grandmother was a Barrett and had followed the tradition and *married* a Barrett! She had always known that, but her grandmother had always brushed it aside as pure coincidence. Why hadn't she wanted Trisha to know the truth? Perhaps because as Diedre had guessed, that she didn't believe that the tradition of the woman inheriting the estate would be honoured in these days. She remembered the shock when she had been confronted by the portrait. It was uncanny, like looking in a mirror and seeing yourself in unfamiliar clothes...

She was suddenly overcome with utter tiredness and committing the unforgivable sin of not removing her make-up she stripped off her clothes and fell into bed.

She slept dreamlessly and woke the next day with a marvellous sense of well-being. She lay for a moment trying to remember why she was so contented—was it because Nigel had asked her to marry him? *Surely, he wasn't serious, although he had seemed so.* He couldn't have fallen in love with her so quickly, then why...the answer came like a douche of icy water—what a fool she was, anyone else would have seen through that apology for a proposal in seconds, but oh no, not little miss head-in-the-clouds Trisha—he only wanted to marry her so that he could continue to live at *Pimento Hill.* Her early contentment was replaced by anger—anger towards herself for being so gullible, anger towards Nigel for deceiving her and yes, anger towards Diedre for being party to the plot—for now Trisha could see how very clever Diedre had been in gaining her confidence and discounting that she had any really strong feelings towards Jason or Hammond...

And yet, Diedre didn't seem to be a devious person. Would she embark on such a course of action knowing that she might die at any moment? She might, she adored her son, she revered the family tradition, the estate was sacrosanct. She couldn't risk Trisha inheriting it and flouting tradition by marrying someone who might neglect its thriving acres and let it all go ruinate—to use a delightful island description. Why had they engineered her coming to the island? She knew nothing of the will...

But the lawyers did, Diedre and Nigel couldn't ignore the will, the contents were too well known to too many people, they had to conform to tradition...

But did they? Legally?

It was all too much; she didn't have to abide by the terms of a will made over two hundred years ago. She would finish the job here, pack up and go home and forget all about it.

She swung her feet to the floor and padded into the bathroom—the memory of the luxurious bathroom and the silken soft rainwater at *Pimento Hill* came back to her—she gave herself a mental shake, this was ridiculous, she was becoming as possessed over *Pimento Hill* as she had been over Jason...

As she *had been* over Jason?

She found with surprise that she could think of Jason without the usual lurch of her heart. She deliberately thought about him and Carla marrying and the prospect left her unmoved...She suddenly laughed aloud and finished dressing with renewed energy.

The next few days were hectic and she had no time to dwell on herself. The whole crew of **YOU: TOMORROW** were deployed in the shooting of the summer edition fashion feature. Most of the shots were done on the beach or on the rocks, great pitted sharply cragged honeycomb rocks which were host to small crabs, which lurked and scuttled in little pools, which caused many shrieks from the models and endless holdups until the offending crustacean had been chased to a pool in another rock.

It was hard work under the hot sun and despite a heavy sunscreen and floppy hat, Trisha acquired a golden tan and her red-gold hair was topped with highlights. The effect on both Jason and Hammond was immediate; they redoubled their attentions to her, so much so that she said reproachfully to Jason:

"Are you being fair to Carla, showing me so much attention?"

"Fair to Carla! What on earth do you mean?"

"Well, you're going to marry her..."

"Marry Carla? I've told you a dozen times that she means nothing to me."

"You have a funny way of showing indifference," she said shortly.

"Whatever gave you the idea that I was going to marry her?"

She hesitated, "Not *what*ever—*who*ever—Carla told me herself and said not to mention it until the deal with her father was final."

"The little schemer," he exclaimed, "I suppose she thought that she'd trap me eventually—thank God the deal has been finalised so I don't need to pay her any more attention. It was all a waste of time..."

"How so? You said that the deal had gone through?"

"Yes, but not to Carla's father—another bidder out of the blue snapped it up."

"Who is the new owner?"

"Haven't a clue," he said carelessly, "So you can forget about fairness and concentrate on me."

She regarded him gravely, his news about Carla would have sent her into a transport of joy a week ago, but now she was quite unmoved. "Jason," she said carefully, "I admit I was hurt and bewildered when you—dropped me—for Carla. But—things seem to have changed—I don't care either way..."

He gripped her shoulders, "I'll make you care again."

"No. It's finished. Quite done with—I like you as a person, I'd like you for a friend..."

His hands dropped, "Who is it, Hammond?"

"No—it's not anybody—just me, I've changed..."

"It's that Barret fellow, isn't it? I saw you together after the showing."

"No, Nigel has nothing to do with it. Although he did—ask me to marry him. I said no."

"Asked you to marry him? You don't know each other."

"That's what I said."

He looked at her curiously, "Was there any truth in that rumour that you were an heiress?"

She hesitated and said firmly, "Of course not, that's all it was, a rumour. Now Jason, shouldn't we get back to work?"

Eleven

The **YOU: TOMORROW** team moved from shooting on the beach and in the hotel grounds to Dunn's River falls, a famous beauty spot and tourist attraction. Because of the latter they could only film early in the day before the falls were officially opened or after the gates were closed for the night. Because of the contrast in lighting between the brilliant morning light and the softer dusk they were able to get some terrific shots.

They were working on an early morning session: the waters gushed down from a height of six hundred feet, tumbling and splashing over huge grey boulders, river stones worn smooth from untold years of being caressed by the cold water from the high hills and surrounding waterbeds.

It was a delight to slither from rock to rock until the river water met the sea and the resultant exhilarating shock of the contrast in temperature inspired the long climb to the top, so as to repeat the experience.

The models were clad in the briefest swim wear—they perched like mermaids on the high stones and gave squeals of delighted alarm as the cold water gushed over them, the spray whipped their sun kissed bodies and the early morning breeze ruffled their hair into damp tendrils. The English models were augmented by two Jamaican beauties, both former Miss Jamaica's—who had come in the top three of earlier Miss World contests. They were excited about being featured in the well-known magazine and they hoped that their modeling careers would be boosted in consequence.

Jason and Hammond worked with concentrated speed, each a master in his medium, catching the natural poses of the girls as they clambered over the wet shining boulders. They were working from a low angle, the bright Nereids against the grey background or sharply etched against the early morning sky. The other members of the team worked from above, using the foaming height of the falls to dwarf the girls, whilst others planned a choreographic session after the naturalists had had their day. Everyone was in swimwear as all the shots were taken either from the water or perched precariously on a high boulder, where the spray drenched man and camera remained continually. Trisha was very conscious of Jason and Hammond's bronzed muscular bodies, but found that she could view them objectively, dispassionately, as she followed them around, making notes of the locality, the models, the swim wear and possible captions.

All too soon, the time allotted to them was up and Jason said, "We're almost through, shall we finish tonight by moonlight or come back tomorrow?"

There was a chorus of, "Moonlight."

"Okay, I checked, the moon's full and overhead by about nine."

"It's going to be cold," one of the models protested. "The water's cold enough now, what's it going to be like after dark?"

"Nonsense! The sun has spoilt you already. Think what it's like in the UK."

That silenced any further objections and the gear was packed into the station wagon just as the gates were opened and the first batch of tourists streamed in, cameras at the ready.

"The competition." Hammond murmured as he steered Trisha towards his rented car.

"Hey there," Jason called. "Trisha's with me."

"She *was*—see you at breakfast."

"You might have asked if I wanted to go with you," Trisha said mildly, although she wasn't sorry to be away from Jason—the memory of her recent feelings for him was very near the surface. She gave a sharp inward sigh.

"What's the deep sigh for?"

She looked surprised, she hadn't realised that it had been audible, "Oh, I don't know—life in general..."

"You promised to tell me what was bothering you—when you returned from *Pimento Hill*."

"I don't remember *promising*—I do remember saying that I didn't want to talk about it until our work here is finished."

He grinned at her sideways, "Stubborn little thing, aren't you?" The grin left his face as he said solemnly, "Trisha, will you marry me?"

Surprise left her speechless for the moment, then she said carefully, "That's very—kind—of you—but no—thank you." She sounded so stilted that she added hastily, "Hammond, I didn't mean to sound—ungracious, unimpressed—it's just that—I'm very mixed up in my emotions—I don't know what—or who—I want."

He shot her a brief look, then back to the winding road, "Still carrying a torch for Jason?"

"No, I'm not. That's all over. He asked me to resume the old footing—I said no."

He gave a short laugh, "Proposals of one sort or another from all sides, eh?" He was silent for a few moments as he negotiated a particularly sharp corner, then said, "You seemed very *friendly* with that chap from *Pimento Hill*—has he captured your heart?"

She felt herself blushing and said hastily, "No of course not, I've only met him twice." She didn't mention that

Nigel also had asked her to marry him—two proposals of marriage and another indefinite one. She certainly was popular suddenly...

"He seems to have worked fast, that kiss he gave you seemed more than cous-friendly," he shot her another sideways glance—but she didn't seem to have noticed the near slip.

"You needn't have watched," she said.

"It was impossible not to, you both seemed to have gone public."

No more than you did, she thought, but decided that it was politic not to mention that incident. She looked at him curiously, there was a note of frustrated bitterness in his voice, but he seemed more angry than disappointed— he'd made no mention of love, just a bare 'will you marry me?' in a fast moving car at nine-thirty in the morning, quite the most unromantic proposal a girl could hope for.

His strange mood seemed to have passed as quickly as it had come as he said cheerfully, "I'm not going to give up. I'll wear you down and keep asking until you say 'yes'."

"Why?'

"Why what?"

"Why do you want to marry me?"

"What a question!" He seemed disconcerted for a moment, then said glibly, "For all the usual reasons: we like each other, we have the same interests, I think that we could make a good life together."

"And where does—love—come into it?"

"Good grief girl, that's taken for granted."

"Not in my book."

He spun the car into the hotel driveway and the tyres screamed on the loose gravel. He slid to a stop under the *porte-cochere* and swivelled in his seat to look at her. "What a romantic you are! A sentimental romantic! You don't seem to be living in today's world, you're back at least fifty years."

She returned his look of exasperation with one of cool appraisal, "If that is so, then we don't have anything in common, do we?"

"Of course we do, when I held you close in my arms and felt you quiver with delight..."

"That is quite different, as well you know," she cut in. "There is more to marriage than 'quivering with delight'." She looked down at her clasped hands with a small frown. She wasn't handling this very well and eyed his set face, "Hammond?"

He looked straight at her, his eyes hard, then they softened as he saw how distressed she was, "Don't look like that, when we get back to London, you'll see things in a different light, this place has cast a spell on you, you're not the same Trisha who came to the island a couple of weeks or so ago."

That was true, she thought, the Trisha who had come to the island was a stupid little ditherer who didn't know her own mind or what—or rather, who—she wanted. Now, she knew her own mind, knew who she wanted—who, through circumstances, was out of reach.

She touched his hand and his own closed firmly over hers, "Trisha? Tell me that you're being coy and playing hard to get?"

She shook her head, "No Hammond, this is for real— but thank you for asking me."

She stepped out of the car and it went off towards the parking area with a screech of tortured tyres. She went up to her room and surveyed herself in the glass. *What is the matter with me?* She asked her reflection. A near proposal from Jason—I exaggerated a little bit about that—a definite one from Hammond and I turn them both down without a second thought. Diedre was right, I was in love with love...

Diedre! I must go and see her before I leave. If Nigel told the truth about her illness, I might never see her again...illness or not, I won't ever see her again.

They weren't shooting again until the evening; she had the rest of the day to herself. She changed quickly, rang Room Service for orange juice and coffee and had left the hotel by ten-fifteen.

As she stepped out of the main door of the hotel, a taxi pulled away from the rank and drew up at her side.

"'Mornin' ma'am. Where to?"

"Good morning. *Pimento Hill* please, do you know it?"

White teeth gleamed in his dark face, "Everybody know *Pimento Hill*, me know it fram me bawn. De Barrett dem, live dere long time, pas' me gran'fader time. Make plenty money now Mr. Nigel come back fram foreign— de pimento berry dem, an' now de flower."

"Since he came back? Back from where?"

"'im go 'Merica, fe wed wit' some flim star..."

Trisha was appalled at the effect the man's words had on her. She felt as if she had recieved a blow to the solar plexus and all the breath had been knocked out of her. She was physically unable to speak for a long moment, then asked in a faint voice, "Married? But his—wife—isn't here?"

"No ma'am, she come and go—de flim tek up she time. Seem like Mr Nigel mek a mistake wit' her."

The driver shot a quick look in his rear view mirror. *Funny t'ing, de lady look so quail w'en me talk bout Mr Nigel.* He gave another quick look and his eyes widened as he recognised her from the newspaper photograph. He gave a silent whistle and thought, *Eh-eh! What goin' on up a de great-house?*

Trisha shrank back into a corner of the seat and let the garrulous driver drone on...

Nigel *married*? And yet he had asked *her* to marry him...was he willing to commit bigamy in order to keep *Pimento Hill*? Diedre had been right also when she said that Trisha would recognise true love when she met it—and what good had it done her? She was confused and near to tears as she stammered, "Please, turn around and take me back to the *Santa Gloria*, I've changed my mind." As she paid the driver, she said, "I'm sorry to have wasted your time."

He touched his cap, "No problem, Miss Barrett, soon pick up another fare."

"How do you know my name?"

"Saw your picture in the paper ma'am."

That wretched article! "I see. Thank you, good morning."

"'Mornin ma'am. Have a nice day."

She kept to her room and spent the rest of the day in an agony of indecision, she should go to say goodbye to Diedre, but she couldn't bear the thought of facing Nigel. Perhaps a telephone call—no, the woman was ill, she might die at any time, she couldn't be so callous and selfish as to consider her own feelings above those of a sick woman. Besides, Diedre had been so kind—added to which was the tenuous—Auntship? Cousinship many times removed between them. That trend of thought triggered off a half memory—something someone had said earlier? No, it was too elusive; she dismissed it from her mind as being totally unimportant.

She went to Dunn's River Falls that evening with a heavy heart, but the promised moon was hidden behind low black scudding clouds and the session had to be abandoned until the next day. She was saved in coming to a decision then as the whole day was spent in making the final shots for the feature, first at the falls, then in Shaw Park Gardens and finally in the town of Ocho Rios itself.

The shooting at Port Royal had been abandoned, as they were constrained for time and had managed to get on film enough variety of locations on the north coast. Suddenly, the trip was over, they were booked out of *Sangster International* on the five-fifteen flight. The sun and the sea, the mountains and the winding country roads would just be memories to mull over, to rejoice over or regret, during the rest of the cold winter that lay ahead.

Trisha spent an hour packing, then called a taxi immediately after lunch to take her to *Pimento Hill*. It was the same driver and he asked, "You sure you wan' fe go ma'am?"

She gave a shaky laugh, "Yes, I'm sure. I won't change my mind again."

She was leaving the island in a few hours, even if she saw Nigel, nothing that he could say would make her change her mind, she was armed against his charm by the knowledge of his marriage. Again, the question intruded: Why had he asked her to marry him when he was already married? If it wasn't bigamy he had in mind, then what? Lure her into living with him and then tell her of his marital status? She tried to push all thoughts of him out of her mind but only succeeded in concentrating her thoughts on him.

She watched the now familiar coastline unfold beside her with a new intensity and an aching heart—would she ever see it again? She had come to love this part of the island in a few short days, she felt so right here...this matter of the inheritance couldn't be taken seriously, surely it was just a myth, people didn't make wills which were honoured down the years—or did they?

The long uphill winding driveway of *Pimento Hill* was negotiated with familiar ease by the taxi driver. "'ere y'are ma'am."

As she paid him she asked, "Will you wait to take me back? I won't be long."

Before he could reply, Nigel's voice behind her said, "That won't be necessary, I'll take you back myself."

She was dismayed at the effect his voice had on her. She swung round and stammered, "Oh no, I couldn't put you to that trouble—I have only a few minutes—I have to be at the airport by three forty-five."

"No problem. I'll take the lady Travis." Nigel handed the man a note, "This should cover the cost of the fare."

Travis touched his cap, "Thanks Mr. Nigel. 'Bye ma'am, have a good flight an' come back to Jamaica soon."

The cab roared off in a white cloud of marl dust, the tyres protesting on the loose surface. Nigel looked down at her gravely, "I second the cabbie's sentiments—but—do you really have to go?"

"Of course I do, I have a job to do." She kept her voice as crisp and impersonal as her thudding heart and a tendency to tremble would allow. "I—came—to say goodbye to Diedre—how is she?"

His gravity deepened, "Not at all well, she collapsed two night's ago and has been in bed ever since. The doctor says that—it's only a matter of time, maybe a day, maybe a week. If a miracle occurs she may rally but he thinks not."

Her agitation in seeing him was overshadowed by distress at his news, "Oh Nigel, I should have come earlier, I did start out, but..."

"Turned back?" She nodded, surprised. "You must learn to meet life—not run away." It was as if he had known the reason for her flight, as if he could read her thoughts. He took her arm and his touch sent a thrill of exquisite pleasure through her body. He must have sensed it for his fingers tightened. He looked down at her and said softly, "Come, Dee will be so glad to see you. But," he added, "perhaps not a quarter as glad as I am."

She was very conscious of his hand under her elbow, part of her wanted to shake it off and say, "Don't touch me like that, don't use that caressing tone of voice, don't look at me with those melting black eyes, you have no right, you are a married man." Another part of her cried out, 'Hold all of me, take me in your arms and kiss me until I faint from sheer ecstasy. What does anything else matter but us?" Her feelings were nakedly apparent—

however, she was convinced that none of her conflicting emotions showed, although her breath came faster than the walk up the short flight of stairs and along the corridor merited.

They entered Diedre's room which was darkened, the curtains closed, only a thin shaft of sunlight glinted from beneath the hems. There was the faint pervasive smell of cologne and disinfectant that spoke of the sick room.

Diedre was propped up against a bank of pillows, her face drawn, dark hollows round her eyes. She raised the lids with difficulty and gradually focused on Trisha. "Trisha? Oh my dear, how good of you to come..."

"I should have come before. I can only stay a moment, I fly—back—tonight." Some inner force made her substitute 'back' for 'home'.

"Must you go?" Trisha nodded. "Then in that case— Nigel darling, bring the black brief case from my dressing room."

Trisha was horrified at the change in so short a time from vibrant flashing eyes and the lilting voice of an ageless beauty, to this shrunken old lady, with a voice barely above a whisper. She bent down and kissed Diedre's brow. "I'm sorry that you're—ill—Nigel should have let me know."

"I wouldn't let him—silly of me when I wanted to see you. I didn't realise though that you were leaving us. I had hoped..." she trailed off.

"Here you are Dee." Nigel came back carrying a small black leather case.

"Open it, you'll see a long manilla envelope in the front compartment. Give it to Trisha. Read it child."

Trisha drew out two documents, one was yellow with age the other crisp and white, she realised as she opened them that they were both wills. She hesitated, "Do you really want me to?"

Diedre nodded and Nigel murmured, "Read them Trisha,

they concern you—wait, you can't see in this light, come into the dressing room."

As she scanned, the closely typed lines of one document, she saw that all that Diedre and Nigel had told her was true, there it was clearly stated '...*I do bequeath to my distant kinswoman, Patricia Topaze Barrett...*'

She was the heiress of *Pimento Hill* and thirty million dollars in cash and bonds. Even by today's rate of exchange that was a lot of money...

There were no strings attached; no mention of marrying a Barrett; no instructions as to how she was to make her will. All her suspicions regarding both Diedre's and Nigel's motives were groundless. She had done them a grave injustice.

Nigel was left nearby *Mahoe Grove*, an estate comparable in size and age to *Pimento Hill* and the rest of Diedre's estate, which was considerable, running to nearly one hundred million dollars. So he hadn't asked her to marry him so that he could keep *Pimento Hill*; he was getting as large a property himself. She was too bemused to puzzle it out further and examined the other document.

This was written in thin spidery handwriting, the ink brown on the page. There was a proviso that the benefactor—Diedre Topaze Barrett—could only inherit the estate if she married a member of a branch of the Barrett family. Diedre had done Trisha the kindness of not including the proviso.

Trisha returned to the bedroom, folded the documents back in their creases and returned them carefully to the envelope with fingers that shook. She looked up to find them both watching her.

"I know that it is unusual to see the will before—the—usual time," Diedre said in a tired voice. "But—I wanted you to have proof—before you left the island."

Trisha was near to tears, "It's very good of you. I don't know what to say."

"No dear, I follow the family tradition," she looked from one to the other, "Not strictly but it so happened that we were lucky that you are who you are." It crossed Trisha's mind that if she hadn't passed muster, that precious tradition might have been ignored, but the doubt died as soon as it was born. "Won't you stay Trisha? It won't be very long."

"Oh Diedre, don't talk like that, it's probably—just a little setback."

"No dear, it's true, it won't be long now," the thin old voice held no bitterness, only a calm acceptance.

Trisha glanced at Nigel, still and watchful at the foot of the bed, then back to Diedre. She couldn't leave her now, her own affairs had to take second place to a dying woman's wishes. She took a deep breath. "Alright, I'll stay but I have to get back to the hotel and explain and get my things."

He nodded.

"Goodbye Diedre darling. I won't be long."

Oh why did she echo Diedre's words? She went out into the corridor and leant against the wall, her legs suddenly weak. She heard a quiet step behind her and turned instinctively, without thought or reason as Nigel took her in his arms and she buried her head in his chest, unresisting in the haven of his embrace.

"It's only a *week* since I saw her—now she's almost unrecognisable," she sobbed.

His arms tightened, "I know it must have been a shock for you. Thank you for saying you'll stay."

"I couldn't leave her like that," she raised her face and he bent and kissed her lips, she had no memory of the cab driver's words—everything but the pulsing moment of sheer searing passion was blotted out. The shock and horror of the last few minutes were swept away on a rising tide of desire that lanced through them both and when he picked her up and carried her along the corridor into the bedroom that she had occupied before; she made no attempt to resist but felt an inexpressible joy at what she knew was inevitable. He laid her on the four poster, took off her dress with a savage tenderness, her bra and pants were tossed aside, his own clothes followed and then he took her in his arms and kissed her throat, her breasts—which thrust towards his avid mouth by their own volition—and at last their mouths were joined in a sweet union. Her body was responding to his caresses in rising rapture and every fibre of her being was alive to his. She gave a moan of pleasure as their desire rose to fever pitch—a crescendo of mounting passion that took command and demanded to be assuaged—she gave a small cry as he entered her and their bodies were as one in an ecstatic throbbing fusion.

Afterwards, cradled against his chest, her fingers lightly stroking the black curling hair, he asked in a wondering tone, "I'm the first?"

"Yes."

"Oh my darling, why didn't you tell me?" He kissed the top of her had and she thought back to Diedre's words '...if you had really loved one of your young men, you wouldn't have hesitated...'

Diedre!

She sat up and exclaimed, "Nigel—how could we? With Diedre so ill?"

He touched her breast with his hand and kissed the nipple before he said lazily, "You really are a pocket Venus..."

She swayed towards him and again they were swept with a searing enchantment that left them spent and breathless. At length, he murmured, "As for Dee, she is the most practical person alive. I think that she will welcome the fact that you and I—have found each other—as they say."

Twelve

Trisha stirred in Nigel's arms and opened her eyes to find him looking down at her with an expression of infinite tenderness. The memory of their lovemaking came back to her in a rush and she gave a voluptuous stretch, she felt no shyness, only an inexpressible happiness that wrapped about her and filled her whole being. Then she realised that the rays of the sun were slanting across the floor and she sat up in alarm:

"Nigel! Look at the time! I should have been back at the hotel ages ago, the others must all have left for the airport."

"Don't worry my dearest, telephone and tell them you're staying. I'll have Martin drive you over to collect your things. I was going to drive you myself, but suddenly I don't want to leave Dee. You do understand my darling?"

"Of course, I'll be back as soon as I can."

He caught her to him for yet another close embrace, until she once more stirred in his arms and murmured, "I must go."

"But you'll be back, there's the whole night before us." His kiss threatened to engulf them again and to send them into further transports of passion, to make them lose all sense of time or place, but with a supreme effort Trisha said, "Please darling—later."

He released her reluctantly; "I can't bear not to have you in my arms, now that you've been there, where you belong, where you'll always belong through all the long years ahead of us."

She hastily showered and dressed, reliving in memory the rapture of the last few hours, her body still tingled from his touch, her lips felt bruised, but she was caught up in a delight that she had never known before...that such a delight could be experienced was beyond the realism of imagination.

She telephoned the hotel and got through to Dolly, who exclaimed, "Where have you been? We've been looking all over for you."

"I'm out at *Pimento Hill...*"

"Oh, the great inheritance..."

"What do you mean?"

"N-nothing, just kidding." The explanation was obviously false but before Trisha could comment, Dolly said hastily, "The flight's been cancelled—engine trouble—we leave the same time tomorrow."

"Not me, that's why I phoned—to say that I'm staying on for a bit."

"What? You can't do that—you're under contract."

"I'm needed here, it's a case of illness. I'll phone Jacqui early tomorrow and explain. I can easily finish my assignment here as at the office, and fax across my copy, so that's no problem. I'm coming in to pick up my things—I'll explain when I see you." Trisha said, then wished she hadn't, she didn't have to explain her actions to Dolly or anyone else. That wasn't true, she had an obligation to the magazine—she couldn't just walk out on them. She had no idea what her future with the magazine was likely to be, but it wasn't a decision that she had to make at the moment.

She went out onto the landing at the top of the double

staircase, the Rolls waited below with Nigel by its side, speaking to Martin. She started down the staircase and Martin touched his cap and said: "Ev'lin', Miss Trisha."

"Good evening Martin."

As she reached the bottom of the stairs, Nigel stepped forward and took her hands in his and regardless of Martin's presence, bent and kissed her lips, "Hurry back," he murmured against her mouth. She nodded and avoiding Martin's carefully wooden expression, got into the car.

The drive to the hotel passed unnoticed, Trisha was aglow with happiness. At last, she had shed all her doubts and indecision—she had found love and knew that Diedre had been right when she said that she would recognise true love when she met it, now the recognition was complete. What utter bliss it was to love and be loved, she felt a supreme contentment that encompassed her whole being...

The fact that *Pimento Hill* was to be hers was overshadowed by Diedre's illness. She couldn't quite grasp that one day—and let that day be far off, she prayed—that she would be the mistress of a huge estate, a wealthy woman, that, from obscurity, she had jumped into a person to be reckoned with, an honoured member of one of the oldest and wealthiest families in the island. It was a heady thought—and on top of it all was the fact that Nigel loved her and they would be together until...

The magic of the afternoon was shattered as reality stepped in and stared her in the face...

Nigel was *married!*

How could she have lost sight of that fact?

Even the shock of Diedre's appearance shouldn't have driven that out of her mind...

Had it been driven out or had she willfully *pushed* it to the back of her mind? Because she didn't want to admit the truth? Because she *wanted* Nigel to make love to her. Because she still wanted to feel the strength of his body crushing hers? Despite her recent knowledge of the shadowy presence of his wife?

She was suddenly possessed by an overwhelming self disgust and condemnation: she had allowed a married man to make love to her, she had given herself to him with wild abandon, in uninhibited passion—oh, what a fool she'd been, taken in by sweet talk and promises that could never be fulfilled—how could he have deceived her so...

But had he? No mention had been made of marriage, the fact that marriage to a Barrett had been a prerequisite for inheritance in the past and such a clause hadn't been included in Diedre's will, pointed to the probability that Diedre did know of his wife, and she, gullible little fool to the last, had thought that Diedre was letting loose the strings that had been binding for over two hundred years.

What was it that he had said? "...Diedre will be glad that we've found each other..." Surely Diedre wouldn't—couldn't—be a party to such a deception? She must know of his marriage and yet she had practically thrown them together. From the short time that she had known Diedre, she would have said that such a course of action was totally out of character. How could one be so wrong about another person?

That brief afternoon of sheer ecstasy which had promised to be repeated time and time again, was already a thing of the past—it had become a shameful episode that would haunt her for months...perhaps forever.

They reached the hotel and she said to Martin in a choked voice, "Don't wait, I've changed my mind, I'm not going back."

He opened his eyes in amazement, "But Miss Trisha, Mr. Nigel—'im seh..."

She was close to tears, "I don't care *what* Mr. Nigel said—I'm *not* going back."

He looked pained, "Very good ma'am," he said stiffly.

He got into the Rolls and drove away, muttering under his breath," Is different me t'ink she is—but no, she jus' like all de other stuck-up white lady dem." Then he remembered the look of stark misery on her face at the end of the journey, in contrast to the one of dreamy rapture at the start, and he murmured, "Is upset she is fe true, but wha' 'appen eena de car to change she so? An' wha' Mr. Nigel goin' seh? 'Im well taken wit' the lady."

Trisha was met at the door of her room by Dolly, determined to get the promised explanation. Her eyes widened as she saw Trisha's expression, "Whatever's the matter, you look as if..."

"It's nothing. Forget what I said about not going back with you all, I've changed my mind..." even as she said the words the thought struck her that she *had* to stay, she had promised Diedre. She couldn't go back on her word, though how she was going to endure the situation was something that she couldn't answer.

There would have to be a confrontation with Nigel—did she have the courage, the *will power*—when faced with him, to resist his magnetism? What she felt for him—still felt, despite his duplicity—made her former feelings for Jason pale to no more than a schoolgirl crush...

She realised that she had been staring unseeingly at Dolly all this time who regarded her with a look of surprised curiosity. "What is it Trisha? What happened at that place to make you behave like this?"

Trisha came back to the moment, "Sorry, I'm in a bit of a daze—please don't ask me why—but no, I can't go with you, not for a few days."

"I wish you'd make up your mind. First, you say you're not returning with the team, then you say you are, then you're not. I don't understand you, you sounded as if you were on cloud nine when you phoned, now you seem to be in the depths of despair."

"Dolly, please. I can't explain." She sat down heavily

on the edge of the bed and in spite of her misery, remembered Dolly's remark. "But you can tell me what you meant by 'the great inheritance'?" Dolly looked uncomfortable, "Come on," Trisha insisted, "Out with it."

"It—it was Hammond who told me about it."

"Hammond? Told you about what?"

"Told me about the huge property in Jamaica and that you were going to inherit it. When the rumour started in the office about you, everybody scoffed and said that such things didn't happen these days, not outside the cover of a book, but Hammond said it was true. He'd lived in Jamaica for some time and knew all about the Barretts and of how the *women* inherited. He'd made enquiries and was convinced that you were from the same branch of the Barrett family and that you were the one who would inherit the property." Dolly paused then added slowly, "He knew all about you before he joined the staff. In fact, we all thought that it was because of you that he wangled his way into the team—just to get to know you."

Trisha got up restlessly and went to the window, this was too much, two blows to her ego in one day, on top of all that had gone before...could she believe Dolly, who was renowned for her spiteful tongue. *Surely she wouldn't go this far unless there was some truth in it? How had the rumour gone all round the office, yet she, the one concerned, hadn't heard a whisper of it? Like the old adage of the wronged husband being the last to know, I suppose.* She turned round and looked at Dolly questioningly, she seemed sincere enough, but she knew that Dolly was adept at appearing sincere—she gave an inward sigh, nobody seemed to reveal their true selves. She returned to the bed and sat down again and said in a bitter voice, "He *knew*—all the time he knew! He just wanted to marry me for my money—for what I was worth..."

Dolly said, "I'm sorry Trisha, but it's better that you find out now. You're not in love with him are you?" Trisha shook her head and Dolly went on, "You're much better off without either of them."

"Them?"

"Hammond and Jason."

"Don't tell me that Jason also...?"

"My poor infant, didn't you realise that Jason took absolutely no notice of you until that rumour began to go round?"

"But I understood that the rumour started long before Hammond joined the staff?"

"It did. Hammond didn't start it but it gained momentum and credence after Hammond arrived and said it was true."

Trisha felt as if she had been winded: to be deceived like that, to accept in good faith all that sworn love and devotion, to find that it was all a sham, a ploy. Now all the little discrepancies which she had noticed began to add up: *Hammond's near anger at her refusal of his offer of marriage, and—yes, she remembered now—how he had almost said 'cousinly' when speaking of Nigel's kiss, then hastily changed it to 'friendly'. And Jason—she remembered his oh, so casual questions on the plane when he asked if the rumour was true, which she hadn't heard about, up to that moment. His actions were understandable now— yet were they? If he had wanted to marry her for her future worth, would he have played such ducks and drakes with her emotions by neglecting her for Carla—unless his story about his relations with Carla were true. More than likely he was so sure of her feelings for him, that he could act as he pleased—and he had been right—she had come running to him, until she woke up to her true feelings...*

None of that mattered now—except the blow to her self-esteem. She had thought that she was desired for herself, not for her possessions...she felt humiliated, like a pawn that had been moved around at will.

She looked at Dolly and asked, "Why didn't you warn

me? Why did you let them make a fool of me? Why are you telling me now?"

Dolly looked uncomfortable, "I didn't warn you, because I didn't really believe Hammond's story. It seemed so improbable, which also answers your second question—if it was only a rumour then they were paying you attention for all the usual reasons..."

"Not if they believed the rumour, or at least thought that they'd put it to the test." Trisha put in bitterly.

Dolly nodded, "Yes, I suppose so. It was only when I read the piece about you in the paper that I believed it and I expect that it also confirmed the facts in Hammond and Jason's eyes. I also found out that the tradition was that you didn't inherit unless you married a Barrett, which lets out both Hammond and Jason..."

She opened her eyes and asked wearily, "So why are you telling me now?"

"I thought that you'd been given the run-a-round too long." Trisha regarded her solemnly and Dolly exclaimed, "Don't look at me like that. I know I have the reputation of being a bitch—and deservedly so at times—but I'm not as bad as I'm painted..."

Her words were interrupted by the shrill of the phone. Trisha picked up the receiver, "Hullo?"

"Trisha, where have you been? I've been looking all over for you."

"Hammond? I've been out at *Pimento Hill*," she said shortly.

"Again? Isn't this becoming a habit?" She didn't answer and he went on, "Have you thought over what we talked about this morning?"

"Oh yes..."

"You have!" he exclaimed eagerly, "You've changed your mind?"

'No Hammond. I know—I understand now why you asked me to marry you. You know all about the Barrett inheritance, you went to the trouble of finding out if I was one of the *Pimento Hill* Barrett's, that's why you came to **YOU: TOMORROW**—that's why you asked me to marry you."

There was silence from the other end of the line. He said, "I don't know how you found out, but it's true—up to a point. It started out cold bloodedly, I admit it, but Trisha, I fell in love with you, I swear it. I don't care if you are an heiress or if you haven't a penny, I love you I tell you."

He sounded convincing enough, but she suddenly remembered the way that he had proposed and how he had called her a hopeless romantic, had accused her of living in the past—surely those weren't the words of a man in love?

"It's too late for that Hammond. If you had taken a little more trouble in your research you could have saved yourself some trouble now, for you would have found out that I would only inherit the property if I agreed to marry a member of the Barrett family. Goodbye."

She replaced the receiver and gave a broken little cry as she dropped her head in her hands.

"Don't take it like that Trisha, they're not worth it. Grief, you look awful. What you need is a drink, I'll ring for one."

Trisha looked up, the events of the afternoon and the subsequent revelations had left her drained. "No, I don't want one, I'll be alright."

Dolly regarded her thoughtfully, then asked, "What did you have to tell me?"

"Tell you?"

"You said on the phone..."

"Oh yes. Yes it's true, I will inherit *Pimento Hill*, but only after a very dear person dies and..."

"I can't believe it," Dolly breathed. "And you have to marry a Barrett? Nigel Barrett?"

It was all suddenly too much and Trisha burst into tears and flung herself on the bed. She didn't hear the quiet tap on the door or Dolly's opening it and the soft exchange of words, then she was being gathered in strong arms and Nigel was saying, "Now, now, what's all this? What is it?"

She thrust against him, "I'm *not* your darling—you..."

"What do you mean? What has happened to bring about this change? When Martin returned without you and said that you were very upset and were not coming back, I couldn't believe my ears. What is it?"

A convulsive sob shook her as she asked, "What about your wife?"

"What wife?'

"The film star."

To her surprise, he flung back his head and burst out laughing, "Where on earth did you hear that?"

"What does it matter?"

"Of course it matters."

He sounded so amused; he acted without any guilt or evasion that she said reluctantly, "It was the taxi-driver."

"Yes, well that figures, trust old Travis to snarl things up. My darling girl, I am not married and have never been."

"But why did Travis say..."

"It all started with one of those strange coincidences—the lady in question stayed at *Pimento Hill* while they shot a few scenes of the film she was in—I wasn't even home at the time and never met her. Later, it was reported in the paper that she—Karen Daley, I think her name was—had married a Nigel Barret—one T mark you—and everyone put two and two together, especially as I was in America at the time of the report of the marriage. It took me months to convince all my friends and acquaintances that it was not me who was the bridegroom—apparently it is still believed in certain circles. That Nigel Barret is twice her age, he is in oil and is able to keep her in the mink and diamonds that she has grown accustomed to wear on the screen."

The relief that swept through her made her want to laugh and cry at the same time. She clung to him, "Oh Nigel, I'm sorry, I was thinking that you had deceived me—I even thought that Diedre was a party to the deception. I didn't know how I was going to face you, how I was going to live with the fact that you were married— I was so miserable..."

"Good," he said briskly, "That means that you do love me."

"Oh yes, yes I do. How can you doubt it?"

He kissed her, softly at first then with growing urgency and a pulsing passion threatened to engulf them, until he drew back his head and said softly, "Not here, no hotel rooms for us. Come on, let's go home and tell Dee the good news."

"I must let the others know that I'm staying on for a bit, or I'll be in danger of losing my job."

"No you won't, unless you sack yourself."

"What on earth do you mean?"

"I was going to wait, but you might as well know now. I bought the magazine."

"You *bought* it?"

"Yes, as part of my wedding present for you—I thought you'd have fun with it. Come my darling, *Pimento Hill* is waiting."

The drive back to *Pimento Hill* passed like a dream to Trisha, she had been through so much in such a short time—the reading of the two wills, the shock of Diedre's illness, finding Nigel then believing that he was lost to her—it was all too overwhelming—and then the latest revelation, that Nigel had bought **YOU: TOMORROW** for her. A new thought struck her, had Jason known the name of the new owner? He had been casual in denying that he did...she brushed the thought away - it didn't matter any more.

Nigel left the Jaguar parked by the outside staircase and they both hurried up to Diedre's room. She took one look at their faces and her own broke into a smile of satisfaction. "You don't need to tell me, it's written all over you. I'm so happy for you."

"It was in danger of being an unhappy ending, Travis had told Trisha that I was married—to a film star."

"Oh no, that old story again, I thought it had died." Diedre held out her hands and they each took one. "I'm feeling a little better, your news is the best medicine in the world, but it may not last. I should like to see you married—how soon can that be?"

Nigel looked at Trisha, a question in his eyes, she answered with a smile and he said, "As soon as I can arrange, tomorrow if possible."

Diedre nodded. "Go and start making the arrangements. Trisha my love, stay with me, I want to talk to you." She patted the side of the bed and Trisha climbed up, still keeping Diedre's hand in hers. Nigel bent and kissed his mother's forehead, then kissed Trisha on the top of her head. Diedre waited until the door had closed softly behind him, then said, "I hoped from the moment I saw you, that you and Nigel would fall in love, that's why I omitted the clause about marriage from my will. I didn't want it to be an obligation—that's what happened to me with Nigel's father and I always regretted it. I had planned to ask you to give up your job and act as my assistant, in the hope that close proximity would do the trick. I was certain that Nigel had fallen in love. He's never acted before in the way he's been acting since he met you—but I wasn't sure about you—and then this happened..." She paused. Her breathing had become laboured and Trisha said urgently,

"Don't talk anymore. Rest a while."

"No, I must say this: there are two unfinished manuscripts in my study. I want you to finish them and send them off to my publishers."

"But—I'm not competent—I'm just a magazine hack, I have no creative ability."

"How do you know? I believe that you have. They are both on disc; it's just a matter of editing. Please do it for me Trisha."

Trisha felt the tears spring to her eyes and, at last, said huskily, "I'll try—but what will your publisher say, will he accept them from me?"

"Yes. I've already written him about him to sound him out in such an eventuality. You wanted to write—now you've got the chance. This may be the push you've needed. I want you to edit as you think fit, don't keep slavishly to my text, I want you to implant your own style on the books. You will do this for me?"

Trisha nodded, "Yes—I'll try," she murmured.

Talking had wearied Diedre, her lids drooped and she slept. Trisha sat there, holding the fragile hand, growing more cramped as the daylight faded and Nigel came softly back into the room.

"She's asleep?"

"Yes."

"Come then my darling."

She withdrew her hand and slipped from the high bed. Outside, he took her in his arms and she was reminded of that same action earlier, she seemed to have lived a whole lifetime since that afternoon.

"It's all arranged," he murmured against her hair. "We'll be married at nine o'clock tomorrow morning. Is that rushing you?"

She shook her head and raised her face to his, "If it was this evening, it couldn't be too soon."

Their lips met in a long kiss filled with the love and contentment that they shared.

Printed in the United States
32926LVS00002BA/136-216